GREAT BRITAIN, FRANCE, AND THE GERMAN PROBLEM
1918 — 1939

GREAT BRITAIN, FRANCE, AND THE GERMAN PROBLEM 1918–1939

A Study of Anglo-French Relations in the Making and Maintenance of the Versailles Settlement

BY

W. M. JORDAN

Originally issued under the auspices of the Royal Institute of International Affairs

FRANK CASS & CO. LTD.

Published by
FRANK CASS AND COMPANY LIMITED
67 Great Russell Street, London WC1B 3BT

Distributed in the United States by
International Scholarly Book Services, Inc.
Beaverton, Oregon 97005

Library of Congress Catalog Card No. 79–171818

ISBN 0 7146 2644 9

This reprint has been authorized by the Oxford University Press.

First edition   1943
New impression   1971

*The Royal Institute of International Affairs is an
unofficial body which promotes the scientific study
of international questions and does not express
opinions of its own. The opinions expressed in this
publication are the responsibility of the author.*

*Printed in Great Britain
By Unwin Brothers Limited
The Gresham Press, Old Woking, Surrey, England
A member of the Staples Printing Group*

FOREWORD

By Professor C. K. Webster

THIS study makes painful but salutary reading. It faces relentlessly certain facts which have produced the world in which we now live. It is the most rigorous analysis of Franco-British differences penned in this country. It is objective, and the author has taken the greatest care to be as fair to France as to Britain. He has digested practically all the evidence published, and, if much more will one day be revealed from the archives, the picture that he draws is a convincing one. His conclusions are solidly based on facts patiently ascertained from the study of many documents.

He does not pretend to give the whole picture. He leaves out, or only sketches in outline, the relation of the two Powers to the League system and to Soviet Russia. By so doing he focuses our attention on reparation, security, and disarmament, the subjects on which such fatal disagreements arose. In no other work of which I am aware has the difference of outlook and its disastrous effect upon action been so clearly revealed.

It is the usual and perhaps wholesome habit of Englishmen to forget past history. But let us remember that the French do not forget. The history of these years will live in their memory. In order that such misunderstandings may not recur, we too must remember it, however different the situation may seem to be when this war is over.

In peace as in war, the best is often the enemy of the good. There is more than one way to victory, but it is essential that a choice be made and consistently followed. Too often, both in war and peace, the choice is too long delayed. Coalitions in war have always been specially liable to develop this weakness. Only patient and skilled diplomacy on the part of statesmen and soldiers can overcome it. Only immediate and recognizable danger of defeat can produce the necessary unity of action.

After 1918 we had a coalition of peace, but how soon it lost its cohesion! The United States fell away immediately. Italian relations with France were fatally impaired by the peace negotiations and by the rise of Fascism. France and Britain remained. During the Great War their relations had been closer than those of any other two Powers. Their statesmen had been in continuous and close association. British armies had fought under a French Commander-in-Chief. If France had borne the main burden of the war in 1914–1916, Britain had in 1917–1918 redressed the

balance. Admittedly the sacrifice had not been equal, since the
war had been fought on French soil, and French casualties were
substantially greater. But Britain had come to the assistance of
France with a strength never imagined possible before 1914, and
alone of the Great Powers of the Alliance had fought throughout the four years of war without faltering. When Foch and
Clemenceau came to London in the early days of December 1918
they were overwhelmed by the popular welcome.

In a short time this close alliance was no longer cordial or complete. Yet France and Britain sought the same end—a Europe in
which both nations could live in safety. "Unfortunately some of
the most irreconcilable differences which array men against each
other turn simply upon the means of accomplishing ends which
both parties equally desire to attain." So wrote Palmerston, and
so it was in this case. Not until the end which they both sought
was unattainable did France and Britain come close together again.
"It was not until March 1936," Dr Jordan points out, "—seventeen
years to a day after the offer of the original British Treaty of Guarantee—that the British Government gave its consent to the Anglo-
French staff conversations which the French had at all times deemed
indispensable." He says little about the years subsequent to the
German remilitarization of the Rhineland—the act which made the
future war inevitable. But he shows more clearly than any other
writer the processes which made that act possible.

Once it had been accomplished, the way to peace lay through an
even greater conflict than that which had previously brought
France and Britain so close together. Its course has been very
different, and the relations between the two Powers have been
severed by the extent of the defeat inflicted on their armies. Yet
perhaps this very fact gives ground for hope. The conquest of
France has caused us to feel this time the full sense of danger which
in 1914–1918 only Frenchmen experienced. Indeed the sense of
irrevocable catastrophe only narrowly averted has pervaded the
whole world. If the nations cannot learn from these experiences
to find common means to a common end, then our Western civilization cannot endure—some would say did not deserve to endure.

Yet we must not forget in reading Dr Jordan's analysis that
Anglo-French relations are only one amongst numerous others.
European security was part of global security, and the war which
we now fight began in Asia and Africa, not in Europe. If Britain
did not realize the danger on the Rhine, France was too apt to think
that she had no need to give to peoples in other continents that
protection which she claimed for herself. Total war is global war,
and the freedom of France is being won in North Africa, on Russian
steppes and Pacific islands, and, indeed, on all the seven seas.

Nor can we obtain sufficient unity in international relations unless there is a unity of purpose at home. Dr Jordan's work concentrates attention on the external manifestations of policy; it is not his purpose to consider the social forces which in part determined them. But unless internal differences are kept subordinate to the imperative necessities of the international problems neither peace nor welfare can be obtained.

LONDON,
February 1943.

PRINCIPAL ABBREVIATIONS

A.J.I.L.	*American Journal of International Law.*
Anglo-French Negotiations .	Papers respecting Negotiations for an Anglo-French Pact. Cmd. 2169. H.M.S.O. 1924.
Baker	Baker, R. S.: *Woodrow Wilson and World Settlement.* 3 vols. New York, 1922.
Chambre: Débats . . .	Journal Officiel de la République Française: Chambre des Députés, Débats Parlementaires.
C.R.L.A.	Conference for the Reduction and Limitation of Armaments.
Gen. Comm. . . .	Minutes of the General Commission. Vols. I–III.
Land Comm. . . .	Minutes of the Land Commission.
Docs.	Conference Documents. Vols. I–III.
Pol. Comm. . . .	Minutes of the Political Commission.
D'Abernon	D'Abernon, Viscount E. V.: *An Ambassador of Peace.* 3 vols. London, 1929–1930.
D.D.	France: Ministère des Affaires Etrangères. *Documents Diplomatiques.*
Eur. Nouv.	*L'Europe Nouvelle.*
H.C. Deb.	Parliamentary Debates, Fifth Series: House of Commons, Official Report.
House	*The Intimate Papers of Colonel House.* Arranged by Prof. C. Seymour. London, 1928.
Lapradelle	Lapradelle, A. G. de: *La Paix de Versailles* (La Documentation internationale). Paris, 1929– .
Lloyd George: *Peace Treaties.*	Lloyd George, D.: *The Truth about the Peace Treaties.* 2 vols. London, 1938.
Lords Deb.	Parliamentary Debates, Fifth Series: House of Lords, Official Report.
Miller	Miller, D. H.: *My Diary at the Conference of Paris, 1918–1919.* With Docs. 22 vols. New York, 1924.
P.C.D.C.	Preparatory Commission for the Disarmament Conference Documents. Series I–X.
Rep. Comm. Report, 1920–1922.	Reparation Commission. Report on the Work of the Reparation Commission from 1920–1922. London. H.M.S.O. 1923.
Stresemann	*Gustav Stresemann. His Diaries, Letters, and Papers.* Edited and translated by Eric Sutton. London, 1935.
Toynbee	Toynbee, A. J.: *Survey of International Affairs, 1920–1923, 1924–* . London, 1925– .
U.S.A. Foreign Relations .	U.S.A.: Department of State. Papers relating to the Foreign Relations of the United States.
Wemyss: *Life and Letters* .	Wemyss, Lady V. W.: *Life and Letters of Lord Wemyss.* London, 1935.

PREFACE

THE present work is the outcome of research commenced five years ago on the Problem of French Security at the Paris Peace Conference. The completion of the work on this subject in the early months of 1940 coincided with an invitation from Chatham House to undertake a study of 'Anglo-French Relations in response to the German Problem' during the inter-war period. The request was made that I should explore the difficulties encountered in Anglo-French relations in the working out of the peace settlement. It seemed evident that no such analytical treatment would be possible save within a range extending from the formulation of war aims in 1914–1918 to the outbreak of the present war. For that reason it was agreed that I should merge the substance of the earlier work in the present Chatham House study.

This note is included in explanation of the scope and the plan of the present work. It is not designed as a complete narrative history. All those aspects of Anglo-French relations which are not directly related to the problem of Germany are of set purpose, for the sake of brevity, excluded. Much is omitted that strictly belongs to the history of this central problem, in order to make possible concentration on those episodes which appear most significant and instructive. I have dwelt on the early years of the period, during which Great Britain and France possessed the initiative in European affairs, and have skipped lightly over the events immediately preceding the present war, when Great Britain and France stood on the defensive. It is not to the closing years that the historian must turn in the search for such guidance as history offers to the understanding of the problems of European settlement.

It is impossible for me to express here my appreciation of the help received from all those by whose advice I have benefited. I cannot, however, refrain from making mention of those to whom I am most indebted: Professor C. K. Webster, whose constant encouragement kept me to my task which pressure of daily work would otherwise have caused me to abandon in its early stages; Professor P. Vaucher, for much helpful criticism; and my wife, without whose never-failing help and understanding this work could not have been continued nor brought to completion.

In accordance with the established practice of Chatham House, complete freedom has been granted me to exercise my own judgment in the writing of this book. Mine accordingly is the entire responsibility for all statements of fact and expressions of opinion.

W. M. JORDAN.

October 1942.

CONTENTS

x

CONTENTS

CHAPTER I

CONCEPTS OF PEACE: 1914–1918

IN 1918 Great Britain and France as Allies achieved, with the aid of the United States, a preponderance of power in Europe, which they retained until the reoccupation of the demilitarized zone by German forces on 7th March 1936. Throughout those eighteen years the divergence of French and British policy with regard to Germany was a primary cause of the failure to establish in Europe the conditions necessary for orderly development. In the present work this one factor in the breakdown of the Versailles settlement is singled out for examination, not from any desire to belittle the influence of other factors, social and economic, but solely on account of the limitations which necessarily circumscribe the range of any detailed and objective study.

The contrast between British and French policy may be stated in various ways. Expressed in the most general terms, the fundamental distinction consisted in the emphasis of the one on consent and of the other on coercion as the mainstay of European peace. The French were deeply conscious that the European settlement would be certainly shaken, and possibly overthrown, as soon as the distribution of power in which it was rooted was modified. Their principal anxiety was to ensure the retention of preponderant power by the upholders of the newly established order. The British, by contrast, were imbued with a conviction of the inevitable fragility of any settlement dependent for its preservation on the backing of superior force. Their inclination was to consent to a process of modification in the search for some permanent basis of friendly understanding.

Many considerations may be advanced to explain this difference in the temper of British and French policy. But among the numerous factors, many of them obscure and disputable, two may be singled out as influential above all others: the first geographic, the second moral, yet itself in some measure the reflection of the difference in geographic position.

In the introduction to *Studies in Diplomatic History*, a collection of memoranda written by Sir James Headlam-Morley as Historical Adviser to the Foreign Office during the first decade of the inter-war period, Sir James dwells on the influence exerted on British diplomacy by the wide dispersal of British interests:

'Like all other countries, England has but a limited amount of power, wealth, public credit, and political influence, and success requires a careful economy of resources. Just because the interests of this country are world-wide, just because there is no continent in which it has not political power and fields of economic enterprise, it is more than any other country exposed to the danger of pursuing conflicting aims and arousing political opposition, and, for this reason, objects which are desirable in themselves cannot all be attained at the same time; there must often be a sacrifice of material advantages, even a withdrawal from spheres of authority where we have established ourselves. . . .

'To this is largely due an element in the history of British policy which is often cause for unfavourable comment. There appears to be an uncertainty of touch, a vacillation and indecision, which is undoubtedly very inconvenient to those other nations who desire to co-operate with us, and which easily may give an impression of weakness.' [1]

Retirement; an appearance of vacillation and indecision; an impression of weakness: these, a Continental observer might not unjustly hold, were the characteristics displayed by British policy towards Europe in the first years of peace. Victory, which for Great Britain signified first and foremost the elimination of Germany as a naval Power, removed what in pre-War years had constituted the essential rivet of the Anglo-French *entente*. On the return of peace, imperial preoccupations diverted the attention of British statesmen from the Continent, whence it seemed that no danger would again threaten Great Britain within the calculable future. The British ideal for Europe during these years of peace was not the creation of a balance of power—that supposedly traditional concept of British policy was consciously rejected; still less was it the retention of preponderant power by the former victors of the War. The British ideal was a Europe whose ordering should command such general assent that the very justice of its arrangements would provide the true guarantee of their maintenance.

While the perplexities of British statesmanship arose from the variety of interests to be adjusted and of objectives to be pursued, the attention of French statesmanship was focused on a single problem of overwhelming import. That problem presented itself under a double guise: on the one hand, a preoccupation strictly self-regarding; on the other, a call to wider responsibilities. The first concern of France—and to this theme it will be necessary to return time and again—was to secure guarantees against renewed invasion. But hers could be no policy of entrenchment in the West; her status as a Great Power and her European outlook, her political traditions and the exigencies of national defence alike forbade it. France stood forward as the protector of the European order against violent overthrow. Yet of the frailty of French power Frenchmen were well aware. It rested not on a natural, but on a conventional basis—on the discriminatory restrictions imposed on Germany in the Treaty of Versailles. Those restric-

[1] Headlam-Morley, Sir J.: *Studies in Diplomatic History*, p. 3.

tions removed, Germany would, in the absence of countervailing safeguards, far outvie in strength all other states on the Continent. Hence the preoccupation of France with the problem of security: how to prevent the natural superiority of Germany in Europe from finding expression in political domination, how to save France in the future from German invasion—two aspects, be it repeated, of a single problem.

The contrast between British and French policy, which resulted from these diverse preoccupations, was accentuated by the difference between the impress of war on the French and the British people. An American writer of recent European origin has remarked that, to the Continental observer of British affairs, 'nothing was more amazing than the hold which the Wilsonian principles were able to gain on public opinion throughout the British isles and the Dominions' in the post-War years.[1] The explanation may well be that Great Britain was the home of Wilsonian idealism, which retained its hold, though in modified form, on wide sections of the British people and exercised a real influence on British policy.

The idealism which inspired the Allied cause in the Great War of 1914–1918 was, in the first instance, the achievement of British Liberalism. In 1914, till the very moment of Britain's entry into the War, the Liberal Press had protested with vigour and solemnity against British participation in the conflict; but from 4th August the British Liberals, with few exceptions, accepted the War, proclaiming the while that it must be fought for higher than material ends.[2] To their influence above all was due the sublimation of the War into an instrument of idealism.

The ideal aims formulated by British Liberalism may be grouped under three heads. The War was conceived, in the first place, as a war to end Prussian militarism. Inversely, it was a war for democracy. Few doubted but that the peace of Europe had been wrecked by an act of wanton aggression. The War then must continue until defeat had discredited for ever in the eyes of the German people their irresponsible rulers, the Kaiser and the Prussian military caste. So the War was a crusade for the emancipation of the German people. 'We are not fighting the German people,' Lloyd George declared to an audience of his Welsh fellow-countrymen in the second month of the War. 'The German people are just as much under the heel of this Prussian military caste . . . as any other nation in Europe. It will be a day of rejoicing for

---

[1] Wolfers, A.: *Britain and France between Two Wars*, p. 216.
[2] See Willis, I. C.: *How we went into the War*. National Labour Press, 1919 (?). Reprinted in Willis, I. C.: *England's Holy War: A Study of English Liberalism during the Great War*. New York, 1928. And Recktenwald, F.: *Kriegsziele und öffentliche Meinung Englands, 1916–1918*.

the German peasant and artisan and trader when the military caste is broken.'[1] In its overthrow was to be found the first promise of future peace. 'Democracy,' Lloyd George declared three years later, 'is in itself a guarantee of peace, and if you cannot get it in Germany, then we must secure other guarantees as a substitute.'[2]

Secondly, the War was a war for the liberation of nations. What had brought the British into the War as a united people was the sense of outrage provoked by the invasion of Belgium. To the realist a vital British interest, the re-establishment of Belgian independence was for all men the requirement of common justice. From the outset, as Elie Halévy observed, the War in the West assumed the character of a war in which the principle of nationality was at stake. Applied to central and south-eastern Europe, that principle shed its conservative character and assumed a revolutionary guise. From the first the British Liberals affirmed the need of the redivision of Europe along new lines. 'What we are fighting for is a new map of Europe'—so wrote H. G. Wells on the tenth day of war.[3] 'Let us then meet fate half-way and admit boldly that we want a new Europe,' wrote another whose knowledge of the Continent was more profound.[4]

Thirdly, the War was viewed as a war to end war. Democratic government throughout Europe, combined with a just territorial settlement, was to provide the surety of peace. The attainment of political independence by each European nation would signify the elimination of the principal cause of war. 'When once the soil of Europe has been divided between equal and free nationalities, it will be possible for every state in Europe to guarantee to all the others its possessions, and wars for European territory will in the nature of things cease, for the causes of them will have disappeared.'[5] A just territorial settlement would thus lay the foundations for the better organization of international relations. 'It is only by working down to the national units that we can work up to the organization within which they might co-operate without friction,' observed the acknowledged exponent of British Liberalism.[6] As to the form of the new organization there was much debate, but on one point general agreement. The semi-permanent division of the European Powers into two hostile diplomatic groups must cease. For the balance of power must be substituted a community of power. The War must end, affirmed *The Nation* on 15th August 1914, 'in the recognition that there are

---

[1] *The Times*, September 20, 1914.
[2] Scott, J. B.: *Official Statement of War Aims*, p. 118.
[3] Quoted Willis, I. C.: *How we went into the War*, p. 92.
[4] Seton-Watson, R. W.: *The War and Democracy*, p. 240.
[5] Headlam, J. W.: *The Peace Terms of the Allies*, p. 6.
[6] Hobhouse, L. T.: *The World in Conflict*, p. 84.

rights and duties which belong to the whole system of States. . . .
It must end, in a word, with the creation of a Concert.' [1]

For the British Liberal the War was thus a war for democracy,
a war for the liberation of the suppressed nations of Europe, a
war to end war. By their writings and propaganda they set the
tone of the declared war aims of Great Britain. The foremost
British official declaration—Lloyd George's speech of 5th January
1918—consisted of an elaboration of these three themes. 'Whatever may have been the objects for which the War was begun'—
to quote the language of the Labour Memorandum on War Aims
of December 1917—it was the determination to secure the realization of these ideals that kept the British nation as a whole nerved
for war.[2]

This interpretation could not but commend itself to the mass
of the French people. Democratic government, the liberation of
nations, the renunciation of conquest, peace between the peoples:
these were ideals which belonged even more to the heritage of
1789 than to the traditions of British Liberalism. Time and again
these ideals were proclaimed in those statements of war aims of
which France was so prodigal in 1917, before the advent of
Clemenceau to power. One example must suffice: Painlevé's
statement of 18th September 1917:

'Disannexation of Alsace-Lorraine, reparation of the injury and the
ruin caused by the enemy, the conclusion of a peace which shall not be a
peace of constraint and violence, containing within itself the germ of
future wars, but a just peace, through which no people, powerful or
weak, shall be oppressed, a peace whereby efficient guarantees protect
the society of nations against any aggression by one among them—such
are the noble war aims of France.' [3]

Yet, despite this bond of common idealism, the havoc of the
War in France was too great to permit the emergence in France
as in England of any belief in a facile and spontaneous reconciliation
with a regenerated foe. A telling description of the moral impress
of the War on France may be found in the opening pages of the
report on Franco-German relations drawn up by Henri Lichtenberger in 1922. The War caused among the French intense
loathing for the enemy, whose merciless cruelty they had felt
heavy upon them, whose methods of war they hated in their heart
of hearts, and whose combative spirit they feared for the future.
They bore in their souls the indelible impression that they had

---

[1] *The Nation*, August 15, 1914.
[2] See the study of Labour opinion in Brand, C. F.: *British Labour's Rise to Power*,
especially pp. 50-100.
[3] *Chambre: Débats*, September 18, 1917, p. 2409. See also Dahlin E.: *French and
German Public Opinion on Declared War Aims, 1914-1918*.

escaped by a desperate effort of their whole being from an enemy who was determined to annihilate them. They had no doubt that, if in a moment of weakness they had wavered, they would have received no mercy from the German victor.[1] That nightmare of apprehension was not easily, and never fully, shaken off in the post-War years. In peace the French continued to feel that they were confronted with a powerful and relentless machine which was being wound up slowly for another spring. Therein lay the origin of the insistent French demand that the elaboration of safeguards against Germany should precede any experiment in reconciliation.

Attention must be drawn, no matter how briefly, to another contrast between the impact of war upon the French and the British mind. What more natural than that men should turn for an explanation of the conflict to an examination of German political thought? Was it not possible, asked the Editor of the *Revue des Deux Mondes* of M. Boutroux, the doyen of French scholars, for him from his knowledge of German life and literature to throw light on the catastrophe through which Europe was passing? Boutroux's article proved the forerunner of a flood of works on '*la mentalité allemande*'; it set the trend of much later writing.[2] One sentence must suffice to indicate the direction of Boutroux's observations: 'German culture differs profoundly from what humanity understands by culture and civilization.' This notion of conflict between the tendencies of German thought and the heritage of European civilization, which in England proved a mere phenomenon of war, took root in the intellectual life of France. In the post-War years it continued the subject of anxious debate. The significance of this continuing discussion of 'Germanism' has been well expressed by the German scholar who more than any other has endeavoured to interpret French civilization to the German people. The very use of the term 'Germanism,' wrote E. R. Curtius, carries the implication that 'the German

---

[1] Lichtenberger, H.: *Relations between France and Germany*, pp. 9–14. The three sentences are taken, with minor alterations, from this work.

[2] Reference may be made to the excellent bibliography of French war literature: Vic, J.: *La Littérature de guerre*. *Manuel méthodique et critique des publications de langue française*. 5 vols. Paris, 1918–23. Boutroux's articles are in *Revue des Deux Mondes*, October 14, 1914 (reprinted as No. 27 in *Pages d'Histoire*); May 15, 1916; June 1, 1917. Charles Andler's veiled comment on Boutroux is worthy of quotation: 'Il y a une tristesse plus grande encore; c'est l'éclipse des vieux maîtres. J'en sais un, notre maître à tous, . . . qui a conquis sa plus authentique et durable gloire à enseigner Leibnitz, Kant et Fichte. . . . Il n'établissait alors d'antinomie entre *Germanisme* et *Humanité*. . . . Ceux qui ont appris de lui . . . assistent avec un silence stupéfait et douloureux à je ne sais quelle tentative de flatter des préventions qui ne sont pas seulement la fumée d'une flamme momentanée d'irritation, mais les prétextes dont se couvrent des puissances sociales occupées, dans la crise même de la patrie, à poursuivre une œuvre sournoise de captation d'influence.' (Andler, C.: *Les Origines du Pangermanisme*, p. viii.)

spirit constitutes an alien body, even perhaps a poison, in the organism of humanity. Germanism is presented as an ever-present threat to France, that is, to human civilisation.'[1] The reaction of France against Germany resulted not only from fear of Germany's overwhelming power but from a sense of dangers inherent in the German outlook on human affairs. In the last of M. Boutroux's articles may be found an apt expression of these mingled feelings:

'It is not the degree of perceptible strength which (Germany) will retain after the War which will be the measure of the perils to which she can again subject mankind; it is the persistence of her craving for domination, aggrandisement, and oppression. If we judge the future by the past, this craving, though hidden, dissembled, and denied, will continue to dominate. The Germany of to-morrow will be conscious of having for years stood against the whole world. Whatever happens, it is improbable that she will deem herself finally vanquished. . . . All measures necessary to reduce such an enemy to powerlessness will need to be maintained for a period which cannot at present be decided.'

Thus in the course of the War two attitudes of mind developed, the one looking forward towards reconciliation with a Germany purged of autocratic rule within the framework of an all-embracing League, the other seeking the assurance of peace in safeguards against the revival of German power. By the intervention of President Wilson the Allied Governments were committed at the close of the War to the conclusion of a peace with Germany which should accord with the principles of Liberal idealism. It remains to trace briefly the sequence of events which culminated in the acceptance by Germany and the Allied Governments of the bases of peace commonly—though by no means correctly—summed up as 'The Fourteen Points.'

From the time of America's entry into the War there dwelt in President Wilson's mind the conviction that, when the time came to make peace, the Allied Governments would be moved by baser motives than those which would inspire the action of his own country under his leadership. 'England and France have not the same views with regard to the peace that we have by any means,' Wilson wrote to his friend and adviser, Colonel House, in July 1917.[2] For this very reason Wilson and House deemed it impolitic in the first months of America's participation to precipitate a discussion of war aims. The division of opinion on ultimate objectives might, they realized, impede the military effort. But as the year drew to its close, Wilson and House revised their

[1] Curtius, E. R.: *Französischer Geist im neuen Europa*, p. 233.
[2] Baker, R. S.: *Woodrow Wilson, Life and Letters*, vii, p. 43.

judgement. The statement of war aims by America and the Allies in a liberal sense would, they were convinced, contribute to drive a wedge between the German people and their rulers. In December, at the Interallied Conference, House strove in vain to secure the acceptance of a broad declaration on peace terms. From this failure sprang the Fourteen Points. If the Allies would not speak together, President Wilson must speak alone.[1]

Wilson's historic speech was delivered at noon on Tuesday, 8th January 1918, to the assembled Houses of Congress. It was the forerunner of others of hardly less fame. For on three later occasions — in a speech to Congress on 11th February, at Mount Vernon on 4th July, and in the Metropolitan Opera House of New York at the opening of the Liberty Loan drive on 27th September—Wilson further proclaimed the necessary foundations of a peace of justice. These later speeches tended more to the enunciation of general principles; only the Fourteen Points laid down the lines of solution for individual problems.

During the night of 3rd October 1918 the German Government sent out an appeal to President Wilson for an armistice. 'The German Government,' the note read, 'accepts as a basis for the peace negotiations, the programme laid down by the President of the United States in his message to Congress of 8th January 1918, and in his subsequent pronouncements, particularly in his address of 27th September 1918.' The note was signed, 'Max, Prince of Baden, Imperial Chancellor.' Max, Prince of Baden, had assumed the office of Chancellor three days earlier. So a change of Government had come about in Germany, and the new Government was reaching out for a peace on the basis of the Fourteen Points. Was this the sign of the advent to power of new political forces in Germany? It is worth while recalling briefly what had happened to bring about this appeal.

On 27th September Ludendorff, the real dictator of German policy, was seized with the fear of an imminent military collapse. All prospect of victory had vanished long since; it disappeared when, on 18th July, the Allies began the counter-attack which brought the last German offensive to an end. Throughout August and the early days of September hope had centred on some temporary triumph of German arms which would provide the setting for the initiation of peace negotiations without humiliation on Germany's part. No such opportunity had come. Military prospects grew ever worse. The German line remained unbroken

[1] *House*, iii, pp. 39, 285; *U.S.A. Foreign Relations*, 1917, Suppl. 2, *The World War*, i, p. 352.

—but Ludendorff despaired of staving off for long a disastrous collapse.

Ludendorff was left with one desire—to save the German army —and, so he judged in his despair, one means for its realization— an armistice which would permit an orderly retreat by the German troops to stronger positions in the rear. He knew full well that Wilson would entertain no appeal from the rulers who bore the responsibility for the conduct of the War. The armistice must be sponsored by a new man, with no damaging past. So at Ludendorff's behest Max of Baden was called in as the puppet to further the latest phase of Ludendorff's conduct of military operations. 'Ludendorff gave the order for parliamentary government to be instituted in Germany and a Prince of Baden carried it out.' [1]

From the moment he learned of the task assigned him, Max of Baden had misgivings about the wisdom of the policy imperiously demanded by the Supreme Command. The urgent appeal to Wilson would, he insisted, be interpreted by Germany's enemies as a sign of weakness. They would become the more intransigeant. Better to proceed with due circumspection; he would first make a speech defining Germany's war aims 'in close but not undignified correspondence' with the Fourteen Points. He would invite all belligerent governments to negotiate on the basis stated. The Imperial Chancellor found himself devoid of power. The position was bluntly expressed in the Crown Council by the Kaiser. 'I am opposed to the offer being made,' the new Chancellor started off. The Kaiser interrupted him: 'The Supreme Command considers it necessary; and you have not been brought here to make difficulties for the Supreme Command.' [2]

Even after the note of 3rd October had been issued, Max of Baden still cherished a hope of mitigating the indignity of the sudden appeal. On 4th October he determined to make a speech to the Reichstag to give the German interpretation of the Fourteen Points. His experts laboured throughout the day on its composition. But his ministers advised against its delivery, and the Supreme Command vetoed it. The speech may yet be read by those who wish to learn what the Fourteen Points meant to the signatory of the German appeal. It is not without importance to bear in mind why from the German side came no interpretation of the Fourteen Points before their acceptance.

Ludendorff's naïve hope of an armistice which would permit the German army to strengthen its position was soon wrecked. The German appeal resulted in an exchange of notes between

---

[1] Rosenberg, A.: *The Birth of the German Republic*, p. 245.
[2] Max of Baden: *Memoirs*, ii, p. 16.

Wilson and the German Government which lasted till 27th October. President Wilson required the German Government to satisfy a series of conditions before he consented to broach officially the proposal of an armistice to the Allied Powers. The first condition related to the terms of Germany's acceptance of the Fourteen Points; President Wilson insisted on a more precise expression of agreement. The second condition related to the terms of armistice. Ludendorff had looked forward to a leisurely retirement of German forces from occupied territory which would permit the withdrawal of military material. He judged that the movement should last two or three months. The Allied Prime Ministers, who were meeting in Conference at Paris in the second week of October, feared that Wilson might fall into the trap. In a telegram to Wilson on 9th October they insisted that the determination of the military terms of armistice should be left to the Allied military experts. Mere evacuation of occupied territories, they pointed out, would permit the enemy to improve his military position; he might withdraw from a critical situation and re-form his units on a shorter front. Wilson's notes to Germany gave the Allies full satisfaction on this point.[1]

In the course of these armistice negotiations Max of Baden's Government had ceased to be Ludendorff's puppet. For Ludendorff had conjured up social forces which he could not control. They brought his power to an end. The army command had gravely misjudged the temper of the nation. Ludendorff had gambled on a speedy armistice. When it was found that only an armistice which registered a defeat of Germany would be accepted, Ludendorff was for breaking off the negotiations. But when the army command had laid bare Germany's weakness the people were in no mood to fight on. On 26th October Ludendorff resigned. Social Democratic and Centre Party Ministers, originally of little influence in the Cabinet, found themselves backed by popular feeling. The German people wanted peace, and first Ludendorff, then Max of Baden, and the Kaiser himself, were swept away by that longing.

When President Wilson received the German note of 20th October, which completed the German acceptance of his conditions, he debated for a time what action to take next. He must proceed to secure the adhesion of the Allies. How was this to be brought about? When, on the afternoon of 22nd October, the subject was discussed in a Cabinet meeting, the President declared, in reply to a comment by Lane, the Secretary of the Interior, that the

---

[1] Lloyd George: *War Memoirs*, vi, p. 3282. See also Foch, F.: *Memoirs*, ii, p. 273; Callwell, Sir C. E.: *Sir Henry Wilson*, ii, p. 135.

Allies 'needed to be coerced, that they were getting to a point where they were reaching out for more than they should have in justice.' [1] The President's decision was to send a final note to the German Government, and simultaneously to forward it, together with the preceding correspondence and a covering note, to the Allied Governments. Thereby Wilson's final communication to Germany became an integral part of his communication to the Allies. The implication of Wilson's action was that the Allies were invited to take the proposal for an armistice into consideration subject to two conditions, firstly their willingness to make peace on the terms put forward in Wilson's speeches, and secondly, approval of the armistice by Allied military experts on the basis of military considerations. Two problems were thereby raised, the first relating to the shaping of the future peace, the second to the content of the armistice. This second problem is taken up in the next chapter.

Wilson and House were agreed that the Allied Governments must be made to accept the Wilsonian bases of peace before the fighting was over. On 17th October House left for Europe in the conviction that this was the main, almost the sole, object of his mission. On arriving in Paris, on 26th October, House cannot indeed have expected any easy acquiescence by the Allies. Five days earlier Balfour had wired to the British *chargé d'affaires* in Washington that the British Government would object strongly to some interpretations of the Fourteen Points. Certain other terms to which the President made no reference would, Balfour added, probably have to be insisted upon. Care must be taken therefore 'to prevent the Allies from being deprived of the necessary freedom of action in the settlement of final terms in the Peace Conference.' Balfour's comments were passed on to Lansing, the American Secretary of State.[2] The French Government appear to have taken no steps to intimate their own misgivings. President Wilson in any event brushed objections lightly aside. There could, he informed House, be no real difficulty about peace terms nor about the interpretation of the Fourteen Points if the Entente statesmen were prepared to be perfectly frank and to have 'no selfish aims of their own.' House, for his part, was willing to sugar the pill. The commentary which was prepared at his behest by way of interpretation of the Fourteen Points was from the Allied viewpoint an accommodating document, and on 29th October he remarked to the Allied Ministers that the President had

---

[1] Lane, F. K.: *Letters*, pp. 293–295; Houston, D. F.: *Eight Years with Wilson's Cabinet*, pp. 307–311.
[2] Baker, R. S.: *Woodrow Wilson, Life and Letters*, viii, p. 479. See also *U.S.A. Foreign Relations*, 1918, Suppl. i, vol. i, pp. 365–367.

'insisted on Germany's accepting all his speeches, and from these you could establish almost any point that anyone wished against Germany.'[1]

Between 29th October and 4th November House met Clemenceau and Pichon, Lloyd George and Balfour, Sonnino and Orlando, in a series of informal conferences to discuss the armistice terms and the Fourteen Points. At the first conference Lloyd George drew attention to the integral connexion of the armistice proposal and the Wilsonian peace terms. If the Allies agreed to the armistice, he commented, they would be bound by those peace terms unless they stated clearly their reservations. Clemenceau agreed after some demur and asked 'that the Fourteen Points might be produced.' When for some time objections to the Wilsonian terms had been pressed, House interjected that, if the Allies refused to accept them, Wilson 'would have no alternative but to tell the enemy that his conditions were not accepted by his Allies. The question would then arise whether America would not have to take up these questions direct with Germany and Austria.' 'That would amount,' said Clemenceau, 'to a separate peace between the United States and the Central Powers.' 'It may lead to this,' House declared with perfect calm.[2] The following day he repeated the threat on finding that Clemenceau was having an elaborate brief prepared setting forth French objections. Thereupon Clemenceau abandoned his opposition. Four days later the Allied reply to President Wilson's note was formally adopted.[3] In consequence of House's threat the Fourteen Points were accepted by the Allied Governments, subject to two reservations only. The first related to Point II on freedom of the seas; the British Government reserved complete freedom on this subject in the peace negotiations. The second related to reparation; the Allied Governments affirmed, and at the same time limited, their legitimate claims to those for damage to civilian life and property. The Allied Memorandum was cabled to Washington on 4th November, and the following day an American note, commonly referred to as the Lansing Note, was dispatched to inform the German Government of this Allied reply.

It is well to recall briefly what were the terms which President Wilson required first Germany, and then the Allied Governments, to accept. They were 'the terms laid down by the President in his address to the Congress of the United States on the 8th January

---

[1] Lloyd George: *Peace Treaties*, i, p. 80.
[2] Aldrovandi, L.: *Guerra Diplomatica*, p. 190; Lloyd George: *Peace Treaties*, i, pp. 75–77.
[3] *House*, iv, chapter 6; Lloyd George: *Peace Treaties*, i, pp. 75–84; Aldrovandi, L.: *Guerra Diplomatica*, pp. 188–195; *U.S.A. Foreign Relations*, 1918, Suppl. i, vol. i, pp. 405–427.

last, and in subsequent addresses.' The Fourteen Points are too well known to need quotation afresh. But it may be noted that the speech of 8th January, which contained the Fourteen Points, was singled out not as of greater consequence than its successors, but as the first of a series. What the President demanded was not just the acceptance of specific solutions, but also the conclusion of peace in the spirit exemplified by his own proposals. Their keynote was impartiality—'even-handed and dispassionate justice,' in the President's sonorous phraseology. There was to be impartial justice in every item of the settlement, no matter whose interest was crossed. Every territorial settlement was to be made in the interest and for the benefit of the populations concerned. All colonial claims were to be impartially adjusted. No punitive damages were to be levied. Guarantees for the reduction of armaments were to be 'given and taken.' All parties were to join in the settlement of each issue. The peace was to be such as all parties could unite to guarantee and maintain. No exclusive alliances were to be permitted within the common family of the League of Nations. These were the principles which the President had laid down. Yet it should be recalled that in his speech of 27th September the President had struck a different note. 'Germany will have to redeem her character not by what happens at the peace table but by what follows.'

CHAPTER II

ARMISTICE AND PEACE: THE SIGNIFICANCE
OF THE MILITARY TERMS

STUDIES of the negotiations preceding the armistice have usually concentrated on the discussions which resulted in the Memorandum of 4th November, whereby the Allied Governments intimated their acceptance, with reservations, of Wilson's speeches as the basis of the future peace with Germany. Historians have paid little attention to the preparation of the document signed on 11th November 1918, which set out the military and naval terms with which Germany was required to comply as a condition of the suspension of warfare. The immediate purpose these terms were designed to serve was to assure the continuance of Allied military and naval superiority during the period of armistice. Their significance extended, however, beyond this limited objective; they were framed with an eye to the more permanent conditions of peace. It is the object of this chapter to examine the political implications of the military and naval terms of the armistice agreement with Germany of 11th November 1918.

It chanced that in the first week of October, when the world was wondering what reply Wilson would send to the German note of 3rd October, the Allied Ministers were meeting in conference at Versailles to consider the situation arising from the armistice which Bulgaria had signed on 29th September. They found themselves faced with the yet more momentous prospect of an armistice with Germany, and to this accordingly they turned their attention. The first rough draft of armistice terms for Germany was drawn up by the British, Italian, and French Ministers on 6th October. For the Western Front they proposed to demand only that the German army should evacuate France, Belgium, and Luxemburg, and withdraw to the other side of the Rhine. They did not stipulate that Allied troops should occupy even Alsace-Lorraine, still less the left bank of the Rhine. It was, however, intended that naval pressure on Germany should be maintained. The blockade was to be continued, while Germany was to be required to cease submarine warfare immediately.[1]

These proposals were drawn up by the Allied Ministers before consulting their military advisers. That step was taken next day, when it was agreed to refer the consideration of armistice terms to the military experts attached to the Supreme War Council. The experts met on the morning of 8th October. General Bliss, the American member, did not attend: he was in bed with a cold. The conclusion reached was that the ministerial proposals were far too weak to provide adequate security for the maintenance of the military ascendancy of the Allies. The military experts put forward proposals of a very different type, for they insisted that the two essential principles of the armistice should be 'the disarmament of the enemy under the control of the Allies,' and the concession of material guarantees for the maintenance of Allied military ascendancy. To the Allied Ministers' demand for the retirement of the Germans beyond the Rhine the experts accordingly made two additions. In the first place they proposed that Germany should surrender 'all arms and munitions of war and supplies between the present Front and the left bank of the Rhine.' In the second place they proposed to require the surrender within forty-eight hours of the fortresses of Metz, Thionville, Strasbourg, Neu-Breisach, and the town and fortifications of Lille.[2]

Meanwhile, Foch also was turning his mind to the subject of armistice terms. 'We are on the slope of victory,' he told Frazier,

---

[1] Lloyd George: *War Memoirs*, vi, p. 3275.
[2] Bliss, Gen. T. H.: 'The Armistices,' *A.J.I.L.*, xvi, pp. 513–514; Newbolt, H.: *Naval Operations*, v, p. 364; Callwell, Sir C. E.: *Sir Henry Wilson*, ii, p. 134.

the American diplomat, 'and victory has sometimes a way of galloping.' On 9th October Foch was called into the conference of Ministers. His proposals diverged markedly from the proposals both of the Ministers and of their military advisers. Foch insisted on three main stipulations. Firstly, evacuation within a time-limit. 'Countries invaded contrary to all right' were to be evacuated by the German army within a fortnight and their population immediately repatriated. Included among these countries were not only Belgium, France, and Luxemburg, but also Alsace-Lorraine. Secondly, the occupation of bridgeheads as a measure of military security. Within a fortnight the Allied armies were to occupy bridgeheads on the Rhine at Rastadt, Strasbourg, and Neu-Breisach. Each bridgehead was to consist of a semicircular zone of territory on the right bank with a radius of thirty kilometres from each bridge as a centre. The object was to secure for the Allied armies 'a suitable military basis of departure permitting us to pursue the War up to the destruction of the enemy force in case the peace negotiations should lead to no result.' At the commencement of October the Allied armies were still too far from the northern Rhine to justify the demand for the occupation of bridgeheads there, but since the Allied armies were nearer the Rhine in the south Foch felt justified in demanding bridgeheads there, so that the Allies could cross the Rhine in the event of the resumption of hostilities. Foch's third demand was the occupation of the left bank of the Rhine as security for the payment of reparation. The Germans were to withdraw across the Rhine within thirty days. In addition to these three primary conditions Foch included certain supplementary terms which do not call for restatement. Most significant is the omission by Foch of the demand for the complete disarmament of the German army, which the military advisers of the Supreme War Council deemed essential. For this demand Foch substituted the requirement that the German army should abandon without destruction all war material which it should fail to remove within the period allowed for the rapid withdrawal beyond the Rhine.[1]

When, two days later, Foch gave Sir Douglas Haig a copy of these draft armistice terms he told Haig that 'his proposals had been warmly welcomed.' [2] But it may be doubted whether Foch's proposals met with such ready agreement from the Ministers. Balfour remarked, when Foch's proposals were read out, that they amounted virtually to a demand for unconditional capitulation. Both Lloyd George and Baron Sonnino thought that not merely Foch but also the Military Representatives were asking too much. Since, however, on 8th October the Conference of Ministers knew

[1] Lloyd George: *War Memoirs*, vi, p. 3277.
[2] Duff Cooper, A.: *Haig*, ii, p. 394.

nothing of the reply which would come from President Wilson in response to the German Note, they concluded that it was not much good at this stage discussing the matter at length. So the Conference broke up without attempting to reach any decision, and the Ministers returned home.[1]

The considerations which went to the shaping of the armistice terms will be the more clearly appreciated if a brief comment is added on the naval terms put forward in the first days of October. The Prime Ministers, in their statement of 8th October, inserted only one naval condition—the immediate cessation of submarine warfare. They added, however, a note that the Allied blockade would not be raised.[2] The naval experts incorporated these two proposals in their draft on 8th October, and they added a few further stipulations. Heligoland was to be surrendered to the Allied Naval Commander-in-Chief of the North Sea. Sixty submarines were 'to proceed at once to specified Allied ports, and to stay there during the Armistice.' All enemy surface ships and naval air forces were 'to be concentrated in bases specified by the Allies and to remain there during the Armistice.' These initial naval terms were indeed modest; the armistice terms eventually signed were far more severe.

After this Allied Conference of 5th–9th October the question of armistice terms was earnestly debated by the British Government. On his return from France Lloyd George reported the discussions to the Imperial War Cabinet. Sir Douglas Haig was summoned to London to discuss the subject with the British Ministers. He crossed on the 18th, and on the morning of the 19th went to Downing Street with Sir Henry Wilson to meet Lloyd George, Milner, and Bonar Law. On Monday, 21st October, a long Cabinet Meeting was held, lasting from 11.15 A.M. until 6 P.M. Lloyd George said it was the longest Cabinet Meeting he had known. Next day, 22nd October, Haig returned to France. Sir Henry Wilson crossed on the 26th, and the Prime Minister shortly after. Negotiations were by then due to commence between Colonel House and the representatives of the Allied countries on the Fourteen Points and on the armistice terms to be offered to Germany.[3]

During this interval between the Conferences at the beginning and the end of October Lloyd George was apprehensive that unconditional acceptance of the Fourteen Points by the Allies might involve the sacrifice of their most important and essential

---

[1] Lloyd George: *War Memoirs*, vi, p. 3278.
[2] Lloyd George: *War Memoirs*, vi, pp. 3275–3276.
[3] Newbolt, H.: *Naval Operations*, v, p. 366; Duff Cooper, A.: *Haig*, ii, pp. 395–399; Lloyd George: *War Memoirs*, vi, pp. 3299–3304; Callwell, Sir C. E.: *Sir Henry Wilson*, ii, pp. 142–143.

war aims. He gave voice to his anxiety at the meetings of the Imperial War Cabinet to which reference has been made. The solution suggested by Lloyd George was that the armistice conditions should be made to approximate as closely as possible to the final conditions of peace. In this way the political aims of the Allies would be safeguarded by the armistice itself. The way would then be open for the acceptance of Wilson's Fourteen Points.

For the British naval authorities Lloyd George's dictum involved a new approach to the problem of naval armistice terms. The First Sea Lord was prompt to point out its implications. An ordinary naval armistice, he said, was one which ensured a cessation of hostilities at sea. For this purpose the naval terms hitherto contemplated—the cessation of submarine warfare, the surrender of sixty submarines, the maintenance of the blockade, and the withdrawal of the German fleet to bases approved by the Allies— would be sufficient. But a naval armistice approximating to the final peace would 'have to deal with the German fleet as an instrument of high policy, not merely as a combative force.' [1] It was on this new basis that the British Admiralty drafted its naval terms of armistice on 16th October. The new proposals included one drastic demand which had not figured among the proposals of the Naval Representatives who on 8th October had viewed the armistice as a simple cessation of hostilities. The new demand was for the surrender of the German fleet, a demand incorporated because, as Wemyss informed Beatty on 26th October, 'so far as the naval terms are concerned it is impossible not to embody terms of peace.' Lloyd George was perturbed by the proposed application of his dictum. Both he and Milner thought the terms proposed too stiff. [2]

It was, however, made equally clear at the Cabinet Meeting on 19th October that the military terms also would depend on the peace terms which it was desired to enforce. The military view was voiced by Sir Henry Wilson and Sir Douglas Haig. But they did not speak in unison. Wilson insisted on the principle of disarmament which the Military Representatives had put forward on 8th October, but he also asserted that in addition the Allies ought to hold assets which would enable them to enforce all the terms which they thought absolutely essential to peace, e.g. the establishment of a Polish state, indemnities for Belgium. To ensure German compliance with such peace terms the Allies ought to occupy German territory up to the Rhine. Bonar Law and

[1] Newbolt, H.: *Naval Operations*, v, p. 366; Wemyss: *Life and Letters*, pp. 398–399.
[2] Wemyss: *Life and Letters*, p. 386; cf. Callwell, Sir C. E.: *Sir Henry Wilson*, ii, pp. 138–139.

Balfour rather agreed with Wilson.[1] But Haig had come to the conclusion that the evacuation of Alsace-Lorraine and its occupation by the Allies were all that could be reasonably and safely demanded. In his opinion it was unnecessary from the point of view of British war aims to go further. Lloyd George and Milner were inclined to agree with Haig. When Balfour spoke about deserting the Poles and the people of Eastern Europe, Lloyd George remarked that we could not expect the British people to go on sacrificing their lives for the Poles.[2]

Of the deliberations among French Ministers on the subject of the armistice, if any took place, nothing is known. Clemenceau, however, took a decisive step on the morning of 24th October, as soon as he learnt of President Wilson's note inviting the Allied Governments to consider the question of an armistice. Immediately Clemenceau summoned Foch and Pétain to Paris. The commanders arrived at the Ministry of War in the course of the afternoon. The Prime Minister instructed them to draw up armistice terms and signified his acceptance of the Foch proposals of 8th October, adding that they should be fortified in view of the progress of the Allied armies since that date. Foch was instructed to call the Commanders-in-Chief of the Allied armies to a conference and to hear their views.[3]

The following day Haig, Pershing, and Pétain met Foch at his headquarters at Senlis. Foch was already aware of the very vital difference of opinion between himself and Sir Douglas Haig, with whom he had discussed the question of armistice terms the previous day.[4] At the meeting at Senlis Foch asked the Commanders-in-Chief to state in turn what they thought should be the armistice conditions. Haig spoke first, then Pétain, and finally Pershing. Marshal Foch did not state with any precision his own views during the Conference itself. He drew up his draft of the armistice conditions after the close of the meeting, and on the afternoon of the following day he took the draft to Paris and handed it to both Poincaré and Clemenceau.

The draft armistice conditions which Foch drew up on 26th October were an elaboration of his draft of 8th October. He demanded still the evacuation of Belgium, France, Alsace-Lorraine, and Luxemburg within a fortnight. The enemy were to evacuate these territories, under conditions of time which would make it impossible for them to remove a large part of the material

[1] Callwell, Sir C. E.: *Sir Henry Wilson*, ii, p. 138.
[2] Duff Cooper, A.: *Haig*, ii, p. 397.
[3] Foch: *Memoirs*, p. 536; Mordacq, Gen. J. J. H.: *Le Ministère Clemenceau*, ii, p. 292; Weygand: 'Le Maréchal Foch et l'armistice,' *Revue des Deux Mondes*, November 1938, vol. 48, p. 16.
[4] Foch: *Memoirs*, p. 356.

of war and supplies that were stored there. Foch specified a minimum quantity of material to be abandoned by the enemy— 5000 guns, 30,000 machine-guns, and 3000 mine-throwers. The left bank of the Rhine was to be evacuated within twenty-two days, whereas thirty days had been allowed by the draft of 8th October. The Allied armies were to occupy bridgeheads at Mainz, Coblenz, and Cologne as well as at Strasbourg. Foch included one proposal not found in the earlier draft: a neutral zone was to be established, forty kilometres wide, on the right bank of the Rhine from the Swiss to the Dutch frontier. Three more days were allowed for the evacuation of this zone. Until the armistice conditions were fully carried out the blockade would be maintained. Foch expected the period to be twenty-five days. He concluded with a statement of the naval terms which he favoured.[1]

Of the three commanders consulted by Foch at Senlis, Pétain alone appears to have shared Foch's views. He gave his opinion that the best way to render the Germans incapable of further fighting was to deprive them of their material. The Germans should be required to withdraw rapidly according to a schedule he had prepared. If this movement were started at once, the Germans would find it impossible to remove their material, especially the heavy guns and ammunition.[2]

These armistice terms advocated by Foch and Pétain were deemed too severe by Sir Douglas Haig. Haig wanted no more than the evacuation of France, Alsace-Lorraine, and Belgium. He proposed that the Allied armies should occupy Metz and Strasbourg.[3] His opposition to the proposals put forward by Foch and Pétain sprang from both military and political considerations. In Haig's opinion, Foch's terms went far beyond what the military situation justified. He feared that, if terms so humiliating as to be unacceptable to Germany were insisted on, the *moral* of the German army would be restored. The German army, he considered, was still capable of retiring to the German frontier and holding a new defensive line for some time after the commencement of the 1919 campaign. In his opinion, the condition of the Allied and Associated armies was not such as to permit a serious offensive which would overthrow the enemy divisions before they reached the line of the Meuse. In the coming months, he believed, the brunt of the fighting would be borne by British troops. A large proportion of the French armies, he had told the Cabinet, would probably be black in 1919.

It was not, however, merely because Haig was rather more

---

[1] *House*, iv, pp. 145–148.
[2] Pershing, Gen. J. J.: *My Experiences*, ii, p. 361; Foch: *Memoirs*, p. 538.
[3] Duff Cooper, A.: *Haig*, ii, p. 397.

pessimistic than Foch in his estimate of military prospects that he supported moderate armistice terms. Behind the dispute between Foch and Haig lay divergent conceptions of the interests for which security was to be sought. For the military terms of the armistice depended on the nature of the peace terms that were to follow. In western Europe Haig envisaged only the restoration of Alsace-Lorraine. Evacuation by Germany would be sufficient to secure the achievement of this aim. Haig reasoned that his own proposals would give the Allies possession of all the territory of which they wished to dispose in the west at the Peace Conference, so that, if the armistice broke down, it would not be necessary for the Allies to attack but for the enemy to do so. Haig desired armistice terms no more severe than those required to give security for the realization of British war aims in the west. 'The British Army has done most of the fighting latterly, and everyone wants to have done with the war, *provided* we get what we want,' he told the War Cabinet on 19th October. 'I therefore advise that we only ask in the armistice for what we intend to hold, and that we set our face against the French entering Germany to pay off old scores. In my opinion, under the supposed conditions, the British army would not fight keenly for what is really not its own affair.' [1]

It was because he believed that the more drastic nature of Foch's terms could not be ascribed to military, but only to political considerations, that Haig opposed them. He denied that the retirement of the Germans to the eastern side of the Rhine, even if the Allies held bridgeheads, would put the Allies in a more favourable military position than if the Germans were left entrenched behind the old frontier of 1870. He expressed this view at the Senlis meeting on 25th October. Perhaps it was to meet Haig's argument on this point that Foch added the further demand for a neutral zone on the right bank of the Rhine. The addition may have removed the basis of Haig's military objections to the conditions advocated by Foch, but of their political implications Haig remained critical. From the Senlis meeting he gathered the impression 'that the insistence of the two French generals on the left bank of the Rhine means that they now aim at getting hold of the Palatinate as well as of Alsace-Lorraine. Pétain spoke of taking a huge indemnity from Germany, so large that she will never be able to pay it. Meantime, French troops will hold the left bank of the Rhine as a pledge.' [2]

It was, however, on military grounds that Foch justified his armistice proposals. He maintained that his proposals alone were adequate to safeguard the military superiority of the Allies during

[1] Duff Cooper, A.: *Haig*, ii, p. 397.
[2] Duff Cooper, A.: *Haig*, ii, pp. 399–400; Pershing, Gen. J. J.: *My Experiences*, ii, p. 361.

the period of the armistice.   When, on 1st November, Foch was endeavouring to induce the British Premier to accept his views, Foch reasoned that Haig's proposals violated the principle that the armistice must not make it possible for Germany to put herself in a stronger military position.   He maintained that the German army would be able, if Haig's proposals were adopted, to retire to the right bank of the Rhine and prepare a strong line of defence. Should Germany at a later date decide to resume the contest, rather than submit to the terms of peace when formulated, her military position would have grown stronger.   'If Germany should break off the peace negotiations, the Allies ought to be in a position to destroy her.'   Only the occupation of bridgeheads would put the Allies in this position.   'Without the bridgeheads we could never be master of Germany.   It was essential first to be master of the Rhine.' [1]

If both Foch and Haig justified their armistice proposals on the grounds of their military adequacy, both were right.   Because Foch had in mind political arrangements to result from the Peace Conference which went far beyond those envisaged by Haig, Haig's proposals were far below Foch's standard of adequacy.   The more drastic peace terms contemplated by Foch might well encounter German rejection.   To enforce them, further military operations against Germany might be necessary.   It was not security against attack during the period of armistice that Foch required so much as security for the exertion of requisite military pressure on Germany to make her accept the peace terms he contemplated.   Included among these was the demand for indemnities.   It was 'as security for reparations to be exacted for the destruction perpetrated in Allied countries' that Foch had demanded the occupation of the left bank of the Rhine in his draft terms of 8th October. [2]

But Foch was not thinking of indemnities alone.   His goal was a Rhineland detached from Germany.   If his ambition was to be realized, it was essential to bring the territory under the control of Allied forces.   No less clearly than Lloyd George did he realize that permanent war aims must be secured in and through the armistice.   'You must strike while the iron is hot.   If France intended to separate the Rhineland from Prussia, there was no time to be lost in shaping the Armistice accordingly.' [3]   Forcible expression to the interconnection of military conditions and political objectives is given in the letter which Foch sent to Clemenceau on 16th October.   What, he asked, was to be the fate of the left bank of the Rhine after reparations had been paid?   'Are we to continue

---

[1] *House*, iv, pp. 122–126.
[2] Foch: *Memoirs*, p. 527.
[3] Quoted Liddell Hart, B. H.: *Foch, Man of Orleans*, ii, p. 414.

in occupation? Are we going to annex a part of this territory, or to favour the creation of neutral, autonomous, or independent states, forming a buffer? Should the armistice make complete reservations at this time as to the fate of these territories? These are questions concerning which it is important that the military commander, whose duty it will be to sign the armistice, and discuss its terms when a request for it has been presented, be informed, after a study of them made beforehand with the Government concerned. For it is certain that the armistice should give us full guarantees for obtaining, in the course of the peace negotiations, the terms that we wish to impose upon the enemy; and it is evident that only the advantages secured to us by the armistice will remain to us; that only the sacrifices of territory agreed to by the enemy at the time of signing the armistice will be final.' [1]

Foch, it has been noted, did not state his own views at the Senlis Conference on 25th October. He listened first to Haig, then to Pétain. The views of the fourth member of the Conference have yet to be discussed. What had Pershing to say? Haig expected that Pershing would back him up. For on 23rd October Haig had entertained Pershing to lunch, and in the course of conversation Haig gathered the impression that Pershing was in agreement with him about the demands which should be made on Germany. Haig was naturally chagrined when at Senlis, two days later, Pershing took much the same view as Foch.[2] On 25th October, as later, Pershing at heart was in favour of continuing the War until a complete victory in the field by the Allies forced Germany to unconditional surrender. But he did not express this view at Senlis, for he had received no clear indication of the proper scope of the discussion. He understood that the conference had been summoned so that the Commanders-in-Chief might be ready to recommend military conditions *if* the Governments decided in favour of the principle of granting Germany an armistice. He could not properly plead that there be no truce at a conference the purpose of which excluded such advocacy. So he proposed the terms which would, in his opinion, yield the most nearly the results which he expected from complete surrender.[3]

Pershing's proposals resembled those of Foch. They were less rigorous in that they would allow Germany thirty days for the evacuation of France and Belgium, exclusive of Alsace-Lorraine, and included no mention of the surrender of arms; they coincided with those of Foch in the demand for evacuation and Allied occupation of Alsace-Lorraine, and the withdrawal of German armies

[1] Foch: *Memoirs*, p. 534.
[2] Duff Cooper, A.: *Haig*, ii, p. 399.
[3] Pershing, Gen. J. J.: *My Experiences*, ii, p. 359; Mott, J. B.: *Twenty Years as a Military Attaché*, p. 266.

to the east of the Rhine and Allied occupation of bridgeheads on the east side of the Rhine. They exceeded Foch's proposals in stipulating the surrender to the control of a neutral Power not only of U-boats, but of U-boat bases, and the unrestricted transportation of the American army across the sea.

From 25th to 29th October, while Pershing was confined to bed with influenza, reflection strengthened his sense of the urgency of continuing the struggle. On 30th October, Colonel Mott, the American Attaché, was interrupted in the enjoyment of his dinner at Marshal Foch's headquarters by a message to go immediately to see Pershing in Paris. Mott found Pershing pacing up and down in a dressing-gown, swearing copiously in the hope of relieving a violent toothache for which the dentist could suggest only an opiate as a remedy—a remedy which Pershing felt bound to reject at a moment when, as he told Mott, 'I have too much need for all my senses.' Pershing handed Mott a memorandum on the military situation. It concluded: 'It is the experience of history that victorious armies are prone to over-estimate the enemy's strength and too eagerly seek an opportunity for peace. This mistake is likely to be made now on account of the reputation Germany has gained through her victories of the last four years. I believe that complete victory can only be obtained by continuing the war until we force unconditional surrender from Germany.' Pershing told Mott to take the message to Foch with the utmost speed. 'There is still time to put into the conditions anything the Allies consider essential.' Mott arrived at Senlis after Foch had gone to bed, and had to wait till next morning, when Foch was on the point of setting off for the meeting of the Supreme War Council at Versailles, before delivering the message. Foch read Pershing's letter attentively. Then, with a backward gesture of the hand which signified difficulties to be brushed aside, Foch replied, 'Tell General Pershing that I am in agreement with his views, and he need not be anxious regarding this matter: what I am demanding from the Germans is the equivalent of what he wants, and when I have finished with them they will be quite powerless to do any further damage.' [1]

General Bliss, the American Military Representative to the Supreme War Council, was not consulted by Foch. Naturally Bliss was excluded from the discussions between the Commanders-in-Chief. But he urged his point of view in a memorandum which he laid before Colonel House on 28th October. The first and only requirement of the military terms, General Bliss maintained, should be to ensure the absolute surrender of Germany. Germany must be made completely incapable of resuming the War. This was what President Wilson desired. Only so could the Peace Conference

[1] Mott, J. B.: *Twenty Years as a Military Attaché*, p. 267.

meet in the assurance that there would be no further disturbance of the peace. Foch's terms, he maintained, did not satisfy this condition. The organization of Hindenburg's army of $4\frac{1}{2}$ million men would be left intact. The German infantry would remain in full possession of its armament, including reserve arms and munitions. The Allies possessed no certain information of the amount of artillery and number of machine-guns in the possession of the German army, nor of the capacity of the German plants to produce new material during the period of armistice. The surrender of the 5000 guns, 30,000 machine-guns, and 3000 mine-throwers demanded by Foch would leave the Germans with an unknown quantity of these weapons. German forces from all theatres of war could be concentrated on German soil in selected positions for national defence. Their spirit would be revived by consciousness that the renewed struggle would be not for aggression but for home defence. If, during the armistice, 'this army can receive its missing armament, either from reserve stores of which there is no absolutely certain information, or from any other source, it is ready to receive it, and then might again become a formidable object to deal with.' The apprehensions of the Allied statesmen in 1919 were to show that these were no fancy fears.[1]

The military terms proposed by Bliss were in a sense more rigorous than those desired by Foch. He concluded his memorandum of 28th October with the statement:

'I, therefore, propose the following:

'First, that the Associated Powers demand complete military disarmament and demobilization of the active land and naval forces of the enemy, leaving only such interior guards as the Associated Powers agree upon as necessary for the preservation of order in the home territory of the enemy. This, of course, means the evacuation of all invaded territory, and its evacuation by disarmed and not by armed or partly armed men. The army thus disarmed cannot fight, and demobilized cannot be reassembled for the purposes of this war.

'Second, that the Associated Powers notify the enemy that there will be no relaxation in their war aims but that these will be subject to full and reasonable discussion between the nations associated in the war; and that even though the enemy himself may be heard on some of these matters, he must submit to whatever the Associated Powers finally agree upon as being proper to demand for the present and for the future peace of the world.'

While Bliss criticized Foch's terms on grounds of military inadequacy, he also was dismayed by what he considered their political implications. Foch's proposals he described as 'partial disarmament by the enemy, accompanied by imposition of certain

[1] Bliss, Gen. T. H.: 'The Armistices,' *A.J.I.L.*, xvi, pp. 516–517; *House*, iv, p. 149.

conditions which apparently foreshadow [and will be regarded by the enemy as foreshadowing] certain of the peace terms.' Bliss realized, like Foch, that the military terms of armistice could be so drawn as to leave their impress on the final conditions of peace, and his conclusion was that the decision about the military conditions could not reasonably be entrusted solely to the military advisers. He wrote to Baker, the American Secretary:

'I do not believe that, in this peculiar case, the question of conditions of a so-called armistice should be left to the military men *alone*. The trouble is that it is not an armistice. It is an absolute surrender that we must have. But in order to get that surrender the conditions which are to follow it should be determined in advance and made known. All of the military propositions for an armistice that I have seen plainly embody or point to the political conditions which will exist after the so-called armistice is agreed to. These political conditions, imposed in the armistice, will be doubtless demanded by the political people in the discussion of final terms. At the same time, these political conditions imposed by military men alone may be such as to keep the world in turmoil for many years to come.' [1]

Why, it may be asked, did Foch not welcome this insistence on complete disarmament and demobilization of the German army? To this question more than one answer has been given. Of the efficacy of disarmament as a guarantee of security Foch in 1918, as in 1919, was sceptical. To him it appeared that the process of disarmament would be impossible of control. An enemy would find loopholes of escape. 'Nothing is easier than to propose and even to impose conditions on paper. It is simple and logical to demand the disarmament of the German armies in the field. But how will you make sure of it? Will you pass through the German armies and occupy before them the Rhine crossings? Demobilization? I am willing. But do you intend to occupy the whole of Germany? For if we do not occupy the whole of Germany, we shall never be certain that demobilization has been carried out.' [2] Faced with the choice of two courses, either to establish the Allied army in a position of unchallengeable military strength or to weaken the enemy army beyond hope of recovery, he chose the former.

It is not unreasonable to suggest that there was yet a further reason why Foch rejected the total disarmament of Germany. Such a course would afford no grounds for the occupation of the Rhineland and of the Rhine bridges which Foch designed to secure as the permanent basis of the security of France. A comment by Bliss in his Memorandum of 28th October had for Foch a barbed

[1] Palmer, F.: *Bliss*, p. 344 (Bliss to Baker, October 23, 1918). See also his cable of 3rd November in Baker, R. S.: *Woodrow Wilson, Life and Letters*, viii, p. 547.
[2] Tardieu: *La Paix*, p. 74.

meaning: 'If we secure complete disarmament and demobilization of the active land and naval forces no other guaranty against resumption of hostilities is needed and the Powers concerned will be guaranteed the attainment of all their just war aims.'[1] For Foch the occupation of the main crossings of the Lower Rhine had not only the merit of providing the jumping-off line for a march to Berlin, but also of making it possible to close the channels of communication between Berlin and the Rhineland.

The study of the conflict of views between Haig, Foch, and Bliss reveals clearly enough that the basic problems of the military terms of armistice were of a political and not of a military order. For Foch the military terms of armistice foreshadowed the peace. But final decisions would have to be taken by the political heads— by the Allied Prime Ministers in conjunction with Colonel House. House arrived in Paris the day after the Senlis Conference. He had come expressly to anchor the coming peace securely on the Fourteen Points. His work has in part already been discussed. In securing Franco-British acceptance of the Wilsonian basis he felt that his mission had been achieved. What was his attitude to the military terms? Did he appreciate the interdependence of military terms and political objectives as did Foch, Bliss, and Haig?

When Colonel House arrived in Paris on 26th October he had little time for reflection. He saw Milner and Haig the same day. In the evening Clemenceau gave him Foch's armistice terms, intimating that they were to be treated as a matter of great confidence. The following morning he discussed the armistice with General Bliss. 'I hope to get to the bottom of the situation before the meeting of the Supreme War Council on Tuesday,' he wired to Wilson.[2] It is safe to say that this laudable and moderate ambition remained unachieved. For Colonel House conceived that his task was to concern himself closely only with securing Allied acceptance of the Fourteen Points. The military terms of the armistice he regarded as purely a military question. On 1st November he expressed his opinion 'that he was not disposed to take from Germany more than was absolutely necessary, but he was disposed to leave the matter in Marshal Foch's hands.' He was equally prepared to accept the lead of the English representatives in naval affairs.[3]

Professor Seymour claims that, though Colonel House accepted the military terms put forward by Foch and the naval terms of the British, 'the entire process of drafting the armistice was none the

[1] *House*, iv, p. 150.
[2] Baker, R. S.: *Woodrow Wilson, Life and Letters*, viii, p. 520.
[3] *House*, iv, pp. 123, 138. For the very different attitude adopted by Wilson, see Baker, R. S.: *Woodrow Wilson, Life and Letters*, viii, pp. 521–523; and Pershing, Gen. J. J.: *My Experiences*, ii, p. 364.

less dominated by the President's policy as laid down in his notes
to Germany.'[1] The claim is hardly well founded. For House
was of the opinion that the political arrangements of the Peace
Conference were ensured by the acceptance of the Fourteen Points.
There is no evidence that he realized the political implications of
the military terms. In his mind the armistice took on the pure
shape of the platonic form. Lloyd George saw differently when he
pronounced the dictum: 'the terms of armistice should contain
as nearly as possible the terms of peace.'[2] Foch saw differently.
'As for the notion . . . that a general works on one side of a
barrier and the politicians and diplomats on the other, there is
nothing more false, or one can even say more absurd. War is
not a dual object, but a unity; so, for that matter, is peace. . . .
The two aspects are clearly and inseparably linked.'[3] Can it be
claimed that the armistice was a great diplomatic victory for the
U.S.A.? The Fourteen Points were enshrined in an Allied Note
for the world's admiration, but concealed in the interstices of the
armistice terms lay the provisions of peace on which France and
Great Britain would insist.

Armistice terms were discussed, along with the Fourteen Points,
by Colonel House, Lloyd George, Clemenceau, and Orlando in the
series of private meetings between 29th October and 4th November.
With them lay the responsibility for the final decision about military
and naval terms. Who were to be their military counsellors? If,
as Foch claimed, the Commanders-in-Chief alone were competent,[4]
Haig would stand against Foch. If the recognized advisers of the
Supreme War Council had a claim to be consulted, Bliss would
plead the cause of disarmament and demobilization. In this trio
of voices there could be no doubt which would dominate. Foch
alone was heard in conference by House and the Allied Ministers.
Haig was not heard in person: his views were stated, or mis-
stated, by the British Prime Minister. General Bliss had only the
satisfaction of presenting his Memorandum to Colonel House on
the morning of 28th October and of hearing the same day that the
Prime Ministers rejected his plea, because Foch insisted that the
Germans would not accept complete disarmament.[5] Discussion
centred on the draft terms presented by Foch. By his initiative
Foch had achieved a considerable diplomatic success. The
question of the occupation of German territory would be well to
the forefront.

The discussion on the military terms between Colonel House

---

[1] Seymour, C.: *American Diplomacy in the World War*, p. 364.
[2] Wemyss: *Life and Letters*, p. 398.
[3] Quoted Liddell Hart, B. H.: *Foch, Man of Orleans*, ii, p. 413.
[4] Foch: *Memoirs*, p. 533.   [5] *House*, iv, pp. 117–119.

and the Allied Prime Ministers is too familiar to need retelling in detail. It may be followed in the easily accessible *Intimate Papers of Colonel House*, to which there is little to add. Lloyd George expressed his opinion that it might be unwise to insist on the occupation of the east bank of the Rhine, but he allowed himself to be won over by Foch. If at any time House had objections, they melted before the sympathy he felt for the claim that French honour required occupation. From what is known of the discussion it would appear that though both Haig and Bliss had insisted on the unreality of considering armistice terms in their military aspects apart from their political implications, and though in fact this view was shared by Foch, the Allied statesmen accepted Foch's terms purely on military grounds. The fate of the Rhineland became the subject of political dispute only after the Peace Conference met.

The final naval terms of armistice, no less than the military terms, bore the impress of political considerations. The naval proposals submitted by the British Admiralty on 28th October marked a real advance on those put forward earlier in the month. The Admiralty now proposed to demand the surrender of all German submarines afloat, of the flagship *Baden*, of ten dreadnought battleships, six battle cruisers, eight light cruisers, and fifty destroyers. Colonel House and the Allied Ministers felt that these terms were too severe. Lloyd George agreed to specify a certain number of submarines to be surrendered; but Admiral Wemyss fixed the number at 160 in the expectation—which proved correct—that this number would cover all the submarines in Germany's possession. Lloyd George agreed also to drop the demand for the flagship *Baden*, and to be content with the internment of the battleships in neutral ports with nucleus crews on board. This arrangement, he suggested, would be more acceptable to the Germans, who would count on the return of the battleships. But Lloyd George stood out for some time against any modification of the Admiralty's demand regarding battle cruisers. 'The Germans have a large number of battle cruisers now, and several more upon the stocks. Consequently, in 1919, they will have as many as all the Allies put together and will even get ahead in the North Sea. . . . These vessels are possessed of great speed, and nothing that the Allies have afloat can catch them.' [1] Eventually, on 3rd November, Lloyd George proposed a compromise: the internment in neutral ports of all the surface vessels which the Admiralty insisted on taking from Germany. This plan, he felt, would safeguard the purposes which the Admiralty had in mind, and was less likely to encounter rejection by the Germans than the demand for the immediate surrender of

[1] *House*, iv, pp. 129–132.

all the vessels in question. But at the last moment, owing to the
uncertainty of finding a suitable neutral port for the internment of
the German warships, a phrase was fortunately added permitting
their internment in an Allied port.[1]

Lloyd George's willingness to tone down the naval terms
encountered bitter criticism from the Interallied Naval Council.
The grounds of their opposition are summarized by the author of
the official British naval history of the war: 'All the Allied Admirals
felt that it would be most dangerous to reduce the terms. They
had been given to understand that the armistice conditions were to
approximate to the conditions 'of peace as closely as possible.
As it was surely axiomatic that the German fleet would be practically
abolished by the Peace Treaty, why should the armistice conditions
be modified? An interned fleet could be used for bargaining at
the Peace Conference; and the Germans would certainly try to
recover it by political concessions.' The American Admiral
Benson alone dissented from this view.[2] To none did Lloyd
George's backsliding appear more lamentable than to Admiral
Wemyss. 'This is dangerous,' he noted in his diary; 'I could agree
if terms of armistice could be different to terms of peace, but this
is not so.' [3]

The armistice terms were finally approved by the Supreme War
Council on 4th November. Four days later they were presented
by Foch to the German envoys at Réthondes. Concessions of
some importance were made to the Germans in the course of the
negotiations. The most important was the grant of six extra days
in which to complete the withdrawal east of the neutral zone,
which was reduced in width to ten kilometres. The armistice was
signed at 5.12 A.M. on 11th November, but was timed from 5 o'clock
in order that it should come into force at 11 A.M.[4]

The military and naval terms may be briefly summarized. The
German troops were to evacuate Belgium, France, Luxemburg,
and Alsace-Lorraine within fifteen days. Within thirty-one days
they were required to withdraw east of the neutral zone on the
right bank of the Rhine. Foch was confident that the rapid withdrawal would make it necessary for the Germans to leave everything
behind.[5] To be on the safe side, however, a provision was included

---

[1] The negotiations on the naval terms may be pieced together from Newbolt, H.:
Naval Operations, v, pp. 370–372, 413–415; *House*, iv, pp. 120–133; Wemyss: *Life
and Letters*, pp. 388, 394; Mermeix: *Les Négotiations secrètes*, pp. 246, 261–264; Aldrovandi, L.: *Guerra Diplomatica*, pp. 206–207.
[2] Newbolt, H.: *Naval Operations*, v, p. 373.
[3] Wemyss: *Life and Letters*, p. 387.
[4] Full minutes of the meetings between Foch and the German envoys are to be found
in *Der Waffenstillstand, 1918–1919. Das Dokumentenmaterial der Waffenstillstandsver-
handlungen*, pp. 1–95. Edited by E. Marhefka. Charlottenberg, 1928.
[5] Wemyss: *Life and Letters*, p. 392.

for the surrender of stipulated quantities of equipment. Allied troops were to occupy the territory evacuated by the Germans as far as the Rhine, and were to hold the Rhine crossings at Mainz, Coblenz, and Cologne, together with bridgeheads at each of these points of thirty kilometres radius on the right bank. The naval conditions of armistice provided for the surrender of all German submarines and for the internment in neutral or Allied ports of six battle cruisers, ten battleships, eight light cruisers, and fifty destroyers. The blockade was to continue.

This survey indicates how the terms of armistice were designed to foreshadow the conditions of peace. The naval terms originally proposed for inclusion in the armistice were altered in the direction of increased severity under the impression that it would be difficult to demand the surrender of the German fleet within the framework of a treaty based on Wilson's points and principles. While the naval terms were thus changed through the impact of Wilsonian diplomacy, it is reasonable to infer that Foch would have demanded the occupation of the Rhineland and the bridgeheads whether or not Wilson's proposals had been brought forward as peace bases. For Foch saw clearly the relation of armistice to peace treaty. It would hardly have been possible to present the demand for the separation of the Rhineland from Germany in the course of the peace negotiations if the territory had not already been brought under military occupation.

Terms of armistice necessarily reflect the relative position of the two contending sides at the conclusion of a struggle. Armistice terms may represent an even finish; or they may signify capitulation of the vanquished. If tantamount to capitulation, armistice terms will be directed towards ensuring two interrelated benefits to the victor: firstly, to guarantee the maintenance of his military superiority, and secondly to vest in him power to impose in due course his conditions of peace. A French scholar, after analysing the armistice of modern times, has reached the general conclusion that from 1871 the conception of armistice has approximated increasingly to that of capitulation, and that it takes on the character of peace preliminaries.[1]

The present survey of the drafting of the armistice of 11th November would suggest the limitations which surround the negotiation of conditions of peace after the conclusion of an armistice which is tantamount to capitulation. For in such an armistice the victors take guarantees for the enforcement of the broad outlines of peace which are in contemplation. And an armistice, if not due to the weariness of the belligerents, is necessarily imposed.

[1] Sibert, M.: *L'Armistice dans le droit des gens*, pp. 42–46.

CHAPTER III

THE CONFERENCE AND THE TREATY

IN the later chapters the course of the negotiations at the Peace Conference on each of the main aspects of the European settlement with Germany is given separate consideration. Since this arrangement breaks up the chronological sequence of the Conference, it may be desirable to preface this chapter by a short composite account of the negotiations in 1919.

On 12th January 1919 the British, French, and Italian Ministers met in Council with President Wilson and Colonel House. The following day Japanese representatives joined in. Thus constituted, the meetings were soon dubbed: 'The Council of Ten'; being composed of two representatives of each of the five Great Powers. In this manner the Peace Conference began.

For the next two months the Council of Ten directed the work of the Conference. During this period little progress was made towards the solution of the main problems of the European settlement with Germany. Other questions, such as those arising out of the administration of the armistice, colonial claims, and the territorial demands of the eastern European states, were brought to the fore. Two months after the opening of the Conference disarmament was the only important aspect of the European settlement with Germany on which final decisions had been reached, though commissions had been set up to consider the future frontiers of Germany with Belgium, Poland, and Czechoslovakia, and to examine the problem of reparation. Why discussion on vital political problems was delayed is not quite clear. For long the responsibility was held to rest on the shoulders of President Wilson, because he insisted that the first task of the Conference should be to draw up the Covenant of the League of Nations. Yet it would seem clear that Wilson's concentration on the Covenant need not of itself have prevented the Council of Ten from proceeding simultaneously with the settlement of such problems as the Rhineland and the Saar. Much time had necessarily to be spent in meeting day-to-day questions concerning the maintenance of order in Europe. Still it is difficult to resist the impression that consideration of the main issues in the German settlement was postponed primarily because so wide a gulf yawned between the views of Clemenceau and those of Wilson and, to some extent, of Lloyd George that Clemenceau deemed postponement the dictate of discretion. Lloyd George himself is said to have gathered the impression towards the end of January that the French were 'marking time so as to delay important questions until after the departure of President Wilson.' [1]

President Wilson left Europe on 14th February to visit the States. In mid-February the first phase in the life of the Conference came to an end. Colonel House acted as the head of the American delegation in his chief's absence. The leadership of the British and French delegations also underwent a change. On 19th February an attempt was made to assassinate Clemenceau. For some days he was confined to his bedroom. About the same time Lloyd George left for London; Balfour remained in Paris as the principal British delegate. House and Balfour did good work, pushing the Conference forward. Then in March, one after the other, the absent leaders returned to their places in the Council of Ten, Clemenceau on 1st March, Lloyd George on 6th March, and Wilson on 17th March. With Wilson's return from America, the Conference entered a new phase.

The new phase was marked by a dual change. The Council of Ten ceased to be the main organ of the Conference. Clemenceau, Lloyd George, Wilson, and Orlando commenced to hold informal meetings on their own. At first neither secretary nor interpreter was present. The conversation was carried on in English, Clemenceau acting as interpreter for Orlando, somewhat to Orlando's discomfort. The meetings came to be dubbed 'The Council of Four.' Soon secretary—Sir Maurice Hankey—and interpreter—Mantoux—were called in. Till the signature of the treaty with Germany the burden of decision on all major questions rested on this restricted Council. The Foreign Ministers and House, deserted by Wilson and the Prime Ministers, constituted the Council of Five, or Council of Foreign Ministers, in which the less important issues were discussed.

The other change which marked the new phase was a change of agenda. The main problems of the settlement with Germany were at last resolutely faced. On 10th March, four days before Wilson's return from America, two small committees were set up, one to go into the question of Germany's western frontier, the other into the question of reparation. Reparation and the Rhineland were constantly before the Council of Four after Wilson's return, and the Saar question was taken up on 28th March.

For three weeks little resulted save an increase of tension, with almost no progress towards agreement on the vital issues of reparation, the Rhineland, and the Saar. House called to see Clemenceau on 20th March after an afternoon conference between Clemenceau, Lloyd George, and Wilson. He asked Clemenceau how they had got on. 'Splendidly,' came the reply. 'We disagreed about

[1] Borden, H.: *R. L. Borden: His Memoirs*, ii, p. 903. Entry in diary, January 21.

everything.'[1] Between Wilson and Clemenceau feeling ran
specially high. On Sunday, 6th April, the American Commission
had a two hours' conference with the President at his house. It
was agreed that the President should tell his colleagues that they
must come to terms, or else he would insist on abandoning the
secret conferences of the Four and having all points of difference
openly discussed in the Plenary Conference. The following
morning Wilson had a cable sent to inquire when his boat, the
George Washington, could be in Brest. So his thoughts were turning
to an abrupt departure. 'I think things will come to a crisis this
week,'[2] wrote General Bliss.

Lloyd George too, in the last days of March, was urging the
need of a peace of moderation. For a brief space Wilson and he
took a common stand. On 22nd March Lloyd George retired
with a few advisers to spend the week-end at Fontainebleau.
In this retreat they drew up the well-known memorandum: 'Some
Considerations for the Peace Conference before they finally draft
their Terms.' It was circulated bearing the date 25th March. In
eloquent pleading Lloyd George put the case for a peace based on
such a will to justice that even the enemy would be forced to
recognize its virtue. With prophetic fervour he foretold that
terms designed to hold the enemy down would call forth a spirit of
revenge. Yet his plea for moderation was somewhat belied by
the comparative harshness of his concrete proposals. Its only
immediate result was a polemic with Clemenceau for which the
honours of artistry must be equally divided. Clemenceau insisted
that, if Germany were to be placated, it would be necessary to revise
the decisions already reached to demand the cession of German
colonies, the surrender of the German battle fleet, and the transfer
of the German merchant fleet. Clemenceau could not follow
Lloyd George in his reversal of the Beatitudes. He felt that the
British Prime Minister, having first secured for his land her in-
heritance on earth, now hungered and thirsted rather late after
righteousness. Lloyd George had hoped to speed the settlement;
when April came he was losing heart.

Yet already in the first week of April the temperature began to
lower. A series of factors combined to produce the change.
Wilson fell ill on 3rd April, and was absent from the Council of
Four till 8th April. His place was taken by the more conciliatory
House, and in Wilson's absence vital decisions on reparation were
tentatively reached. Lloyd George veered over towards the
French view on reparation in response to a parliamentary gale
blowing up from Westminster. The Saar problem moved evenly
towards a solution on 9th April. Agreement was delayed longest

[1] *House*, iv, p. 405.   [2] Palmer, F.: *Bliss*, pp. 387-388.

on the question of the occupation of the Rhineland. Eventually, on 15th April, Wilson agreed to a compromise solution of this question also, possibly in order to facilitate the acceptance of the necessary American amendments to the League Covenant. Lloyd George had just left for England to defend his conduct of the negotiations in the Commons debate on 16th April. Returning to France almost immediately, he seems to have had little option but to accept the plan of occupation on which Wilson and Clemenceau had agreed. Time was pressing, for on 14th April the announcement had been made of the decision to invite the Germans to Versailles.

'Neither summer nor a peace treaty seems ready to appear.'[1] So wrote a member of the American delegation on 25th April. In fact, however, work on the various parts of the Treaty was well advanced, but men absorbed in the preparation of one section had little knowledge of how the labour of others was proceeding. On 29th April the German representatives arrived, and in the following days the various sections of the Treaty were hastily assembled. On 6th May the terms were communicated to the representatives of the lesser states in a plenary session of the Conference, and on 7th May they were formally presented to the German delegation.

There followed a period of uncertainty whether Germany would agree to sign the Treaty. The German delegation protested against the conditions of peace in a series of notes, culminating in a final memorandum of 29th May. The German criticisms, and fear that Germany would renew the War rather than sign the Treaty without modification, led Lloyd George to open a vigorous campaign for the revision of the Treaty terms.

On 1st June, a Sunday, Lloyd George held a meeting of the British Cabinet in Paris. He summoned the British Ministers from London for the purpose. The Dominion Premiers, too, were present. Lloyd George invited criticism of the Treaty; he had, he said, no fear of changing his views when it could be shown that the information on which his earlier decisions had been based was unsound. The British Ministers agreed that Lloyd George should press for concessions to Germany in four respects—the frontier with Poland, the Rhineland occupation, reparation, and admission to League membership. At his request Lloyd George was authorized to tell his colleagues in the Council of Four that the British Empire would not join in making Germany accept the Treaty without revision. 'Clemenceau,' said Lloyd George, 'would not enter upon any discussion unless he was forced. M. Clemenceau was a man with a sense of justice, but he was in a position of very

[1] Shotwell, J. H.: *At the Paris Peace Conference*, p. 294.

great difficulty in view of the opinion which was behind him.
Still, if he knew that he had either to face his own extremists or
to march forward without the British Empire he would be willing
to discuss.' [1]
The British conference lasted throughout Sunday and was
continued on Monday morning. That afternoon Lloyd George
informed Wilson and Clemenceau of its resolutions. 'So far as
the British public is concerned,' he said, 'it has made up its mind
that it wants to get peace and is not so much concerned about
the precise details. . . . The whole of those he consulted were
unanimously agreed that, unless certain defects in the Treaty were
put right, they could not advise that the British army should be
allowed to march or that the fleet should take part in the blockade.'
Clemenceau gave the reply that his colleagues heard so often:
'We Frenchmen understand Germany and the Germans better than
you. The more concessions we grant them, the more they will
ask for.' Lloyd George in reply threatened to return to England
and place the matter before Parliament unless Clemenceau agreed
to alterations in the conditions of peace. Finally it was decided
that Clemenceau, Lloyd George, and Wilson should each consult
members of their respective delegations. [2]
The consultations would appear to have taken place the following
morning; and the Council of Four turned again to the question
of revision on Tuesday afternoon. It is not intended here to
relate the course of the discussion on the following days. Suffice
it to say that Lloyd George's struggle met with but partial success—
greatest in the matter of Germany's eastern frontier, least perhaps
in that of reparation. If Lloyd George had expected support from
Wilson, he was disappointed. In the Council of Four Wilson lent
Lloyd George little support. 'I am ready,' said Wilson to his
colleagues on 3rd June, 'to modify the clauses which can be shown
to be unjust, but not to sacrifice our decisions to the desires of the
Germans.' [3] It was to Wilson that Clemenceau appealed when, in
a last despairing rally, Lloyd George on 25th June came of a sudden
to the Ministry of War to announce that he could not sign the
Treaty, for the Rhineland occupation was unacceptable to England. [4]
In face of Wilson's intransigeance Lloyd George had at last to
give in. Three days later the Treaty of Versailles was signed.

When Henry White, the American plenipotentiary, received
members of the Chamber of Deputies, he was pained and shocked

[1] Lloyd George: *Peace Treaties*, i, pp. 687–720.
[2] *Miller*, xix, p. 277; Tardieu, A.: *Le Sleswig*, p. 246; *Baker*, ii, pp. 111–112;
Anglo-French Negotiations, p. 106.
[3] Tardieu, A.: *Le Sleswig*, p. 249.
[4] Mordacq, J. J. H.: *Le Ministère Clemenceau*, iii, p. 317.

to discover that they honestly feared that 'in a few years Germany would once more fall upon them.' Among Frenchmen this fear was universal. 'The war,' wrote another member of the American delegation, 'has destroyed all confidence in Germany's good faith on the part of even liberal France.' [1] The potential military power of Republican Germany haunted France no less than had that of Imperial Germany. Foch was expressing the general conviction when he wrote:

'. . . Now that the Hohenzollerns have gone, in circumstances peculiarly damning to that dynasty and, indeed, to any military monarchy, the danger of a return to the imperial system must at least be remote. But a republic built up on the same principles of militarism and the centralization of power, and taking the whole of Germany in hand, will be no less dangerous and will remain no less a menace to peace. Experience shows that it would not be difficult to give that character to a republic in a country soaked with the Prussian system, Prussian methods, and militarist doctrines—a country in which discipline and the centralization of power, thanks both to the national temperament and to tradition, are still the basis of society. More than that: republican Germany, unhampered by the difficulties which the existence of the small principalities undoubtedly created for the Empire, is likely to derive increased strength from her unity and from the vitality and energy of a people henceforth in closer relationship to their Government.'

Excessive confidence in Germany's democratic future, Foch added, should not be permitted to 'jeopardize our doctrine of liberty and justice, our very existence itself, so long as a revulsion of feeling, a sudden reaction, may once again hurl against us in a fresh war vast numbers of men, trained to arms, and capable of being transformed at a moment's notice into a mighty army.' [2]

Behind this apprehension lay the knowledge that the position of France rested on precarious foundations. Time would favour the defeated enemy, so much the stronger in population and industrial resources. Victory had been achieved by a narrow margin, and not by the arms of France alone. It was the victory of an alliance, and at the touch of victory alliances throughout history have had a way of crumbling. The defection of Russia had removed the main basis of France's pre-War policy, and the menace of a Russo-German combination cast its shadow ahead. In course of time France might look to the new states of eastern Europe to fill Russia's vacated rôle, but till they had stabilized their position they would remain liabilities rather than assets. 'Western Europe,' concluded Foch, 'must rely on its own resources in order to frame its destiny

[1] Nevins, A.: *Henry White*, p. 379. Shotwell, J. H.: *At the Paris Peace Conference*, p. 92.
[2] *Anglo-French Negotiations*, pp. 20–21.

and secure itself against the possibility of a renewed German aggression.'[1]

The frankest expression of French policy on the eve of the Conference is to be found in Clemenceau's speech in the Chamber of Deputies on 29th December 1918.   He spoke extempore: it had not been his intention to intervene in the debate, but in response to a challenge from Albert Thomas, Clemenceau proceeded—as he put it—to 'think aloud':

'During these years, we have laboured, we have suffered, we have fought, our men have been struck down, our towns and our villages have been devastated.   Every man-says rightly: "We must see that it does not happen again."

'I think that too!   But how?

'There was an old system, which seems condemned to-day and to which I do not fear to say that I remain to some extent faithful at this time: countries organised their defence.   It was very prosaic.   They tried to have good frontiers.   They went armed.   It was a terrible burden for all peoples. . . .

'I was saying that there was this old method of solid and well-defended frontiers, armaments, and what is called the balance of power. . . . This system to-day seems to be condemned by very high authorities. Yet I would say that if this balance, which has been spontaneously produced during the War, had existed earlier; if, for example, England, America, France, and Italy had agreed in saying that whoever attacked one of them was attacking the whole world, the War would not have taken place. . . .

'So there was this old system of alliances, which I am not for giving up—I tell you that openly—and my dominant thought in going to the conference is that nothing must occur which shall separate in the post-War period the four Powers which have come together in the War.   For this Entente, I shall make every sacrifice. . . .

'Still, Messieurs, when I speak of international guarantees which have not yet seen the light of day, and which perhaps will be more difficult to set up in reality than in writing or speeches, I am at liberty to say that if France is left to look after her own defence—for she above all doesn't want to see invasion again—I for my part accept with joy every addition of supplementary guarantees which is afforded us.   I go even further. If it is decided that these supplementary guarantees are such that we can make sacrifices of military preparation, then as far as I am concerned I will make them with pleasure, for I am not bent on imposing unnecessary charges on my country.'[2]

How France sought to provide for her defence is well known. She proposed to hold, with the support of Allied forces, an advanced military frontier on the Rhine, backed by a nominally

[1] *Anglo-French Negotiations*, p. 21.
[2] *Chambre: Débats*, December 29, 1918, pp. 3350–3352.   Clemenceau: *Discours de Paix*, pp. 15–34.

independent Rhineland Republic. Since this proposal met with vigorous opposition from Great Britain and the U.S.A., it proved incompatible with the first principle of Clemenceau's policy—the maintenance of the Entente. When, therefore, as alternative provision for the security of France, a British and American pledge of military assistance was offered, Clemenceau abandoned this proposal, though not until he had procured British and American assent to a temporary occupation of the Rhineland.

In the last days of August the Treaty was subjected to anxious scrutiny in the Chamber of Deputies. Had France been made secure against future attack? A sense of misgiving prevailed. Germany's armaments were to be limited; but the limitation was to be subject to no permanent control. Why, indeed, had Germany been left with an army at all? Why not just a gendarmerie? The left bank of the Rhine was to be demilitarized, together with a strip fifty kilometres wide on the right bank; but was the maintenance of this demilitarized zone assured? In the Saar the frontier of 1815 had been restored, not the stronger frontier of 1814. The Rhineland was to be occupied by Allied forces for fifteen years; but the provision for the evacuation of territory at the end of each period of five years made the protective value of the occupation doubtful. From the Right, from the Centre, and even from the Left came criticism of the failure to secure a permanent military frontier on the Rhine. The British and American Treaties of Guarantee were greeted with satisfaction; but would they, without subsidiary military conventions, prove efficacious against the danger of invasion? A close examination could not fail to reveal the fragility of the structure raised for the defence of France. How, demanded Albert Thomas—Socialist leader, future Secretary of the I.L.O.—could this 'sum total of insufficiency . . . constitute a solid security for the country'? [1]

Then, in 1920, came the news that Clemenceau's sacrifice had been in vain. The American Treaty of Guarantee had miscarried. In consequence, the British Treaty of Guarantee would not come into force.

It is necessary to pause over these ill-fated treaties. The original intention appears to have been the signature of a tripartite treaty; but President Wilson explained to Lloyd George that he deemed it wiser to conclude one treaty between the United States and France, and one between Great Britain and France. When Balfour drafted the British note which formally pledged Great Britain to conclude the Treaty, he inserted a provision making the entry into force of the British treaty conditional on the ratification of the American treaty. President Wilson surmised that this

[1] *Chambre: Débats*, August 29, 1919, p. 3662.

proviso had passed unnoticed by the French; but since Balfour's note was read with care both by Clemenceau and by the astute Tardieu, the accuracy of this surmise may be questioned. Unhappily the American Treaty of Guarantee was enmeshed in a common fate with the Treaty of Versailles, which in March 1920 fell victim to a deadly mixture of party rancour of Republican against Democrat, of Senatorial assertion against the Presidency, and of personal hostility to President Wilson—with an element of the traditional objection to foreign entanglements thrown in. It was the ironic fate of the American Treaty of Guarantee to be negotiated in Paris by a delegation which viewed it with disfavour, only to lapse through the activities of those whose leader, Senator Lodge, viewed it favourably. For Senator Lodge was prepared for the Treaty of Guarantee, but condemned the Covenant, while the more influential members of the American delegation at Paris wanted the Covenant, but condemned the Treaty. They feared that a special guarantee for France would throw doubt on the value of the pledges contained in the Covenant; Senator Lodge, though objecting to a general system of guarantees, was ready to accept the separate Treaty with France.[1]

It is commonly recognized that the failure to maintain the Anglo-French Treaty was a blunder of the first magnitude. There developed among the French a strong feeling that France had been deserted by her fellow-victors in a situation of acute peril. The British recoil was ascribed to the narrowest promptings of national egoism. The Treaty of Versailles, said the French, assures to Great Britain benefits which are both solid and indisputable. The destruction of the German fleet and the transfer of the German colonies are accomplished facts which it would be senseless for Germany to seek to impugn. This advantageous position constitutes a temptation for Great Britain to revert to a policy of isolation and to shake off her responsibility for watching over the execution of the Treaty. France is now left to bear alone the brunt of German resentment. She must insist on the payment of reparation; she must protect the new settlement against disturbance by Germany—for these are conditions of her stability, and indeed of her very existence.

Though, then, the Treaty of Versailles was greeted in France with misgiving, French opinion in the main rallied to its support. Its clauses, if firmly upheld, would provide a guarantee against any renewed bid by Germany for the domination of the Continent.

[1] *Anglo-French Negotiations*, pp. 95, 104–105; *Miller*, i, pp. 294–295. For the American Senate's rejection of the Treaty of Versailles: Holt, W. S.: *Treaties defeated by the Senate*, pp. 301–303; Fleming, D. F.: *The United States and the League of Nations*. On Lodge: Nevins, A.: *Henry White*, pp. 405, 450; Cambon, J.: 'La Paix,' *Revue de Paris*, November 1937, p. 28.

What seemed essential to the French was that Germany should be given no grounds to hope that she would be allowed to call in question the state of affairs which had resulted from the victory of the Allies. Insistence on strict adherence by Germany to the terms of the Treaty became the characteristic French attitude. For this reason the clamour against the Treaty which developed in Great Britain, combined with—as it seemed to the French—the somewhat enigmatic attitude of the British Government with regard to the question of treaty revision, may well be held to have constituted an even more potent cause of division between Great Britain and France than the formal abandonment of the Anglo-French Treaty.

In Great Britain opinion condemnatory of the Treaty of Versailles grew rapidly in volume and intensity in the six months which intervened between the signature of the Treaty and its entry into force. The debates in the Commons on 3rd July and 21st July appeared to bear out Lloyd George's diagnosis of his countrymen that they wanted peace and were not much concerned about the details. But the Commons had ceased to mirror faithfully the feelings of the British people; its composition reflected the passions of December 1918, not the cooler mood which had already begun to set in. *The Spectator* might declare: 'The Peace is a good peace; it is what it ought to be—a dictated peace' [1]; but from this judgement Englishmen of liberal opinion dissented in increasing numbers. The attack on the Treaty was led by the small but talented group in the Union of Democratic Control in whose judgement the Treaty bore out the suspicions which they had entertained throughout the War of the purity of Allied intentions. Three days before the signature of the Treaty the Annual Conference of the Labour Party had carried a resolution, introduced by Ramsay MacDonald, then a leading member of the Union, demanding the 'immediate revision by the League of Nations of the harsh provisions of the Treaty . . . as a first step towards the reconciliation of the peoples and the inauguration of a new era of international co-operation and good-will.' [2] Six months later the campaign for treaty revision received a sudden and unexpected impetus from the publication of J. M. Keynes' *Economic Consequences of the Peace*. 'A thunderbolt,' commented *The Nation*. Few books indeed have been received with such acclaim. When Parliament reassembled in February 1920 the Opposition was emboldened to move an amendment to the Address regretting that 'Your Majesty's Ministers have not recognized the impracticability of the fulfilment by our late enemies of many of the terms of the Peace Treaties.'

[1] *The Spectator*, May 10, 1919.
[2] Labour Party: *Report of Annual Conference, 1919*, pp. 139–142.

In this revulsion of an influential section of British opinion against the Treaty of Versailles, two strains may be distinguished: the wrath of the idealist at its iniquity, and the scorn of the economist at its insanity.   This distinction, it must be added, is just a matter of convenience for the purpose of exposition.   For, by a strange perversity, many of those who throughout the War had proclaimed their devotion to the principle of self-determination now tended to invoke that principle only in criticism of the new German frontiers, while deploring for economic reasons its acceptance as a basis for the political re-division of Europe;   and those whose primary concern was with economic reconstruction lapsed not infrequently into vague invocations to Peace which appeared to spell, so it seemed to the French, no more than a pusillanimous recoil from the responsibilities of victory.   'The economic restoration of Europe should to-day be our first concern,' declared Mr McKenna. 'If we neglect it, our whole foreign trade will contract and decay. . . . What Europe needs at the present time is Peace!   Not merely the peace of pacts and treaties, but peace born of the spirit of peace, when the nations "shall beat their swords into plough-shares."' [1]   Justly aghast at the horrors of the blockade, revolted by the passion and resentment which war had left in its wake, it was not easy for Englishmen to understand that 'war and peace are both affairs of power.' [2]

To range over the criticisms directed against the individual clauses of the Treaty would necessitate too wide a digression;   nor is it essential to do so.   For the burden of the protest against the Treaty went beyond mere criticism on points of detail.   That the Treaty had been conceived in the wrong spirit—this was the more general and the more trenchant charge.   Had not the German people, at the behest of the Allies, thrown off the yoke of autocracy? Why then had the crimes of the old régime been visited on the new? Why had no gesture of reconciliation been extended to democratic Germany?   Was it not the real source of evil that the motives of the old diplomacy had prevailed with the Allied leaders?   Their trust had been placed in arbitrary safeguards against the recrudescence of German power.   They had withdrawn German territory from German rule—by the institution of the Saar régime, 'an act of spoliation and insincerity' [3];   by the establishment of Danzig as a Free City, mere 'disguised annexation'[4] ;   and especially by the incorporation of West Prussia in Poland—all national mutilations which German nationalism would for ever resent.[5]

[1] *The Economist*, May 7, 1921.
[2] Percy, Lord Eustace: *The Responsibilities of the League*, p. 59.
[3] Keynes, J. M., now Lord Keynes: *Economic Consequences of the Peace*, p. 76.
[4] Henderson, A.: *The Peace Terms*.
[5] *Foreign Affairs* (Union of Democratic Control), August 1919.

They had denied the right of self-determination to the Germans of Austria; they had even placed millions of Germans under the Czechs. Germany alone among the Great Powers had been disarmed, and by her exclusion from the League was to be branded as an outlaw among the nations. This then was no peace of justice and of right, such as would win the assent of the German people; it was not, in the language of the pulpit, the vehicle of.a healing spirit.[1] It was peace by preponderant military power. It would not endure, for its maintenance would depend on the continuance of a great military alliance, vigilant, determined, united, and indefatigable.[2] It was not to a peace of this nature to which men of liberal mind had looked forward. Their vision had been of a regenerated Europe, purged of all militarism, knowing neither national oppression nor the rivalries of great states, its peoples inspired by common hopes, its statesmen working together in friendly agreement. This vision, for four years a pillar of cloud by day and of fire by night, had broken on the threshold of the new age.

In similar fashion the economic argument against the Treaty passed beyond criticism on questions of detail to an indictment on grounds of principle. It received its classic presentation in the work of J. M. Keynes; later commentators were content to reiterate the case presented in his famous work. Two passages of the *Economic Consequences of the Peace* contain the essence of Mr Keynes' thesis. Firstly: that 'round Germany as a central support the rest of the European economic system grouped itself, and on the prosperity and enterprise of Germany the prosperity of the rest of the Continent mainly depended.' The second: that 'the German economic system as it existed before the War depended on three main factors: I. Overseas commerce as represented by her mercantile marine, her colonies, her foreign investments, her exports, and the overseas connection of her merchants; II. The exploitation of her coal and iron and the industries built upon them; III. Her transport and tariff system. The Treaty aims at the systematic destruction of all three.'[3] Conclusion: the Treaty was incompatible with the economic prosperity of Europe. 'While this Treaty stands unrevised,' commented one who followed in Mr Keynes' footsteps, 'there can be no resumption, save on the puniest scale, of the activity which, in the generation before the War, had made Germany the workshop of the Continent.'[4] Mr Keynes' own proposals were not immoderate. The demand on Germany for reparation, which the Treaty left indefinite, should

[1] See Jacks, L. P.: 'Why We are Disappointed,' *Hibbert Journal*, October 1919.
[2] Brailsford, H. N.: *After the Peace*, p. 63.
[3] Keynes, J. M.: *Economic Consequences of the Peace*, pp. 14, 60.
[4] Brailsford, H. N.: *After the Peace*, p. 21.

be reduced to the sum of £2000 million. This reduction should be made more acceptable to the Continental states by British renunciation of all claim to cash payments from Germany and by the all-round cancellation of war debts. More debatable from the Continental viewpoint was the proposal for a Free Trade Union comprising the whole of central, eastern, and south-eastern Europe, with, perhaps, the United Kingdom and other countries which might choose to join.

Merely to recall these central economic themes is to overlook the inward significance of Mr Keynes' work. Why should it have provoked from a French jurist the cry: 'Not a Frenchman but will feel deeply hurt on reading this work. France is not understood by Anglo-Saxon pacifists'? [1] 'Les pacifistes anglo-saxons ne comprennent pas la France'—the cry reverberates through the ensuing years during which English policy became the despair of reasonable Frenchmen as French policy became the despair of reasonable Englishmen. The explanation of M. de Lapradelle's distress may perhaps be found in the political philosophy in which the economic criticisms advanced by Mr Keynes were embedded. It was, where political issues were concerned, a philosophy of easy optimism, based on the conviction that the single-minded pursuit of economic ends would suffice to induce the European nations to put aside their national feelings and give themselves over to 'thoughts and hopes of the happiness and solidarity of the European family.' The revival of economic activity was the only worthy goal; all else was foolish endeavour. This was the creed which Mr Keynes expressed in language of telling force and fascinating brilliance. The 'real' policy of M. Clemenceau on 'unreal' issues —what did this mean but that questions of national security mattered nothing? Was it wise to proclaim Article 10 as one of the 'two disastrous blots on the Covenant'? Were the labours of the Council of Four just 'empty and arid intrigue'? Was the peace in fact a Carthaginian peace? [2] Mr Keynes' insistence on the paramount importance of economic questions, combined with his emphasis on the reintegration of the German economic system, provoked distrust in the minds of the Continental statesmen: insistent belittlement of the political problems of European settlement had as its consequence the alienation of all those whose co-operation was indispensable if plans of economic recovery were to be worked out and carried through.

Perhaps this chapter may most fittingly conclude with a quotation from a work which failed to attain the popularity of its sensational

[1] Lapradelle, A. G. de: 'Les Conséquences économiques de la Paix,' *Revue politique et parlementaire*, June 10, 1920.
[2] Keynes, J. M.: *Economic Consequences of the Peace*, pp. 5, 139, 243.

contemporary, yet which, by its breadth of thought, maturity of judgement, and sobriety of language, remains, and is likely to remain, without peer as a commentary on the European scene of that day viewed from British shores. The peroration of Lord Eustace Percy's imaginary speech by a British statesman pleading for the maintenance by Great Britain of the power which would enable the country to discharge its responsibility for the 'ordered police work of the settlement' was addressed to those who were vociferous in their opposition to any such prolongation of the British political and military effort. That opposition, Lord Eustace Percy's statesman concluded, 'has already been widely voiced, precisely by those . . . who have been ever ready to respond to the cry for liberation coming from remote peoples; who desired, above all other things, to make this war, if it had to be fought at all, a war of revolution in the cause of nationality. It is their policy which has now come to fruition; a new system of States based on the principle of nationality has been created in Europe; will they now have the courage to go forth and labour in the fields they have sown till they have garnered the grain of peace, or will they retire to their fireside and leave others to reap a harvest of new bloodshed and misery?' [1]

CHAPTER IV

THE VICISSITUDES OF POLICY AND OPINION:
1920–1930

SINCE the history of Anglo-French relations is the kernel of the history of Europe between the two World Wars, it has been related in outline in countless general works. The primary purpose of the following chapters is not to narrate the history of Anglo-French relations, but to elucidate the problems encountered in the making and maintenance of the Versailles settlement. Since it will be necessary to return again and again to some episodes, in order to consider them on each occasion from a different angle, it may be desirable to explain the arrangement which has been adopted. The present chapter traces the vicissitudes of policy and opinion during the first decade. The arrangement of the remaining chapters is based on the distinction which may be drawn between the actual problems at issue and the methods by which they were handled. Chapters V, VI, and VII deal with questions of method during the first decade: Chapter V reviews the working of the inter-Allied agencies set up to watch over the execution of the Treaty;

[1] Percy, Lord Eustace: *The Responsibilities of the League*, p. 58.

Chapter VI deals with the problems raised by the enforcement of the provisions of the Treaty; Chapter VII is concerned with the experiment in diplomacy by conference during the decade which followed the War. After these three chapters on questions of method, the major problems of the period—reparation, disarmament, security, and territorial questions—are taken up one by one. The main purpose of these chapters is to provide an analytical presentation of French and British viewpoints. The chapters on reparation, on the disarmament of Germany, and on the Rhineland question are each prefaced by a chronological record of the negotiations. No historical narrative is included of the negotiations relating to general disarmament and collective security, because the general history of these questions has already formed the subject of many works.

The first three years of peace were years of uneasy co-operation. The Treaty entered into force on 10th January 1920. Within three months a disastrous embroilment of Anglo-French relations threatened when French troops occupied Frankfort in retribution for the German violation of the demilitarized zone. At the Conference of San Remo, which followed shortly after, a somewhat deceptive reconciliation was achieved, but the practical understanding then reached about the policy to be followed towards Germany enabled a superficial concord to be maintained for the next two years, despite mutual suspicion and intermittent tension. By the close of 1921 the need had become apparent of a more complete accord on basic problems: neither country could hope to secure the satisfaction of its essential interests without the co-operation of the other. At Cannes, in January 1922, Lloyd George and Briand exchanged their well-known memoranda on the conditions of a closer association. Their discussions terminated abruptly with the return of Briand to Paris to face his critics in the Chamber. On 12th January he resigned; Poincaré, the advocate of intransigeance towards Germany, of independence towards England, replaced him as Prime Minister. The acrimonious contention on the subject of reparation which marked the remainder of the year 1922 culminated in the Franco-Belgian occupation of the Ruhr at the outset of 1923.

Throughout these years British and French statesmen were well aware of the critical situation that would arise through the failure of the two countries to stand firmly together. Against France, Great Britain was impotent in European affairs. The British army had been rapidly demobilized: what remained of it— 300,000 men in 1920—was scattered about the various parts of the Empire where disturbances threatened—64,000 in India and Aden

43,000 in the Near and Middle East, 50,000 in Ireland, and just over 100,000 retained in Great Britain, as much in view of social unrest as to provide an imperial reserve. Troops could ill be spared for European responsibilities; by the end of 1920 the British army on the Continent was restricted to 13,000 men on the Rhine. France by contrast was superficially well equipped to impose her own policy on European questions. Her formidable army was now without rival on the Continent. But France remained aware that only the arrival of aid from overseas had saved her from crushing defeat. She justly feared that a rift in the Entente would stimulate German resistance to the fulfilment of the Treaty. The wiser of her statesmen pointed to the perils of isolation in the future, and urged that she would prove to have overreached her power if she sought to act on her own. Alone neither Great Britain nor France could carry through a European policy.

Yet the disparity of British and French military power in Europe undoubtedly sharpened the intermittent brawls which disfigure the history of Anglo-French relations during this period. Great Britain, lacking more direct means of influencing the course of affairs, succumbed to the temptation of addressing irresponsible homilies across the Channel to a troubled and sensitive neighbour. France, feeling that anyhow she was being left to bear alone the odium of enforcing a treaty that was not after all exclusively her handiwork, was prone to act with small regard for the views of her ally. 'National egotism,' commented a French observer, 'is not necessarily less irritating when it takes the form of deeds without words, than when it takes the form of words without deeds.'[1] The Upper Silesian plebiscite affords one of several illustrations of the tension which resulted from the clash of these two modes of national self-assertion. At Paris it had been agreed that the four Great Powers should contribute equally to the forces needed in the plebiscite areas.[2] Unhappily the American contingent was withheld in consequence of the failure of the U.S.A. to ratify the Treaty. To Clemenceau's intense dismay, Lloyd George intimated in January 1920 that Great Britain also would be unable to make any contribution to the plebiscite forces. In the outcome, the dispatch of two British battalions, one to Allenstein and one to Danzig, was conceded, but these were withdrawn before the end of the year.[3] For Upper Silesia the French provided ten and the Italians three battalions. The French found themselves in the nettling situation of bearing the primary responsibility for the maintenance of order in pursuance of a plebiscite which they had not desired and the out-

---

[1] 'The Case of France,' by a French Correspondent, Round Table, June 1920.
[2] Wambaugh, S.: Plebiscites since the World War, i, p. 219.
[3] Callwell, Sir C. E.: Sir Henry Wilson, ii, p. 225; 129 H.C. Deb., June 1, 1920, col. 1755.

come of which threatened, in their judgement, gravely to disserve the interests of France. Four British battalions were indeed moved to Upper Silesia in March 1921 for the actual holding of the plebiscite, but they were withdrawn the following month for service in Ireland. In May the Franco-Italian force was faced with a Polish insurrection, in the course of which the Poles succeeded in occupying the territory to which they laid claim. Englishmen rightly concluded that the Polish insurrection had been organized in the confident expectation that the French would make no serious effort of repression. Lloyd George declared in the Commons that either the Allied forces present in Upper Silesia should restore order—he could not, he added, insist on this course since no British troops were there—or else the Germans themselves should be allowed to take action. Briand retorted the following day that the presence of a strong British force would be of more value than any amount of good advice; if Germany attempted to interfere, he added, 'she would be giving rise to the most regrettable incidents from which France could not disinterest herself.'[1] Though British reinforcements were sent to the area before the end of the month, the Allied forces were unable to regain complete control of the area till the beginning of July.

Of course, Anglo-French relations were disturbed by causes more profound than the disparity of power consequent on the dispersion of British interest. The aims of the two countries could not be easily reconciled. Their incongruity is familiar; the point need not be laboured here. Great Britain sought to end the paralysis of European trade by promoting the financial and economic recovery of Germany. This preoccupation decided the British attitude on reparation. Great Britain came to deplore also any action which threatened to dislocate the German industrial structure; thus the retention by Germany of the industrial triangle of Upper Silesia appeared preferable to its partial or complete transfer to Poland. France, however, viewed the rehabilitation of Germany with marked apprehension. Her policy was dominated by considerations of security; and security, as she understood it, involved the steady maintenance of the discriminatory restrictions and territorial provisions of the Treaty of Versailles. The financial stability of France was dependent on the receipt of reparation; but France feared that Germany, her prosperity once restored, would refuse the payment of reparation and even seek to destroy the political order which was the expression of her defeat.

In the judgement of most Frenchmen the moment of that seemingly inevitable challenge belonged to the near rather than the distant future. It could be held back, they believed, only if

[1] 141 *H.C. Deb.*, May 14, 1921, col. 2382-2385; *The Times*, May 16, 1921.

the Allies displayed their determination to counter it by measures of constraint whenever and wherever it appeared. Here was the fundamental cleavage between Great Britain and France—a cleavage in the political outlook of the two countries. The negotiations for an Anglo-French Pact of December 1921–July 1922 served only to emphasize this contrast. The supreme objective of French policy was the stabilization of the European settlement. This purpose France designed to achieve by tightening the bonds between the states interested in its maintenance. She was determined to conclude agreements for mutual military assistance with the smaller European countries which shared her fears of Germany, but as the corner-stone of her system she desired a close military alliance with Great Britain—only however if it expressed the common intention of the two countries firmly to maintain the new order created by the treaties.[1]   This conception of European peace based on the domination of an alliance of which France would remain the spearhead consorted ill with the spirit of British policy. British policy was guided above all by anxiety to bring to an end 'the division of the European nations into two mighty camps.' The view expressed by Lord Curzon was shared by the country as a whole—that a military alliance along the lines desired by France would have the fatal result of provoking the formation of 'rival and, it might be, hostile combinations between other Powers (conceivably even between Germany and Russia).' [2]   The British Government was willing to go no further than to pledge British aid to France in the event of the invasion of French territory. When the project of an Anglo-French pact was debated in the Commons, even this limited commitment was viewed favourably only by a small group of Conservative M.P.s.

These contrasts of policy will be amplified in later pages. But it may be well to insist here that British policy reflected faithfully the disposition of the British people, as did French policy that of the French. There exists no better description of how France felt in 1922 than that which Professor H. J. Laski contributed to *The Nation* after a brief visit in the spring of that year. He wrote:

'In France, whatever else be lacking, unity at least there is. . . . Few seem to doubt the approach of a new war; at least be it made

[1] Frenchmen of Briand's cast of mind envisaged the conclusion of some additional arrangement with Germany on the lines of the Washington Agreements—perhaps a consultative pact combined with projects of economic reconstruction and with voluntary recognition by Germany of the demilitarized zone; but only by way of supplement to a network of alliances between the beneficiaries of the settlement. See *Anglo-French Negotiations*, p. 123; *D.D. Documents relatifs aux négotiations concernant les garanties de sécurité contre une agression de l'Allemagne* (Paris, 1924), p. 93 ; and the remarkable articles by Philippe Millet in *Eur. Nouv.*, December 24, 1921, and May 27, 1922.   [2] *Anglo-French Negotiations*, p. 158.

ertain that France will fight from a position of advantage. Germany
s still a figure uniquely evil, the origin of all wrong and suffering,
•rosperous in fact, and falsely declaring herself bankrupt to win the pity
f soft-hearted England. Yet not entirely soft-hearted. For, having
lestroyed the German fleet, England has no menace to confront; while
he France that lost a million of her sons will soon, perhaps isolated, be
efending once more her heritage of freedom and justice. Everywhere
he mood is one of self-pity. The foreigner cannot measure the sacrifice
'rance has made; he cannot grasp the strength of those subtle forces
hat make for dissolution. He does not realize the need of enforcing
he lesson of justice written into the clauses of Versailles. If there is
isharmony in Europe, it is because Versailles has not been enforced.' [1]

To this concise account there is little to add, save perhaps to
tress the passionate conviction of the French that bare justice
equired the payment of reparation, because Germany had planned
nd precipitated the War.

No summary statement can portray with equal fidelity the more
omplex contemporary state of British opinion. Though hatred
f Germany ebbed rapidly, resentment lingered. Even at the
utset of the Ruhr occupation, feeling in England was divided;
he southern counties sided with the French—so the British
Ambassador in Washington informed the American Secretary of
tate—while in the Midlands, especially in Labour circles, anti-
French feeling prevailed. [2] It is possible here to recall only those
endencies of popular thought which contributed powerfully to
he estrangement of the two countries—tendencies which were
lominant, it must be added, only in Liberal and Labour circles and
n the Nonconformist churches, yet which spread beyond their
onfines. The mental atmosphere of England evoked in the
Frenchman almost a sense of bewilderment. The Englishman—
o he felt—had dismissed the danger of war from his mind. Peace
vas thought of and spoken of as a moral condition that must
pring from a universal sense of brotherhood—an attitude at
ariance with the French conception of peace attainable only by
he elaboration of juridical arrangements and military guarantees.
trictly pacifist doctrine—that force must be renounced in every
hape or form—received widespread acceptance. The Treaty, of
vhich there was much criticism and far too little defence, was
ondemned above all for its alleged mutilation of the German
ation. Its revision forthwith was demanded. Rightly or wrongly,
Germany was credited with having experienced a real political
ransformation. If nevertheless signs were perceived of the
esurgence of Junker influence, the reaction was attributed to the

[1] *The Nation*, May 6, 1922.
[2] *U.S.A. Foreign Relations*, 1923, ii, pp. 52–54.

pressure of French militarism, a militarism—to quote one ugly ye
characteristic example of vituperation—worse than that of Hohen-
zollern Germany, 'resting on the savagery of negro conscripts and
the egoism of little half-barbaric allies.'[1] Conclude an alliance
with such a nation? It would but encourage and confirm her in
her policy of vengeance.

The most convincing evidence of the contrast between the
British and French outlook is to be found in the perplexity of the
British Labour and French Socialist parties when they endeavoured
to formulate a common viewpoint on European affairs. In consequence of the 'fundamental and serious divergence of opinion
between the two parties, especially on the question of the desirability
of defensive alliances, a conference of party representatives met in
May 1922 to discuss frankly the state of public opinion in the two
countries.[2] The report epitomizes in terms of studied moderation
the Anglo-French polemic of the years 1920–1922.

The British delegates spoke as follows:

The financier and the unemployed workman in Great Britain
find themselves in agreement on one question. They both desire
the speedy and complete revival of British trade. The pacific
foreign policy of the British Government is directed towards that
end, for the economic reconstruction of Europe is a matter of life
or death to the British people. The British feel that France is the
real obstacle, because the French appear to see in Germany only a
future army of invasion. Then, too, Great Britain is no longer
really interested in reparation, whereas the French seem willing to
push their demands in a manner which points to the economic
enslavement and political dismemberment of Germany. To the
British mind French policy is militaristic. France is not in any
real danger—so at least the British people feel—save perhaps for
a danger of her own creation. French policy is responsible for
the growing influence of anti-democratic forces in Germany. The
Germans will be driven in despair into the arms of any other
country willing to help them. France is trying to maintain peace
in Europe by establishing an equilibrium of military force. That
will inevitably bring about new combinations and future wars.
Now is the time to begin a new era in foreign policy. The errors
of the past must not be repeated.

The French Socialists replied less assertively, intent rather to
explain the motives of their countrymen than to vindicate the
policy of their Government. They said:

There is a simple explanation of the difference between the British
and the French points of view. The North Sea is wider than the

---

[1] *The Nation*, February 14, 1920.
[2] *Labour Party: Report of Annual Conference, 1922*, pp. 29–35.

Rhine, and the German fleet is at the bottom of the sea. France is dominated by the fear of the rapid economic recovery of Germany; Germany would then regain her military strength and might be bent on revenge. But France is not imperialistic in the true sense of the word; not even among the reactionaries is there any desire for aggression or expansion. There are indeed people in France actuated by the idea of overstressing the demand for reparation in order to find motives for extending the political influence of France —but they form a negligible minority. Then a strong feeling exists in France that the country will go bankrupt unless help comes from outside. With it goes a general belief that Germany can pay, but that France is being left in the lurch by her allies, especially Great Britain. The average Frenchman thinks the British selfish. They have taken the German colonies and the German mercantile marine. They have got rid of the German navy. Now, therefore, the British have not the same interest as the French in making Germany pay. The arguments of the militarist elements are reinforced, too, by the belief that Germany is trying to rebuild her military machine, and that a strong army is necessary to compel her to pay what she has agreed to pay. In France the strength of the German militarist party is not under-estimated. Really there are two Germanys. The Government in France can—and does—play upon French fear of Germany. French socialists have to combat this fear on the lines that France must be guaranteed security, only by means of an international organization to guarantee the security of all nations.

The growing tension between Great Britain and France in 1922 must be viewed against this background of conflicting opinion. To Englishmen it appeared no more than reasonable that the renewed offer to France of a British guarantee against German invasion should be conditional on the modification of French policy. The memorandum of 4th January 1922, presented by Lloyd George to Briand at Cannes, stated the conditions: French co-operation in plans of European reconstruction; an economic understanding with Russia; the elimination of naval rivalry; the co-ordination of British and French policy in the Near East.[1] But in France the feeling prevailed that at successive conferences Lloyd George had already wheedled French Prime Ministers—first Clemenceau, then Millerand, and lastly Briand—into a series of concessions, each involving the curtailment of French rights under the Treaty. Where, Frenchmen questioned anxiously, would the process end? They greeted the British guarantee as a lollipop designed to ensure the subordination of French to British policy.

---

[1] A first draft of the Cannes Memorandum stated these conditions more bluntly. Briand's intervention resulted in the publication of a toned-down version. See Riddell, Lord: *Intimate Diary*, p. 142; *D'Abernon*, i, p. 247.

Poincaré's assumption of the Premiership symbolized the determination of France to enforce and maintain the Treaty at all costs—with Great Britain if British co-operation could be procured without the sacrifice of French rights and without detriment to the ascendancy of France over Germany; if not, then without Great Britain. The conclusion is warrantable that when, at the end of 1922, Poincaré decided to proceed to the occupation of the Ruhr, his general purpose was to demonstrate that France alone was strong enough to maintain the Versailles settlement.

At the outset of the Ruhr occupation the British Government announced that, though able neither to approve of nor to participate in the occupation, it would avoid any action which might embarrass France. Behind this policy of 'benevolent neutrality' lay awareness of the comparative impotence of Great Britain. To the Opposition speakers—E. D. Morel, J. R. MacDonald—who came forward as the champions of the European balance of power, Bonar Law replied that, to follow the course they advocated, it would be necessary 'to prepare ourselves for the possibility of enforcing our will upon France by war.' As long as the French believe that 'their pressure will have its effect on Germany,' he added, it will remain 'useless, in my view, for us to offer our services.' [1] The failure of Lord Curzon's attempted mediation in the summer proved the soundness of that view. Lord Curzon desired to associate Great Britain with France in the offer of conditions which would induce Germany to abandon passive resistance. But the termination of the struggle through British mediation would have defeated Poincaré's purpose; mediation would be regarded by Germany, he felt, as proof of the inability of France to dispense with British aid; for this reason he insisted on the unconditional submission of Germany. The exchange of notes between Curzon and Poincaré concluded with Curzon's outspoken note of 11th August 1923 and Poincaré's equally pointed rejoinder of 20th August 1923. German resistance to the occupation, though momentarily stiffened by this controversy between the quondam allies, collapsed at the end of the following month when the inability of Great Britain to help had become apparent.

Superficially Poincaré's triumph was complete. In the following months the French hold on the Ruhr industries tightened; under the aegis of the occupation in the Rhineland and the Ruhr, separatist bands grew active. But Poincaré's victory had no meaning unless France remained ready to enforce the Treaty again by independent action—if necessary, by similar action—in the future. Henceforward France lacked certainly the will to do so, and—though this may be disputed—almost certainly the power.

[1] 161 *H.C. Deb.*, March 6, 1923, col. 369-370.

For the struggle had exhausted France only less than Germany. This circumstance procured for Europe what in retrospect may be discerned as a period of truce. In 1924 adversity gave France and Germany a common interest in the discovery of a way of escape from the quandary to which their mutual antagonism had brought them. The collapse of the currency, the menace of political disintegration, the French grip on the German economic system obliged Germany to assent to a reparation settlement she would earlier have refused. France, seemingly at the zenith of her power, found her own position undermined by financial weakness. The Ruhr occupation, though momentarily yielding a trivial profit, was bound, if continued unchanged, to become before long a renewed source of embarrassment to the Treasury. French finances, deranged even before the occupation, had reached a precarious condition; a precipitous depreciation threatened unless foreign loans were forthcoming. France could no longer flout the opinion of the banking world. These conditions made possible the elaboration, with American co-operation, of the Dawes Plan. Its acceptance had as a result the dismissal of the reparation problem from the political arena from 1924 to 1929.

In 1924 Anglo-French relations as well as Franco-German relations experienced a decisive modification. In France the electoral victory of the Cartel des Gauches placed the Radical Socialists in power; the new Premier, Edouard Herriot, succeeded Poincaré on 1st June. Herriot looked forward to a friendly understanding with a democratic Germany, to the renunciation of 'the policy of isolation and of force,' to the extension of the influence of the League of Nations, and to the conclusion of security agreements within the framework of the League. In Ramsay MacDonald, who, combining the offices of British Prime Minister and Foreign Secretary, had replaced Lord Curzon at the end of January, Herriot found a not uncongenial collaborator. MacDonald had signalized his assumption of office by his endeavour to set Anglo-French relations on a friendlier footing through the exchange of personal letters with Poincaré—an action illustrative of MacDonald's conviction that international problems would prove susceptible of solution by 'the strenuous action of good-will.' But perhaps more decisive of the trend of Anglo-French relations was the change which governmental responsibility effected in MacDonald's attitude to the Treaty. He, one of the foremost advocates of Treaty revision, found that to work even with Herriot he must acquiesce in the principle of the sanctity of the Treaty. In the Franco-British Memorandum of 9th July 1924 MacDonald conceded that the violation of the provisions of the Treaty 'would lead to the collapse . . . of the permanent foundations on which rests the peace so painfully achieved . . . and would tend not to prevent, but to inaugurate, fresh conflicts.'[1] As by magic, the annual motion for the revision of the Treaty, which had hitherto figured among the resolutions of each annual Labour Party conference since 1919, disappeared henceforward from the agenda. The token of British recognition that Franco-British co-operation was dependent on British participation in the enforcement of the Treaty was the retention of British troops in the Cologne zone to ensure the more complete fulfilment of the military terms. To this action MacDonald assented, though it fell to his successor to carry it out.[2]

When, five days later, the Franco-British Memorandum of 9th July 1924 was debated in the House of Commons, Austen Chamberlain rose 'to say a word or two about the policy which my Friends and I would recommend to the consideration and attention of the Prime Minister for the future.' The speech which Austen Chamberlain then delivered outlined with remarkable fidelity the foreign policy which he was to pursue as Foreign Secretary from October 1924 to June 1929.

'What is the policy which we would follow? In the first place, we would frankly accept and uphold the Versailles Treaty and its subsidiary or collateral Treaties as the basis, and the only possible basis, for the public law of Europe.

'In the second place, we would make the maintenance of the Entente with France the cardinal object of our policy. We would do that both to give confidence in the stability and the execution of the Treaties and to prevent fresh causes of difference arising between ourselves and our Allies. Let me say that, making that our aim . . . we should feel . . . that there was a similar obligation on the part of our Allies to make the maintenance of that Entente the cardinal article of their policy and to meet us in the spirit in which we were prepared to meet them. Thirdly, we should make the observance by Germany of her obligations a not less cardinal feature of our policy in foreign affairs, and, in return, if Germany frankly accepted and loyally fulfilled the obligations as now presented, we should be prepared to respect the integrity of Germany and to welcome her back into the comity of nations; and always, like His Majesty's Government and like every party in this House, we should seek to secure, wherever it be possible, associations with the United States of America in such ways and under such conditions as may at any moment alone be possible to the American people.'[3]

With this forecast of his policy may be coupled a sentence from Austen Chamberlain's speech in the House on 5th March 1925: 'No real progress will be made until we can . . . give that measure

[1] *Cmd.* 2191.
[2] See p. 81. Cf. the Franco-British reconciliation at San Remo, p. 71.
[3] 176 *H.C. Deb.*, July 14, 1924, col. 109–110.

of security and stability to Europe as she is now constituted, upon which all progress in human affairs, all recovery of national life and all commercial and economic prosperity must depend.' [1]   Economic prosperity dependent on the stability of Europe as *now* constituted —this was new language from a British Foreign Secretary.   Austen Chamberlain pressed home from conviction the lesson that MacDonald had perforce learnt—that the cause of peace was not furthered by the vain talk of Treaty revision.

Austen Chamberlain's first task was to exorcise the fear of Germany which still prevailed in French minds.   Herriot avowed his anxiety to MacDonald and Chamberlain: to MacDonald—'If there is another war, France will be wiped off the map' [2]; to Chamberlain—'I look forward with terror to her making war upon us again in ten years.' [3]   Hitherto two avenues had been explored in the search for a solution of the problem of French security: both were blocked in the spring of 1925.   An exclusive Anglo-French Pact, though seemingly favoured by Austen Chamberlain, was even more unpopular in the country at large in 1925 than it had been in 1922.   Since 1922 a solution along other lines—regional pacts within a general treaty of mutual assistance—had been sought at Geneva.   The history of the abortive negotiations is familiar—Lord Cecil's four propositions of July 1922; the League Assembly Resolution 14 of September 1922; the Draft Treaty of Mutual Assistance, hammered out in the Temporary Mixed Commission and presented to the Assembly in September 1923, only to encounter rejection by the Labour Government in July 1924; the Geneva Protocol, worked out by the Third Committee of the Assembly in September 1924, on the basis of the suggestions thrown out by Herriot and MacDonald in the debate of 4th–6th September; and the rejection of the Protocol by the Conservative Government in March 1925. Stresemann's project of a reciprocal pact of security for the Rhineland offered a welcome escape from the impasse which threatened to develop.   At his first meeting with Herriot, Austen Chamberlain informed him that the German proposal provided the only basis on which Franco-British negotiations for a solution of the problem of security could proceed. [4]   Though profoundly disappointed, Herriot agreed.   But his successor Briand found some consolation in Chamberlain's anxiety to conduct the ensuing negotiations in a manner expressive of the continuance of the Entente.   It is customary to record that the agreements which resulted marked 'the real dividing-line between the years of war and the years of

[1] 181 *H.C. Deb.*, March 5, 1925, col. 707.
[2] Suarez, G.: *Une Nuit chez Cromwell*, p. 165.
[3] Petrie, Sir C.: *Life and Letters of Austen Chamberlain*, ii, p. 263.
[4] 270 *H.C. Deb.*, November 10, 1932, col. 561.

peace.' The Treaties, initialled at Locarno on 15th October 1925, were signed in London on 1st December.

'Locarno was not the end, but the beginning,' declared Sir Austen Chamberlain in his first public statement after his return to England.[1] The omens which pointed to the transfiguration of European politics through the pervading influence of the new spirit of reconciliation were not indeed wholly belied by the course of events; the mutual trust of Briand, Chamberlain, and Stresemann remained the dominant political factor in European affairs for the next three years. Yet by 1929 there prevailed the uneasy feeling that Locarno had failed to fulfil its promise. It had relieved but not removed French fears of Germany; the Treaty signed by Great Britain was more a British than a French solution of the security problem—more a pact of understanding than, from the French viewpoint, an effective Treaty of Guarantee. So the search for security went on. In Germany disillusionment was intense and widespread. The signature of the Locarno Treaties had yielded forthwith a galaxy of minor concessions—the relinquishment by France of the demand for a permanent Commission of Inspection in the Rhineland, the evacuation of the Cologne zone, modifications in the régime of the Rhineland occupation so extensive as to transform its character, and a pledge to reduce the army of occupation.[2] Yet the German Government had deemed it politic to convey to its citizens a false impression of disappointment.[3] But in the later professions of discontent there was no pretence. The fulfilment of the promised reduction in the Allied army of occupation was unwarrantably delayed; by the time it was completed—towards the close of 1927—Germany had begun to count on complete evacuation. The question of evacuation was linked with the elaboration of a final plan of reparation payments; the negotiations were protracted. Before their completion the Locarno triumvirate had broken up. In June 1929 the guidance of British foreign policy passed from Chamberlain to Arthur Henderson. In October Stresemann died. Briand alone remained. By the first year of the second decade of peace the Locarno spirit had disappeared.

[1] Chamberlain, Sir A.: *Peace in Our Time*, p. 83.
[2] For the alleviations in the administration of the Rhineland, see *The Times*, November 19, 1925.
[3] *Stresemann*, ii, p. 232; *D'Abernon*, iii, p. 207.

CHAPTER V

THE AGENCIES OF ALLIED CO-OPERATION

IN the immediate post-War years the imminent dissolution of the Anglo-French Entente was announced with unwearying reiteration in the columns of the English Radical Press. In the midst of one such prognostication a Liberal journal proceeded to define the Entente as 'a disposition, though scarcely an obligation, to act together in the main issues of European policy.'[1] So regarded, the Entente was indeed breaking down. The formal bonds of alliance, though nominally maintained by the continuing state of war with Turkey, had virtually been severed on the ratification of peace with the principal enemy. And of disposition towards common action there was little trace, save perhaps with regard to the reduction of the German armed forces, for the viewpoints of the two peoples were as poles asunder.

Yet, if the Treaty of Versailles was to be carried out, the collaboration of Great Britain and France was essential. For the conditions of the Treaty could be fulfilled only in the course of years. Plebiscites remained to be held; boundaries to be delimited. German armaments had to be brought down to the level set by the Treaty. The Rhineland would remain under Allied occupation for some fifteen years; perhaps more, perhaps less. New problems would incessantly arise in the making of reparation payments. These and other matters would constantly call for decisions taken by the Allies, not singly, but as a body. To meet this need several Allied organizations had been set up through the agency of which it was intended that such decisions should be reached. The question arises: to what extent were these organizations able to function as effective instruments for the co-ordination of Allied policy despite the disintegration of the Alliance in the early twenties? Not all the bodies set up are brought under review in this chapter. About the Boundary Commissions little information is available. The Plebiscite Commissions have been treated in two truly magisterial works.[2] Only those bodies active in the political field call for consideration here: namely, the Supreme Council, the Conference of Ambassadors, the Military, Naval, and Air Commissions of Control, the Reparation Commission and the Rhineland High Commission.

The Supreme Council was an institutional outgrowth of the War. Experience early demonstrated the value of supplementing the

---

[1] *The Nation*, May 13, 1922.
[2] Wambaugh, S.: *Plebiscites since the World War*, Washington, 1933; and *The Saar Plebiscite*, Cambridge, Mass., 1940.

ordinary channels of diplomatic correspondence by direct and personal intercourse between British and French Ministers. The ministerial conferences held intermittently from July 1915 onwards culminated in the formation in November 1917 of the Supreme War Council, composed of the Prime Ministers of France, Great Britain, and Italy, together with one other Minister of each country. The United States was represented only occasionally for political purposes, though permanently maintaining a military delegation to the Council headed by General Bliss. The political heads of Government came together in the Supreme War Council to examine the problems arising in the conduct of war not in the light of their separate national interests but from the viewpoint of the common purpose of achieving victory. Reporting on its work to the American Government, General Bliss wrote: 'Matters of gravest importance to the safety of the world were settled with cordial unanimity in a few minutes which, did they have to be handled by diplomatic dispatches, through the hands of jealous general staffs and of suspicious Cabinets . . . would have taken precious days or weeks.' The political chiefs were assisted by an advisory body of military experts entrusted with the continuous study of developments on all fronts. Their function was 'to advise the Supreme War Council as a whole, and not merely as the representatives of their respective nations on the Council.' In war the Council was found an effective agency for the co-ordination of Allied policy.[1]

After the armistice the Supreme War Council, with the addition of Japanese and permanent American representatives, maintained its identity alongside the machinery of the Peace Conference, and on the ratification of peace with Germany emerged as the Supreme Council *tout court*. From 1920 to 1923 conferences of the Principal Allied Powers continued to be held to deal both with those questions, particularly of the Near East, in respect of which no settlement had been achieved in 1919, and with the major problems arising in the execution of the completed treaties. The French Prime Minister, Millerand, looked forward indeed early in 1920 to the resumption of normal diplomatic methods of negotiation, but the multiplicity of the issues and the personal aptitudes of the British Prime Minister combined to compel the continuance of the conference method.[2] Unhappily 'diplomacy by conference' failed as a means of main-

---

[1] 'Report of General Bliss on the Supreme War Council' in *U.S.A.: Foreign Relations: Lansing Papers, 1914–1920*, ii, pp. 198–302; Hankey, Sir M.: *Diplomacy by Conference*.

[2] *Chambre: Débats*, March 26, 1920, p. 578. For a description of the informal procedure of the Supreme Council, see *U.S.A: Foreign Relations, 1921*, vol. i, pp. 63–64. See also Maurice, Sir F.: *Lessons of Allied Co-operation, 1914–1918*. Part III deals with the Supreme War Council.

:aining harmony between the Allies after the return of peace. This question is taken up again in a later chapter, but one comment may be made here. After the return of peace the Supreme Council had at its command no subordinate organizations charged with the continuous study of the problems of peace comparable with the military and economic bodies whose creation had been essential for the prosecution of war. Divested of its satellites, the Supreme Council shed its character as an agency for the patient elaboration of a truly allied policy, and became nothing more than an intermittent series of conferences at which, commonly in a blaze of publicity, an English policy was pitted against a French policy with the result that, to avoid the avowal of a rift in the Entente, hasty compromises were devised which in the long run provoked dissatisfaction in England and exasperation in France.

The Supreme Council differed from the Supreme War Council not only by its attenuated organization but by its changed composition. Owing to the failure of the United States to ratify the Treaty, the American representative attended its meetings only in the capacity of an observer instructed 'to express no opinion and to take no action on any subject . . . but to report the proceedings to the Department.' ¹ Belgium, on the other hand, made good a claim to representation. During 1919 Belgium had been represented on the Supreme Economic Council by M. Jaspar. In March 1920, hearing that the Supreme Council itself was discussing economic problems, Jaspar paid a surprise visit to London and sought from Austen Chamberlain an explanation how it came that the Council had taken up the study of economic problems, which would affect Belgian interests, without having invited Belgian participation. Lloyd George, approached by Austen Chamberlain, agreed that Jaspar should join in. Thereafter Belgian collaboration in the Supreme Council was retained, though restricted to questions of direct concern to Belgium. Thus at Paris in August 1921 the Belgian representative was excluded from discussions on Upper Silesia, but took part in the proceedings on other questions.² From 1920 to 1924 Belgian statesmen exercised an invaluable mediatory influence between France and Great Britain.

Since the Supreme Council met only intermittently, to deal with matters of high policy, the establishment of some permanent organization to deal with the multifarious questions of a minor nature which would arise in the execution of treaties was essential. For this purpose the Conference of Ambassadors was set up in January 1920. It consisted of the British, Italian, and Japanese

---

¹ U.S.A.: *Foreign Relations*, 1920, i, p. 2.
² See Terlinden, C.: 'La Belgique aux conférences interalliées,' *Revue Générale*, January 15, 1922.

ambassadors in Paris, together with a French representative who presided, while a Belgian representative was entitled to be present for the discussion of matters affecting Belgium.[1] As a rule, meetings were held once a week. In the supervision of German disarmament the Conference was assisted by the Inter-Allied Military Committee of Versailles, whose function was to submit advisory reports on military questions. Within the limitations of its authority the Ambassadors' Conference was instrumental in ensuring the presentation of a united Allied front towards Germany. Stresemann later impugned it as 'a sort of penal committee established against Germany.'[2] The Conference was indeed reproached in England with a leaning towards French views. This reputation may be ascribed primarily to the necessity of a strict adherence by the ambassadors to the letter of the Treaty, and partly perhaps to a natural tendency on their part to adopt an attitude favourable to the country to which they were accredited. But the Conference was powerless to promote unity of views on the critical issues of policy which were brought before the Supreme Council, with which it appears to have had no organic connexion.

Among the functions of the Conference of Ambassadors was the supervision of the Inter-Allied Military, Naval, and Aeronautical Commissions set up in accordance with the provisions of the Treaty to control within Germany the reduction of the German army and navy and the abolition of the German air force.[3] Of these bodies the Military Commission came to play the most significant rôle in Anglo-French relations. The principle of Allied solidarity received consistent expression in its organization. From 1920–23 decisions were taken by majority vote. The German Government was required to address to the Commission in the first instance all communications concerning the application of the military clauses. The vital centres of the Commission's activity were the district committees responsible for the visits of inspection in the various localities of the Reich. The personnel of each district committee was inter-Allied in character. The officers of the Military Commission were fortunate in their ability to work together in singular harmony; their labours were not impeded by that divergence of purpose between the Allies which developed in spheres of policy other than German disarmament.

Such divergence of purpose greatly lessened, though it did not wholly nullify, the utility of the two other bodies which call for

---

[1] 134 *H.C. Deb.*, November 4, 1920, col. 587.   A valuable study of the Conference of Ambassadors is now available: Pink, G. P.: *The Conference of Ambassadors.* Geneva Research Centre, Geneva Studies, vol. xii, Nos. 4–5, February 1942.   It has not been possible, however, to utilize Dr Pink's study in the preparation of this work.

[2] *Stresemann*, iii, p. 159.   [3] See p. 145.

consideration here—the Reparation Commission and the Inter-Allied Rhineland High Commission. The Reparation Commission was a permanent executive body charged with the administration of the reparation provisions of the Treaty. Though inter-Allied in composition, the Commission was not, in law, the mere agent of the Allied Governments. Its decisions were final; they could not be rescinded by governmental action. The Commission owed its independent status to the intention of the American delegation at the Peace Conference that it should be the instrument for dealing with reparation in accordance with economic rather than political considerations.[1] A combination of factors accounts for the failure of the Commission to serve this purpose. The absence of an American delegate undermined the Commission's prestige; American membership would have enhanced the Commission's authority as the agency through which the United States participated in the handling of the reparation problem. The American withdrawal disturbed, too, the distribution of voting power within the Commission; the French Chairman's privilege of a casting vote acquired in a body of four a significance which it could not possess in a body of five. Though the privilege was rarely exercised, the knowledge that it lay in the background is said—with what justification it is impossible to determine—to have often overshadowed the course of discussion. Moreover the appointment by France of politicians such as Poincaré and Barthou instead of financial experts as chief delegates compromised its character as an agency for carrying through reparation along sound financial lines. And, perhaps for this reason, the British Government from the outset sought to push the Commission aside and to seek a reparation settlement by direct negotiation with the German Government.

Yet, though debased in practice, the conception of the Reparation Commission was eminently sound. Within the limitations of its authority it provided the machinery for the adaptation of the reparation provisions to the exigencies of financial and economic conditions. Thus it made a plentiful and judicious use of the power of making exceptions to Article 248, the strict application of which might have paralysed German financial administration.[2] Nor in the more crucial task of modifying Germany's total liability to her capacity to pay is it apparent that anything was gained by transferring the discussion from the seclusion of the Commission to the noisy dispute of the Supreme Council. It is true the Commission had no authority to cut down the amount demanded for reparation—a power with which the Americans alone had sought to endow it; but there was nothing to prohibit the Commission from discussing such reduction, and even recommending it if

[1] For the origin of the Reparation Commission, see pp. 106-107.   [2] See p. 121.

unanimity could be attained. 'It was frequently a cause for amazement,' wrote its secretary in later years, 'that the Governments did not take advantage of the Commission's Treaty independence by seeking shelter under it; it would apparently have been ordinary political perspicacity for the Governments to wash their hands of the business by allowing and encouraging the Commission to enunciate unpalatable truths and take unpopular measures which would have been fatal to any politician.' [1]   The wisdom of such a procedure received recognition when, in November 1923, at the instigation of the American Secretary of State, the reparation problem was referred for examination to the Dawes Committee of Experts.

Much more than the Reparation Commission, the Inter-Allied Rhineland High Commission proved in practice a grotesque distortion of the aspirations of its all too idealistic creators. To appreciate its history, its origin must be examined.

When, in April 1919, it was decided to occupy the Rhineland for fifteen years, it became necessary to regulate the future relations of the military with the local population and the local administrative authorities.   For, when an army is stationed in such circumstances on foreign soil, the subordination of the native police and local authorities to the army command becomes imperative in order that the Commander-in-Chief may take all measures necessary for the security of his troops.   Custom, based on numerous precedents, requires that the Commander-in-Chief should be the supreme representative of the occupying state in the occupied territory, and that a condition of martial law should be maintained.   Such a military régime had prevailed in the Rhineland throughout the period of armistice.   The British and French military authorities favoured the continuance of this régime after the return of peace, and proposals to this effect, drafted by Generals Twiss and Weygand, were submitted to the Council of Four on 11th May 1919.   But they met with fierce criticism in American quarters.   Noyes, the American member of the Inter-Allied Rhineland Commission, protested in a letter to Wilson that the military proposals would lead to 'unendurable oppression of six million people during a period of years.'   He advised the preparation of a new plan on the following basis:—

I. As few troops as possible concentrated in barracks or reserve areas with no 'billeting,' excepting possibly for officers.

II. Complete self-government for the territory with the exceptions below.

[1] McFadyean, Sir A.: *Reparation Reviewed*, p. 35.

III. A Civil Commission with powers:
> (a) To make regulations or change old ones whenever German law or actions—
>> (i) Threaten the carrying out of Treaty terms, or
>> (ii) Threaten the comfort or security of troops.
> (b) To authorize the army to take control under martial law, either in danger spots or throughout the territory, whenever conditions seem to them to make this necessary.

Noyes' object was to minimize military interference with German civil life and administration. To this end he recommended the establishment of a Civil Commission to take the place of the Commander-in-Chief as the supreme representative of the Allied Governments in occupied territory. At Wilson's suggestion a Committee was set up by the Council of Four on 29th May to draw up a new plan based on the principles put forward by Noyes. This Committee, which consisted of five members, including Lord Robert Cecil and Louis Loucheur, drew up the convention known as the 'Agreement with regard to the military occupation of the territories of the Rhine.'

Under the provisions of this Rhineland Agreement, which was signed by the German delegation on 28th June 1919, an Inter-Allied Rhineland High Commission was constituted as the supreme representative within occupied territory of the Allied and Associated Governments. By the terms of the Agreement, the Commission was to consist of four representatives of Belgium, France, Great Britain, and U.S.A.; but the defection of the U.S.A. resulted in a membership of three, though until January 1923 the General-in-Command of the American army of occupation was present at meetings of the Commission. The powers of the Rhineland Commission, and the way they were exercised, will be dealt with at a later stage. What calls for attention here is the failure of the Rhineland Commission as an instrument for the co-ordination of Allied policy in the Rhineland.

By a curious irony, within the Committee which drew up the Rhineland Agreement the only zealous advocate of Noyes' plan was the French representative, Louis Loucheur. The caustic criticisms of Foch and Weygand were so telling as to turn Lord Robert Cecil into an opponent of the scheme. The American representative was but a lukewarm supporter. Indeed, though the Rhineland High Commission was of American parentage, in parturition its life would have departed but for the solicitude of M. Loucheur. Loucheur insisted on the contrast between the occupation of France in 1870–1873 and the projected occupation of Germany. After the Franco-Prussian War there were stationed in France the troops of only one country, Germany. From 1919 the armies of four states—so it was expected—would occupy German soil. Differences of tradition and policy would lead to the pursuance of different policies in the areas occupied by troops of different nationality. 'We need to be certain,' urged Loucheur, 'that the principles which are going to be adopted in one zone of occupation shall be similarly followed in the others.' The Dorten incident, indeed, had just shown that a critical situation might develop unless some supreme organization was set up which would enable the Allied representatives to exchange views and take action as a unit. Noyes had this in mind when he put forward his suggestions.[1]

Though in theory the authority of the Rhineland Commission extended over the whole of the Occupied Territory, in practice the Commission presented, from the first moment of its organization, little more than a façade of Allied unity. This was perhaps an inevitable consequence of the division of the Occupied Territory into four areas: the Belgian around Aachen, the British around Cologne, the American around Coblenz, and the French extending from Mainz southwards into the Bavarian Palatinate. Within each area the Representatives of the High Commission actually in contact with the German local authorities and with the German population were all of the same nationality as the troops occupying that area. They were responsible not to the High Commission as a body, but to their own national commissioners. Each commissioner appears to have possessed little knowledge of and almost no control over the activities of the Representatives of the High Commission outside the territory occupied by the troops of his own country. The disintegration of the High Commission was further accentuated by the arrangements made for the enforcement of the Commission's Ordinances, which were binding on all persons and authorities, Allied and German, within the Occupied Territory. Each Allied army organized special courts within its own area of occupation, before which offenders against the ordinances were brought. Thus sheriff and judge, as it were, escaped the unifying control of the High Commission and assumed the livery of their respective countries.

The impotence of the High Commission as an instrument of co-ordination is exemplified above all by the contrast between British and French policy in the Rhineland in 1923–1924. Yet as early as February 1920 the American observer—P. B. Noyes himself—lamented to the Acting Secretary of State that 'three-quarters of the territory is French and it is very hard to know what

---

[1] *Miller*, xix, pp. 485–494; *Baker*, iii, pp. 255–256; Allen, H. T.: *Rhineland Occupation*, pp. 85–88; *Peace Conference, 1919: Commission interalliée de la rive gauche du Rhin, procès verbaux et documents.* For the Dorten incident, see p. 178.

s taking place.'[1] The onset of the Ruhr occupation revealed how uperficial was the supposedly unitary character of the occupation. Thus the 'special ordinances,' passed by the majority vote of the French and Belgian Commissioners, by means of which the measures of coercion introduced by military decree in the Ruhr were applied to the Rhineland, remained a dead letter in the British area of occupation. So, too, in January 1924, the French objected 'on technical grounds' to a proposal to send an officer of the British section of the Commission to inquire into the separatist movement in the Palatinate; in consequence the British Government resorted to the expedient of instructing the British Consul General to conduct an investigation.[2] When the High Commission, in February 1924, appointed an Inter-Allied Committee to investigate in the Palatinate the measures to be taken there for the restoration of order, its action marked the resumption of the Commission's control over the whole occupied area.[3]

A survey of the agencies of Allied co-operation after the War of 1914–1918 is eloquent of the powerlessness of institutions to effect the co-ordination of policy when changes of political temper supervene among the peoples concerned. The Reparation Commission and the Rhineland Commission were split by the Anglo-French cleavage of view. It may be that had the Reparation Commission been accorded from the start full powers for working out a practical solution, and had it been left to function without governmental interference, it might have robbed the reparation problem of its venom; but, even so, no such development could have ensued save within a framework of Anglo-French agreement on questions of security. The essential task was to keep the two countries in step in matters of high policy; and here the Supreme Council failed ignominiously. That failure may doubtless be traced in part to defects of procedure and to the idiosyncrasies of the principal actors; but, by and large, it must be ascribed to the mental chasm which opened between the peoples of the two countries. In such circumstances there was no remedy save in the growth of mutual comprehension; nor was this fully achieved until the danger which had brought them together in the past again loomed on the horizon.

[1] U.S.A. Foreign Relations, 1920, ii, p. 293.
[2] 56 Lords Deb., January 15, 1924, col. 45.
[3] For the Rhineland High Commission, see Tirard, P.: La France sur le Rhin; Rousseau, J.: La Haute Commission Interalliée (Mainz, 1925); Alléhaut, M.: Les Libertés dans les pays rhénans; Reynolds, B. T.: 'The Occupation of the Rhineland,' International Affairs, May 1928; Parkes, N.: 'British Summary Courts in the Rhineland,' Nineteenth Century, April 1930. Cornier, C.: Le Statut de l'occupation rhénane (Paris, 1934) has not been available. See also below, p. 75.

CHAPTER VI

THE ENFORCEMENT OF THE TREATY

IT'S a faultless Treaty. Like the legendary mare, it possesses every virtue but one: it hasn't the breath of life in it.'[1] In these words Briand expressed the growing disquietude of the French in 1920 and the early months of 1921 at what seemed to them the dilatory and partial application of the Treaty. First one provision of the Treaty—that on which the British public had set its heart in the election of 1918—had been virtually jettisoned. Confronted by the refusal of the Netherlands Government to surrender the Kaiser, the Allies had perforce to abandon their project of trying him 'for a supreme offence against international morality and the sanctity of treaties.' Then another provision had been modified in practice to meet the protests of the German Government. The Treaty required the delivery for trial by Allied military tribunals of German subjects accused of having committed acts in violation of the laws and customs of war. The German Government declared their inability to enforce the arrest and surrender to the Allies of the accused persons, and suggested that they should instead be tried before the Supreme Court of the Reich at Leipzig. Though the Allies agreed to this procedure, the German Government continued to take refuge—to quote Lord Curzon—in 'evasion, procrastination, and delay.'[2] More immediately injurious to French interests were German shortcomings as regards coal deliveries and disarmament. In the first months of 1920 the coal deliveries effected by Germany fell considerably below the quantities demanded by the Reparation Commission, while the continued existence in Germany at the close of 1920 of militia formations and of police units organized on a military basis indicated, in the view of the French Government, a fixed determination to evade the disarmament clauses. Finally, the British and French Governments both inveighed against the apparent reluctance of the German Government to address itself resolutely to the problem of reparation. To anxious French minds the Treaty seemed menaced with infantile paralysis.

German dereliction brought to the forefront a problem which had received all too little consideration during the negotiations in 1919, but which for more than a decade was to remain a cardinal

[1] *Chambre: Débats*, February 4, 1921, 2me séance, p. 225.
[2] 45 *Lords Deb.*, May 5, 1921, col. 210–214. For a full account, see Toynbee: *Survey,* 1923, pp. 96–99; Lerner, K. von.: 'Die Auslieferung der deutschen Kriegsverbrecher,' in Schnee, H., and Draeger, H.: *Zehn Jahre Versailles*, i, pp. 15–29; and documents in *Cmd.* 1325.

element in Anglo-French relations. How were the Allies to enforce compliance with the Treaty provisions if Germany appeared unwilling to carry them out? It was in the nature of the Treaty of Versailles to raise insistently the issue of sanctions, for whereas a treaty which ensures equal benefits to all its signatories may evoke their spontaneous collaboration in its application, a treaty which consecrates the claims of victors gives promise of life only in proportion to their power and will to enforce its terms. Hardly had the Treaty entered into force before the Allies found themselves confronted with the alternatives of either modifying the Treaty in order to pave the way for friendlier relations with Germany, or of resorting to coercion in an effort to maintain the Treaty in its integrity. This choice of policies imposed itself most clearly in regard to reparation. The Franco-British controversy on this question owed much of its acuity to awareness on both sides that its handling would influence decisively the general trend of Allied policy.

In Great Britain the stability of any settlement imposed and maintained by superior force soon became the subject of misgiving. The inclination of British statesmen was to seek through negotiation to find some basis of amicable understanding with Germany. The most succinct statement of their attitude is to be found in the Notes written by Lord Curzon during the controversy with France over the occupation of the Ruhr. Lord Curzon wrote in the famous Note of 11th August 1923:

'His Majesty's Government hold the opinion that an undertaking freely entered into, because acknowledged to be just and reasonable, stands, in practice, on a different footing and offers better prospects of faithful execution, than an engagement subscribed under the compulsion of an ultimatum, and protested against at the very moment of signature, as beyond the signatory's capacity to make good.' [1]

Though the exigencies of the Entente caused British policy to deviate on occasion from the course suggested by this pronouncement, it expressed faithfully the spirit which the British Government sought to breathe into Allied policy from the very first months of 1920. To the British mind the Treaty of Versailles was tainted at its source because it had been imposed on Germany at the point of the sword. MacDonald, when bringing the London Conference on the Dawes Plan to a close, sought to underline the departure from the procedure of 1919. 'We are now offering,' he declared, 'the first really negotiated agreement since the War; every party here represented is morally bound to do its best to

---

[1] *Cmd.* 1943, p. 55.

carry it out, because it is not the result of an ultimatum.' [1] In the same spirit the Treaty of Locarno was acclaimed in England because it resulted from a Conference at which the nations 'who had been enemies met on a footing of perfect equality, free to give or to refuse, to undertake or not to undertake.' [2] In one sphere after another, first reparation, then disarmament, and finally frontiers, Englishmen sought to substitute for the Treaty other undertakings 'freely entered into, because acknowledged to be just and reasonable.'

To the French the British inclination towards conciliation for long appeared perilous and premature, more likely to evoke in Germany a systematic resistance to the execution of the Treaty than to contribute to the pacification of Europe. Their feeling, intense in the early years though weakening as the years passed by, was that time must be allowed for the consolidation of the new settlement, and that the course of wisdom was to impress Germany with a sense of the irrevocability of the Treaty. In their attitude to the Treaty Frenchmen differed but little: they saw in it their essential safeguard for the future, and the safeguard too of the new states of eastern and central Europe with whose fate their own seemed linked. When respect for the Treaty was at issue, men so dissimilar as Poincaré and Herriot spoke the same language. Replying to Lord Curzon, on 20th August 1923, Poincaré wrote: 'If France insists on the Treaties being carried out purely and simply, she does not do so through a sort of juridical attachment to the letter and spirit of diplomatic documents. . . . She apprehends that a most dangerous precedent would be created by a breach of the Treaty of Versailles. The Treaties of Saint-Germain, Neuilly, and Trianon would soon share the same fate, and the whole of the new Europe would be shaken to its foundations.' Just so Herriot told the German Ambassador on the eve of the London Conference in July 1924 that his 'irrefragable principle would be that there should be no alteration in the Treaty of Peace. He thought that such an attitude would be to the advantage of later generations, as he would thus avert the risk of war, which was indissolubly bound up with any cutting down of the Treaty.' [3]

This spiritual antagonism between British and French policy was in large measure responsible for the embitterment of Anglo-French relations in the course of the reparation controversy from 1920 to 1924. To regard that controversy solely as a dispute on a financial and economic problem is to view it in a false perspective. For the debate on reparation formed also the field of battle between the opposed British and French conceptions of the future place of

---

[1] *Cmd.* 2270, pp. 96–97.
[2] Chamberlain, Sir Austen: 188 *H.C. Deb.*, November 18, 1925, col. 421.
[3] *Stresemann*, i, pp. 365–366.

Germany in the polity of Europe. Conciliatory methods of negotiation were not for the British Government simply a means towards a financially sound reparation settlement, nor was coercion for the French Government directed merely towards the maintenance of existing reparation obligations. Conciliation was for the British Government an end in itself, as was coercion—the constant display of superior force—for the French Government; for the one desired to alleviate and the other to perpetuate the war-bequeathed distinction of victor and vanquished. Sanctions must be regarded not merely as measures ancillary to the collection of reparation, but as a substantive issue in Franco-British relations.

The history of sanctions may then with good reason be detached from the history of reparation, though the two are closely inter-twined. The study falls naturally into two sections. The first relates to the measures of coercion applied in the years 1920–1923, which resulted in the reconsideration of the problem of sanctions at the London Conference on the Dawes Plan in 1924; the second is devoted to the Rhineland occupation as a guarantee of the execution of the Treaty. The Rhineland occupation as a measure of security is treated in Chapter XV.

Sanctions for the enforcement of reparation payments were authorized by Paragraph 18 of Annex II of the reparation section of the Treaty. The celebrity attained by this paragraph in 1923 justifies quotation of the text:

'The measures which the Allied and Associated Powers shall have the right to take, in case of voluntary default by Germany, and which Germany agrees not to regard as acts of war, may include economic and financial prohibitions and reprisals and in general such other measures as the respective Governments may determine to be necessary in the circumstances.'

This loosely drawn paragraph had its origin in a Wilsonian paraphrase of a French proposal. In March 1919 Klotz, the French Minister of Finance, put forward a proposal that German default in the payment of reparation should be met by 'total or partial financial and economic blockade,' or by the occupation of additional places of strategic importance, or by 'territorial occupation which would put the [Reparation] Commission in command of financial or industrial revenues requisite for the discharge of the German debt.' This presage of Poincaré's productive pledges proved acceptable to none save the French. But when the time came for defining the powers of the Reparation Commission, Klotz secured the assent of his British and Italian colleagues in the Committee entrusted with the task to a more modest proposal— that the Allied Powers should assert their right, in the event of voluntary default, to apply specified measures of coercion, tanta-mount to the interdiction of communications and economic inter-course, the seizure of German goods and the prohibition of financial facilities. The Allies were moreover to reserve the right to apply other measures not specified. But when the matter came before the Council of Four, on 23rd April, President Wilson, in line with the American members of the Committee, insisted on the deletion from the Treaty of all reference to specific measures of coercion, and proposed the formula contained in the paragraph quoted.[1] No purpose would be served by dwelling on the controversy to which the interpretation of this text gave rise. It may well be remembered as a classic example of the untoward consequences of improvisation in drafting.

After the Treaty had entered into force, the problem of sanctions first arose not in connexion with reparation, but in connexion with the demilitarized zone. On 13th March 1920 the legitimate German Government was chased from Berlin by reactionary Reichswehr elements whose immediate object was to prevent the carrying out of the military terms of the Treaty. The triumph of the insurgents was short-lived; a general strike paralysed their authority, and on 17th March their leaders fled the land. So ended the 'Kapp Putsch.' But the insurrection gave rise to an unfortunate hang-over in the Ruhr, where so-called communist elements, which had risen in the first place against the reactionary insurgents, remained under arms. The disturbed area was in the demilitarized zone, within which Germany was debarred by Article 43 of the Treaty from maintaining troops. The Allied Governments had indeed sanctioned the retention of 17,000 troops in this zone until 10th April 1920; but it was claimed that these forces were in-adequate to repress the revolutionary movement. On 15th March 1920 the Allies were asked by the Kapp Government to sanction the entry of additional troops into the zone; two days later the request was repeated by the legitimate German Government from Stuttgart. While the British and American Governments favoured compliance, the French Government judged—rightly it would seem—that the Reichswehr were bent on preventing any peaceful local settlement. The French Government denied the necessity of military action, but were prepared to grant permission for the entry of additional German troops on condition that Allied forces should at the same time occupy Frankfort and Darmstadt as a pledge for the withdrawal of the German troops as soon as the revolutionary movement had been put down. The British Govern-

---

[1] See Annex VIII, Chapter IV, of Klotz's draft of March 28, 1919, in Klotz, L.: *De la Guerre à la Paix*, pp. 215-249; Burnett, P.: *Reparation at the Paris Peace Conference*, i, pp. 976, 998, 1006, 1099-1102.

ment opposed any such condition; Lord Derby refused even to discuss the question in the Council of Ambassadors. So a fortnight passed. On 3rd April 20,000 German troops advanced into the demilitarized zone without authorization. Three days later, without giving the other Allied Governments prior information of his intention, Millerand sent French forces into Frankfort. They were withdrawn on 17th May, when the Reichswehr had evacuated the demilitarized zone.[1] Shortly after the Frankfort incident, the Supreme Council met at San Remo (19th–26th April 1920). There Lloyd George pressed for a Conference with the Germans. As the price of French acquiescence, Millerand exacted British agreement to the principle that before the holding of any such Conference the Allies should reach agreement concerning the measures of coercion to be applied against Germany should occasion arise.[2] During the following months this principle of prior agreement on sanctions was scrupulously observed. The Allied Governments announced on 26th April their determination 'to take all measures, even to the extent, if necessary, of an occupation of German territory, which will have the effect of ensuring the execution of the Treaty.'[3] At the end of June agreement was reported to have been reached to occupy the Ruhr if Germany did not give effect without delay to the military clauses.[4] The occupation of the Ruhr was openly threatened in order to bring about the signature by the German representatives at the Spa Conference (5th–15th July 1920) of the protocols respecting coal deliveries and disarmament; and the same threat was inserted in these protocols as a penalty for failure to observe their provisions. A most elaborate scheme of sanctions was drawn up at the Paris Conference (24th–30th January 1921) to be applied if Germany should refuse to comply with the Paris Resolutions on reparation and disarmament.[5] A month later Lloyd George and Briand took counsel together on the question of sanctions at Chequers (27th February 1921) in preparation for the second Conference with the Germans (London, 1st–14th March 1921), and again at Lympne (23rd–24th April 1921) in preparation for the Allied Conference of London (29th April–5th May 1921).[6]

[1] For this incident, see *The Times*, March 24–April 13, 1920; speech by Millerand on April 13, *Chambre: Débats*, April 13, 1920, 2me séance, pp. 723-727; and speech by Briand nine years later in *Chambre: Débats*, November 8, 1929, p. 3052; *U.S.A. Foreign Relations*, 1920, ii, pp. 297-327; *Cmd.* 1325, Docs. 72, 76, 92, 95; Ronaldshay, Lord: *Curzon*, iii, pp. 231-233.
[2] *Chambre: Débats*, 2me séance, April 28, 1920, p. 1446.
[3] *Cmd.* 1325, p. 95.
[4] *U.S.A. Foreign Relations*, 1920, ii, p. 394; Whitlock to Secretary of State, June 30, 1920.
[5] *The Times*, January 31, 1921.
[6] *Eur. Nouv.*, March 19, 1921.

Lloyd George's assent in April 1920 to the formulation in advance of the measures of coercion against Germany was doubtless inspired by confidence in the prospect of reconciling Allied and German views in the course of successive conferences. The frustration of this hope at the London Conference of March 1921 left Lloyd George no recourse other than the application of sanctions in accordance with his pledge to the French. Sanctions were then applied not on account of any specific breach of the Treaty, but on the grounds that the dilatory and partial execution of its terms, and in particular the failure to put forward a satisfactory offer for reparation, evinced the purpose of Germany to evade her obligations.[1] The Allies occupied Duisberg, Ruhrort, and Düsseldorf; they established an Allied customs cordon between occupied and unoccupied Germany; they diverted to the Reparation Commission the customs revenue collected on the external frontier of the occupied territory; and they imposed a tax on German imports into Allied countries.

These measures were successful in eliciting a more adequate reparation offer, but it was rejected by the Allied Governments. Briand arrived at the London Conference (29th April–5th May 1921) pledged to demand the occupation of the Ruhr without further ado. The British Ministers pleaded in favour of sending Germany revised proposals accompanied by the threat that the Allies would occupy the Ruhr if Germany refused to accept them. Between the British and the French the Belgian representatives exercised their mediatory rôle. They pointed out that French troops would not be ready to move into the Ruhr until the preparatory measures of mobilization had been completed on 12th May, and that delay might well be used for a final approach to Germany as the British desired.[2] Briand acceded to this suggestion. On 5th May the German Government was informed that unless within six days the German Government accepted the requirements of the Schedule of Payments regarding reparation, and of the Paris Note of 29th January regarding disarmament, the Allies would occupy the Ruhr. This ultimatum precipitated a change of Government in Germany. The new Cabinet formed by Dr. Wirth accepted the Allied terms on 11th May, and so narrowly averted the Ruhr occupation.

The submission of Germany having been achieved, the British

[1] See conference speeches by Lloyd George, March 3 and 7, in *Times*, March 4 and 8, 1921; also statements to Commons on March 3 and 10, 1921: 138 *II.C. Deb.*, col. 2016; 139 *H.C. Deb.*, cols. 753 et seq. Cf. also Mem. of British Embassy to U.S. Dept. of State, March 14, 1921: 'In view of the failure of the German Government to accept the Paris decisions respecting Reparation or to make a satisfactory counter-offer, the Inter-Allied Conference sitting at London has decided to apply the following sanctions to Germany' (*U.S.A. Foreign Relations*, 1921, vol. ii, p. 36).
[2] *Chambre: Débats*, May 24, 1921, p. 45.

Government desired to cancel forthwith the operation of the sanctions imposed in March. Their maintenance appeared an unwise rebuff to the new Chancellor, who displayed both good will and energy in carrying out the Treaty. The export levy was indeed transformed by the Schedule of Payments into a method of collecting reparation payments with the co-operation of the German Government. The French Government refused at first to raise the other sanctions, conscious of the vehement protests which their withdrawal would provoke in the Chamber of Deputies. But on 13th August 1921, at the last session of the Conference of Paris, Loucheur surprised the British by proposing the termination of the economic sanctions, while Briand agreed to cancel the military measures at an early date.[1] The customs cordon was in fact raised on 1st October 1921, but owing to the replacement of Briand by Poincaré the Ruhr towns remained under military occupation until August 1925.

Here it is well to pause to consider the problems raised in 1920–1921 by the necessity of coercion for the enforcement of the Treaty. The crucial problem was whether action might be taken against Germany only by the Allied Governments acting together, or whether each Allied Government was free to act on its own. The French Government advanced the claim to take independent action; the British Government appears to have contested, in 1920, not the legality but the political expediency of this claim.[2] Circumstances had brought about a change in the French attitude between 1919 and 1920. During the Peace Conference the French delegation had displayed the greatest anxiety to ensure Allied solidarity in the applications of sanctions. 'Il ne faut pas de politique séparée,' declared Klotz, on 11th March 1919, in the Third sub-Commission on Reparation. 'Germany must always find facing her a consortium of all the Entente nations.' To this end Klotz had sought to set up within the League of Nations a Financial Section, empowered to interpret the financial and economic clauses of the Treaty and to call upon the Allied and Associated States to put measures of coercion into operation.[3] The pale reflection of this French proposal in the Treaty was the power confided to the Reparation Commission of making recommendations as to the action to be taken in the event of German default. But though the Commission might recommend, it was for governments to

---

[1] Allen, H. T.: *Rhineland Occupation*, pp. 214, 244.
[2] On October 28, 1920, Austen Chamberlain stated in the Commons that in the opinion of the British Government each Government was clearly entitled by Paragraph 18 of Annex II to decide for itself what action to take in pursuance thereof (133 *H.C. Deb.*, October 28, 1920, col. 1921).
[3] Lapradelle, IV (*Réparations*), ii, pp. 899, 901–902; Lapradelle, VII (*Commission financière*), pp. 346–349, 373; *Miller*, xvi, pp. 476–478.

decide.   In the first weeks of 1920 French suspicions of British
compliance towards Germany gave rise to the feeling that French
rights under the Treaty would be jeopardized if their enforcement
depended on British participation.   So France came to claim the
right of independent action; of this claim the occupation of Frankfort was symbolic.   In these circumstances the British Government
invoked in its turn the principle of Allied solidarity, but rather to
hold France back than to ensure common action for the enforcement of the Treaty in the future.   Lloyd George made public his
emphatic condemnation of the French by way of a statement by
Philip Kerr on 8th April 1920, to representatives of the provincial
Press.   Lord Curzon protested to the French Ambassador that
what France had done was 'incompatible with the mutual understanding and that common action upon which the stability of the
Alliance and the security of Europe alike depended.' [1]   Lord
Derby was instructed to take no part in the proceedings of the
Conference of Ambassadors on German questions until an assurance
had been received that France would in future act only in concert
with her Allies in all matters relating to the execution of the Treaty.
Millerand gave this assurance.   By virtue of the understanding
reached just afterwards, at San Remo, the British Government
counted on subordinating the French predilection for sanctions to
its own policy of friendly negotiation with Germany, while the
French Government reckoned to ensure British participation in
measures of coercion against Germany.

Anglo-French negotiations could indeed proceed, given the
contrast of outlook between the two countries, on no other basis
than that of trading French assent to the British policy of accom-
modation against British assent to the French policy of coercion.
Thereby Allied policy acquired the character of an unstable compound of which the constituent elements alternately exercised the
predominating influence.   A policy of sanctions was pursued
pari passu with a policy of conciliation by conference.   This
antinomy within Allied policy would have been followed by no evil
consequence—indeed, might have been beneficial—had the object
of Allied policy been to obtain German compliance with reasonable
demands capable of execution.   The French and British viewpoints
were not incompatible, but rather supplementary.   For if, on the
one hand, it was necessary to overcome French hesitation to appear
at the Conference table with the Germans for fear that discussion
should reveal division in the Allied ranks, on the other hand, it was
necessary to remind the British, now shrinking from the sound of
arms, that in the last resort the provisions of a treaty must be
enforced if they are not to be indefinitely whittled away.   The

[1] Ronaldshay, Lord: *Curzon*, iii, pp. 232–233.

source of tragedy lay in that Allied policy was directed towards securing, by parley or by force, German assent to the performance of the impossible in the matter of reparation. The Allies, having first stripped Germany of her transferable wealth, expected forthwith periodic payments which could not be made save after a period of economic and financial rehabilitation, the primordial necessity of which neither French nor, at this stage, British policy took account. As long as this limitation to German ability to meet Allied demands was overlooked, the British policy of negotiation with Germany could not avail to reconcile German offers with Allied expectations, with the result, already related, that in March 1921 British statesmen were called upon to honour the bond which bound them to the policy of sanctions should their own policy be barren of results. Sanctions were then applied for reasons which defied precise explanation, and in the outcome brought about the signature of an agreement which proved impossible of execution.[1]

The imposition of sanctions in March 1921 revealed the existence of a serious lacuna in the terms of the Treaty—or rather in the supplementary Rhineland Agreement. The Supreme Council had ordained the establishment of a customs cordon between occupied and unoccupied Germany. Inevitably the duty of organizing the cordon devolved on the Inter-Allied Rhineland High Commission, the supreme representative of the Allied Governments in the occupied territory. But the Commission could exert authority over the German population and the German authorities only by the issue of ordinances; and the scope of its ordinance-issuing power had been defined, and so limited, by the terms of the Rhineland Agreement. The Agreement authorized the issue of ordinances so far as might be necessary 'for securing the maintenance, safety and requirements of the Allied and Associated forces.' This definition had indeed proved extremely elastic; it gave the Commission—to quote the conclusion of its American legal adviser —'practically *carte blanche* in the way of enacting legislation.' [2] All questions bearing on the maintenance of public order—strikes, the food supply, public meetings, etc.—had from the start been brought within the Commission's legislative sphere on the plea that any public disturbance would compromise the safety of the troops. But the Commission was not endowed by the Rhineland Agreement with any authority to issue ordinances to ensure the execution of the Treaty. This omission moreover was not accidental. The first draft of the Rhineland Agreement—a document of British and not French origin—did indeed provide for the exercise of such

[1] See p. 108.
[2] Ireton, R. E.: 'The Rhineland Commission at Work,' *A.J.I.L.*, vol. 17, 1923, p. 463.

power by the Commission. Urging the adoption of this provision in the Committee which drew up the Agreement in June 1919, Lord Robert Cecil commented: 'I think what is needed is a civil authority with power to ascertain whether the Treaty terms are being observed and carried out. If in five years' time Germany refuses to carry out these terms, either as a whole or in part, the High Commission will have the right, by means of an ordinance, to close the frontier between the occupied districts and the rest of Germany, and so bring pressure to bear to see that she respects her obligations.' But Loucheur, supported by Foch and Weygand, protested that the Commission would thereby come to interfere too closely in German internal affairs. Cecil acknowledged the validity of their criticisms, and in consequence the Committee reported that 'to vest in the High Commission power to issue ordinances for the carrying out of the Treaty might give rise to an important extension of its action, and it asks the Council of Four if this was really their intention.' This provision was, in consequence, struck out by the Council of Four.[1] Nevertheless, the Supreme Council turned inevitably to the Rhineland Commission to apply the measures of coercion decreed in March 1921, and the Commission acted in the only way it could act—by the issue of ordinances—in order to give effect to the decisions of the Supreme Council. So too in 1923, though without the concurrence of the British Commissioner, the High Commission enforced in the Rhineland by the issue of 'special ordinances' the same measures of coercion as were applied by military authority in the Ruhr.

Throughout 1921 the French acquiesced, though with growing impatience, in the co-ordination of French with British policy. In debate after debate, each more stormy than its predecessor, Briand dwelt on the necessity of keeping in step with Great Britain. Isolated action by France, he foresaw, would be singularly dangerous politically, and would in the end jeopardize the economic and financial position of France. 'It is not enough for France alone to determine to carry out the Treaty in accordance with her own interests. Constant discussion with the Allies is called for, for it is always necessary to come to some agreement; else everything comes tumbling down.'[2] Briand's replacement by Poincaré in January 1922 resulted from the widespread feeling that his policy was threatening to tie France to British leading-strings. The note of revolt was first clearly sounded by Poincaré in his speech on 24th April 1922, at Bar le Duc, where he reasserted the right of France to act independently in applying sanctions against Germany

---

[1] *Peace Conference, 1919: Commission interalliée de la rive gauche du Rhin*, pp. 23–25, 31, 86–88.
[2] *Chambre: Débats*, October 18, 1921, pp. 17–18.

for the enforcement of reparation claims. According to Poincaré's interpretation of the famous Paragraph 18 of Annex II of the Reparation section, France would be entitled, in the event of voluntary default duly declared by the Reparation Commission, to apply not only financial and economic measures but to take military action against Germany, while Germany would be debarred from considering such steps as an act of war. At the end of 1922 Poincaré proceeded to procure from the Reparation Commission the declarations which would legitimate, in his view, an advance into the Ruhr. On 26th December 1922 the Reparation Commission declared Germany to have voluntarily defaulted in the delivery of timber to France during 1922; on 9th January 1923 Germany was declared in default in respect of coal deliveries to France. On both occasions the Commission's decision was taken by the majority vote of the French, Belgian, and Italian delegates against the vote of the British delegate, Sir John Bradbury. These decisions were the prelude to the Ruhr occupation, which commenced on 11th January 1923.

The vicissitudes of the Ruhr occupation fall outside the scope of this chapter. Here attention must be directed to the re-examination of the problem of sanctions for the enforcement of reparation payments which was necessitated by the liquidation of the Ruhr occupation at the London Conference, 16th July–16th August 1924. The Conference was summoned for the purpose of considering the measures necessary to put the Dawes Plan into force. The Dawes Committee—the financial experts who had devised the Plan—had reported that its success would depend on the adoption of suitable precautions to ensure that sanctions should not be imposed 'except in the case of flagrant failure to fulfil the conditions accepted by common agreement.' Behind this warning lay one cogent consideration. The purpose of the Plan was to make possible the payment of reparation by the re-establishment of German credit, and this not just in the near future, but forthwith. For the Plan itself entailed immediate flotation of a foreign loan to provide the means for the payment of reparation in the coming year. No such loan could be raised unless the financial world received some assurance that henceforward German financial stability would not be undermined by the application of sanctions in the political interests of France.

One indispensable condition of the success of the Dawes Plan was, then, the introduction of safeguards against any arbitrary declaration of default by the Reparation Commission in the future. The Treaty provided, be it recalled, for sanctions against Germany in the event of a declaration by the Commission that Germany had voluntarily defaulted in the payment of reparation. But in the view of the British Government, shared by British and American bankers, the Commission had become just 'an instrument of Franco-Belgian policy'; it had on the eve of the Ruhr occupation seized —to quote Sir John Bradbury's allegation—'on certain failures which, in view of the volume of the financial obligations under the Treaty, were almost microscopic,'[1] as a pretext for action prompted in large measure by motives little related to the desire for reparation. It was one of the major tasks of the London Conference to prevent the repetition of such action while, of course, leaving the way open for the application of sanctions in the event of a refusal by Germany to continue reparation payments while able to pay.

Agreement was reached at the Conference on two safeguards, the one terminological, the other procedural in character. Had a test case ever arisen, the former safeguard would almost certainly have proved illusory. The Allies concluded an agreement not to impose sanctions except in the circumstances referred to in the Dawes Report. The relevant passage has already been quoted; its virtue lay in the substitution of the words 'flagrant failure' for 'voluntary default.' Flagrant default, the British Prime Minister informed the Commons, was a 'large, general default,' one which indicated the existence of 'a conspiracy in high places to throw off obligations.' But, despite MacDonald's elucidation, the new term was no more precise, no less open to dispute, than the old.[2] Special interest attaches, however, to the adoption of the word 'flagrant,' since later it passed into the Locarno Treaty of Guarantee.

The second safeguard was found in a new procedure designed to ensure, in the future, impartial consideration of the question whether circumstances calling for the application of sanctions had arisen—i.e. whether flagrant default had taken place. In the course of the negotiations which preceded the London Conference the British Government had advanced a proposal to entrust the declaration of default to some body other than the Reparation Commission—the Financial Committee of the League was suggested —the objective character of whose findings would command general assent. This proposal to set aside the Reparation Commission, tantamount to an amendment of the Treaty, provoked a storm of criticism in France, before which the British Government deemed it wise to bow. A journey by MacDonald to Paris, occasioned by the French protests, resulted in a Franco-British agreement that the Reparation Commission should retain the powers it derived from the Treaty of Versailles, but that efforts should be made to secure the presence of an American on the Commission whenever the question of German default came under

[1] *Rep. Comm. Report, 1920–1922*, p. 253.
[2] See *Stresemann*, i, p. 378; and *Cmd.* 2270, p. 73.

consideration. But this arrangement provided no final solution, for the powers of the American representative remained undefined. For a few days the Conference was paralysed by a deadlock between the bankers and the French representatives. In the outcome it was agreed that if the Reparation Commission with the addition of an American citizen should fail to reach a unanimous decision on the question of default, any member of the Commission who had participated in the vote might appeal to an arbitral commission composed of three impartial and independent persons, under an American chairman, whose decision should be final.[1]

This agreement to settle by arbitration any dispute between the Allies on the question of default remedied what experience had proved a serious gap in the provisions of the Treaty. No proposal, however, was ever again made to declare Germany in default; in consequence, no occasion ever arose for the reference of such a proposal to arbitral settlement. But, mainly at the instigation of the French Prime Minister, Herriot, provision was made by the agreements concluded in 1924 for the arbitral settlement of a wide range of other disputes which might arise in the working of the Dawes Plan, and these further arbitration provisions proved of real value in practice. Most significant were those for the settlement of disputes on questions of interpretation. A significant departure was made from the practice of the Treaty, which had vested the power of interpreting the reparation provisions in the Reparation Commission, an exclusively Allied body from whose decisions there was no appeal. Impartiality in the interpretation and application of the Dawes Plan was ensured by agreements for arbitration in the event of disputes between the German Government on the one side, and, on the other, the Reparation Commission and the officials appointed to supervise the working of the Plan. 'It ought to be recognized,' commented the eminent British Legal Adviser to the Commission when reviewing these changes, 'that it is indispensable to include in every treaty or international arrangement a carefully drawn and all-embracing clause providing for the judicial or arbitral settlement on legal principles of differences arising in the course of the execution of a treaty, whether those differences are as to the interpretation of the text or as to the application of the text to external circumstances.'[2]

As 'guarantee for the execution of the present Treaty by Germany,' the Treaty of Versailles prescribed the occupation of the Rhineland for fifteen years. If the provisions of the Treaty were faithfully carried out by Germany, the northern section of

[1] Cmd. 2184; Cmd. 2191; Cmd. 2270, pp. 115–116; Times, July 25, 1924.
[2] Fischer Williams, Sir J.: 'A Legal Footnote to the Story of German Reparations,' British Year Book of International Law, 1932, p. 37.

the occupied area, which included Cologne, was to be evacuated at the end of five years, and the central section, which included Coblenz, at the end of ten years. Evacuated territory might be reoccupied either during or after the expiration of these fifteen years if Germany should refuse to observe her reparation obligations, while should Germany before the end of fifteen years comply 'with all the undertakings resulting from the present Treaty,' the occupying forces were to be withdrawn immediately.

The study of the enforcement of the Treaty necessitates consideration of the question to what extent these provisions proved effective as a guarantee for the fulfilment of the terms of peace. It should be borne in mind that the occupation clauses were the outcome of the prolonged wrangle on French security, and not the result of any careful consideration of the problem of treaty enforcement. Until the conclusion of the Locarno Treaty, the French, unlike the British, viewed the occupation of the Rhineland more as a measure of security than as a guarantee for the execution of the Treaty. French policy regarding sanctions was therefore strongly influenced by the desire to consolidate the Rhineland occupation as a military safeguard against Germany, while wellfounded apprehension that military sanctions would strengthen the French hold on the Rhineland was undoubtedly in large measure responsible for British reluctance to proceed to their application.

The inadequacy of the occupation provisions as a guarantee for the fulfilment of the Treaty is indicated by the critical character assumed by the problem of sanctions from 1920–1924. The scheme of occupation proved in practice too rigid. The psychological and financial burden which it imposed lay on Germany as a dead weight; it could not constitute—to quote Jacques Seydoux' expressive phrase—'la menace immédiate qui oblige à àgir et à exécuter.' The experience of the post-War years demonstrated that the enforcement of the disarmament and reparation clauses required a more flexible system of guarantees, making possible the relaxation or intensification of pressure according as Germany pushed forward or held back in the fulfilment of Treaty obligations. The Treaty contained no provision—or, at least, no clear provision—for making the occupation bear either more or less heavily on Germany during the first five years. Though the fact of occupation made possible the exceptional measures of coercion applied in 1921–1923, the Allied Governments could seek legal justification of their action only, as in 1921, in a general right to use force short of war to compel respect for Treaty obligations, or, as in 1923, in a debatable interpretation of an obscure clause among the reparation provisions.

In 1925, at the end of the first quinquennial period, the Allies exercised their right to delay the evacuation of the Cologne zone. German failure to comply with the military clauses constituted the ostensible justification of the postponement [1]; the French were indeed seriously perturbed by German shortcomings in the matter of disarmament. Though in Great Britain the military situation in Germany caused little disquietude, the alignment of Great Britain with France on this question was a tacit condition of the Franco-British *détente* of 1924. Accordingly the British Government consented to postpone the withdrawal of the Allied forces in order to enforce the more complete execution of the military terms. But in their reluctance to assent to the evacuation of the Cologne zone the French Government was manifestly influenced by the knowledge that this movement would go far to nullify the military value of the occupation.[2] In these circumstances Sir Austen Chamberlain, while insisting that the evacuation of the Cologne zone should be conditional only on German compliance with the military clauses of the Treaty, sought to meet the French demand for security by means other than the continuance of the occupation. The requisite supplement to the security of France was contributed by the Locarno Agreements, the conclusion of which enabled Sir Austen Chamberlain to procure the evacuation of Cologne in December 1925, as soon as an agreement had been reached with Germany regarding the execution of the military clauses. Thereafter the principle that the occupation was exclusively a guarantee of the execution of the Treaty ceased to be in dispute.

Primarily the occupation remained a guarantee for the payment of reparation. It had been instituted especially for this purpose. The time-honoured method of extracting an indemnity is to station an army on enemy soil and to withdraw it in proportion to the payments made. Such a course provides an inducement to the conquered state to pay as rapidly as possible in order to get rid of the foreign troops. This was the procedure to which Germany had resorted in 1871; this too was the manner in which Poincaré proposed to carry through the evacuation of the Ruhr after 1923. But the Rhineland occupation was not so regulated, for in 1919 the immensity of the bill precluded the acceptance of the customary arrangement. British and American opposition was adamant against any proposal to make the occupation coterminous with the payment of reparation, for such a proposal opened up the forbidding vista of an occupation of indefinite duration, before the political implications of which British statesmen inevitably recoiled. So the term of fifteen years was set, subject to the provisions for withdrawal and reoccupation already noted.

[1] See p. 137.   [2] See p. 188.

Military occupation proved at best an uncouth guarantee of financial payments of the magnitude demanded by the Treaty. Germany could not follow the example of France after the Franco-Prussian War—raise loans to pay off the debt and so secure speedy evacuation; for the financial world had no belief in German capacity to pay the sums demanded. The difficulty of enforcing payment by the direct exploitation of industrial resources under military protection was amply demonstrated by the Ruhr occupation; the riches of a modern community depend 'on the voluntary exercise of mental capacity and are not forthcoming at the lash of physical coercion.'[1] The first condition of systematic payment was in fact a process of financial reorganization which military occupation was calculated to impede rather than promote. For the Treaty gave the cost of occupation priority over all other payments required from Germany, and at the outset the sums actually received from Germany were barely sufficient to meet this first charge. Only in March 1922 was the cost of occupation limited by an Inter-Allied agreement to a definite sum—namely, 240 million gold marks.[2] Even this sum excluded the cost of the unlimited services and furnishings which could be exacted by the armies of occupation under Articles 8–12 of the Rhineland Agreement—a vicious system 'which must have made the Rhineland approximate to an Army Council's dream of Paradise.'[3] One merit of the Dawes Plan was that for the first time it included within a single sum for each year all the costs of all the armies of occupation together with all payments on account of reparation and restitution.

This settlement of the question of cost did not exhaust the untoward influence of the military occupation on reparation. It reappeared in the negotiations which resulted in the substitution of the Young for the Dawes Plan. For four years the Dawes Plan provided a working solution of the reparation problem; admittedly a temporary solution—yet in 1928 no compelling financial considerations dictated revision of the Plan, nor was there any unanimity of opinion in Treasury circles in favour of such a course. Revision was effected not in consequence of general agreement that the time was ripe for the elaboration of a permanent settlement; it came about through the interconnection of reparation and military occupation.

The evacuation of the Rhineland was the immediate goal of Stresemann's policy in 1928. The German Chancellor, Hermann Müller, broached the question to Briand at Geneva in September.

---

[1] Fischer Williams, Sir J.: 'A Legal Footnote to the Story of German Reparations,' *British Year Book of International Law, 1932*, p. 37.   See also pp. 127-130 below.
[2] See *Toynbee, 1920–1923*, p. 167.
[3] McFadyean, Sir A.: *Reparation Reviewed*, p. 82.

Briand would seem to have replied to Müller as Poincaré had replied to Stresemann a month before; that the occupation was a guarantee of reparation payments, and that therefore the question of evacuation could only be settled in connexion with the question of reparation and debts.[1] Though denying the legitimacy of this view, Müller could not but agree to a *de facto* connexion. He had then no reason to recoil from the prospect of a final settlement based on a re-examination of Germany's capacity to pay. The Agent-General for Reparation Payments held the view that Germany would do well to rid herself of the trammels of the Dawes Plan before an economic crisis supervened. Müller took the decisive step. After conversations at Geneva—conversations attended, as Snowden later reminded the Commons, by no Finance Ministers— it was announced, on 16th September 1928, that agreement had been reached to open official negotiations for the early evacuation of the Rhineland and to set up a Committee to prepare a final reparation settlement. Only then did it become apparent that German capacity to pay would not be the touchstone of the new settlement. The price of evacuation promised to be high. Though tempted to draw back, Stresemann had no choice but to proceed; retreat would stultify his entire policy. From the negotiations the Young Plan emerged; it foundered in the world economic crisis, which the Dawes Plan might have weathered.

The conclusion of a professedly permanent reparation settlement in 1929 resulted in the evacuation of the Rhineland five years before the date assigned by the Treaty. Thenceforward the military restrictions imposed on Germany were backed by no material guarantee. The Treaty contained no provisions for Allied action to prevent German rearmament. Article 213 authorized the League Council to institute by majority vote only an investigation; it was silent on the question of action to follow. When German rearmament had become notorious, in the spring of 1933, General Temperley, questioned by Sir John Simon, advised the reoccupation, if necessary, of the Rhine bridgeheads [2]—a precautionary measure for which Clemenceau had sought without avail to make provision.[3] When Germany openly repudiated the military and air clauses, in March 1935, the Council of the League, at the instance of Great Britain, France, and Italy, solemnly reproved this unilateral repudiation of international obligations and referred to a Committee the examination of economic and financial measures which might be applied in the event of further repudiation. The labours of the Committee proceeded no further than an examination of French

[1] *Stresemann*, iii, p. 383.
[2] Temperley, A. C.: *The Whispering Gallery of Europe*, p. 249.
[3] See p. 147.

proposals for cutting off the supply of arms and war material to any state committing 'a breach of an undertaking of concern to international security.'[1] The next such breach occurred on 7th March 1936, when German troops re-entered the demilitarized zone.

When Bonar Law first read the conditions of peace he warned Clemenceau that 'the fifteen years' occupation is as incapable of protecting France as it is of guaranteeing the execution of the Treaty.'[2] The history of the Rhineland occupation bears out that judgement. The occupation provisions constituted a fitting capstone to the many unhappy compromises which shaped the Treaty of Versailles. The Treaty was distinguished by lack of balance between the obligations imposed on Germany and the guarantees instituted to ensure their observance. It was constructed on the assumption that, after a brief span of time, the defeated state would act as its own gaoler for the convenience of the victors. In 1919 Great Britain and the U.S.A. joined more or less heartily with France in imposing on Germany discriminatory restrictions, financial burdens, and territorial curtailments which Germany was bound to resent. But the French alone were prepared to make provision for the registration and punishment of violations—provisions indispensable if the Treaty was to be maintained; and the French alone possessed the will—though not, as the event proved, the power—to carry through the Treaty in the spirit in which it had been made. The British and American authors of the Treaty shrank from the distasteful problem of Treaty enforcement. It involved more extensive interference in the internal affairs of Germany than they approved; it offended against their conception of the future organization of international relations. The consequence of Anglo-American fastidiousness was to project into the ensuing years a long-drawn-out dispute concerning the legality of the guarantees and sanctions which were indispensable if the Treaty was to be enforced. 'Only those treaties which states consider to be to their advantage will be kept regardless of special sanctions'[3]; from this conclusion, warranted by a study of the broad problem of treaty enforcement, the history of the Treaty of Versailles affords no grounds for dissent.

[1] For a summary of the work of this Committee, see Engel, S.: *League Reform*, pp. 31–33 (Geneva Research Centre: Geneva Studies, XI, Nos. 3–4).
[2] Tardieu, A.: *Le Sleswig et la Paix*, p. 249.
[3] Wild, P. C.: *Sanctions and Treaty Enforcements*, p. 210.

CHAPTER VII

CONCILIATION BY CONFERENCE

AS French policy in the first years of peace found expression
in the elaboration of guarantees and sanctions, so British
policy is represented by the series of conferences which mark the
years 1920–1922. They were the means whereby the British Government sought not only to keep the victorious Powers in friendly
contact but to promote closer relations between them and the
principal enemy state. The Council of the League of Nations, the
intended instrument of such a policy, was powerless to serve this
purpose owing to the exclusion of Germany from membership of
the League. The association of Germany with the Allied Powers
could in consequence be effected only by grafting German representation on to the Supreme Council. The first step in this direction
was taken when, at San Remo, in April 1920, Lloyd George
persuaded his colleagues to invite the German Ministers to meet
the Allies in conference at Spa. The immediate object of the
policy thus initiated was to obtain 'German co-operation in the
execution of the Treaty . . . so far as possible through direct
communication between the German Government and the Allies.' [1]
This chapter is concerned with the development of this policy of
conciliation by conference.

Reference has been made in the preceding chapter to one concession—prior agreement on measures of coercion—exacted by
Millerand as the price of French assent to this policy. Millerand
also secured Lloyd George's acceptance of the principle that, before
meeting the Germans in conference, the Allied Governments should
reach precise agreement between themselves on all subjects of
discussion. This principle was adhered to for the next five years.
Every conference with the Germans till 1925 was preceded by
Inter-Allied or Anglo-French negotiations to ensure the presentation
of a common front to the German delegation. The first conference
with the Germans at Spa (5th–16th July 1920) was preceded by
Anglo-French conferences at Hythe (15th–17th May 1920) and
Boulogne (21st–22nd June 1920), and by the Inter-Allied Conference
of Brussels (3rd July 1920). The second conference with the
Germans, held in London (1st–14th March 1921), was preceded
by the Inter-Allied Conference in Paris (24th–30th January 1921).
The Cannes Conference (6th–13th January 1922), the later meetings
of which were attended by Rathenau, was preceded by Anglo-
French conversations (18th–22nd December 1921) to fix the condi-

[1] *U.S.A. Foreign Relations*, 1920, ii, p. 435.

tions of a partial moratorium on reparation payments. The London Conference on the Dawes Plan (16th July–16th August 1924) was divided into two stages, to the first of which the German Ministers were not invited. Finally, Chamberlain and Briand took care to reach agreement between themselves in 1925 about the project of a security pact before entering on the negotiations which culminated in the Locarno Agreements.

French success in establishing the principle of Allied agreement in advance of any discussion with the Germans may be measured by the contrast between the attitude of Lloyd George in 1920 and that of Ramsay MacDonald in 1924. At San Remo in April 1920 Lloyd George desired to summon the Germans to meet the Allies there and then; at the Inter-Allied Conference on the Dawes Plan Ramsay MacDonald, after weeks of consultation between Allied experts and Ministers, still counselled that 'until we come to a successful measure of agreement to show that we are not going to quarrel amongst ourselves, it would be exceedingly bad policy to have any representatives of the German Government here,' [1] But the rider added by Millerand to Lloyd George's policy deprived the early conferences of their conciliatory character. Both before the Spa and the London Conferences Allied reparation plans were drawn up to provide bases of comparison with any offers made by Germany; the first project, the Boulogne Plan of May 1920, was kept secret, but the second, the Paris Proposals of January 1921, was given out for publication. The German representatives on their side were expected to initiate the proceedings by the presentation of correspondingly detailed proposals. The failure of the Conferences of 1920–1921 may in some measure be attributed to this baneful procedure, which accentuated the antagonism of the parties by ranging them on opposite sides in defence of their respective plans.

Unwise publicity accentuated the perils of this hazardous procedure. In 1920 a powerful, perhaps irresistible, reaction set in in favour of 'open diplomacy.' Despite the Wilsonian prescription of 'open covenants openly arrived at,' the rule of secrecy had been followed in the making of peace; and the criticisms levelled against the Treaty gave rise to the belief, both in England and France, that its negotiators would have been better advised had they taken the public more widely into their confidence. Publicity commenced with the Spa Conference: Lloyd George could justly claim that there never had been an international conference at which so much, not merely of the decisions, but of the actual discussions, had been given to the Press.[2] The consequence was to lessen yet further

[1] Riddell, Lord: *Intimate Diary*, pp. 186–187; *Cmd.* 2270, p. 37.
[2] 132 *H.C. Deb.*, col. 477, July 27, 1920.

the chances of compromise and agreement. The knowledge that his words would be blazed abroad caused each delegate to modulate his speech less to the needs of diplomatic negotiation than to the demands of inflamed opinion in his own country; and no position, once publicly assumed, could be abandoned thereafter without humiliation.

The first conference with the Germans at Spa (5th–16th July 1920) was a fiasco. The German Chancellor Fehrenbach had announced his satisfaction at the prospect of meeting the Allies in discussion 'argumentatively and face to face.' In fact he was given no such opportunity. Discussion between the Allies in the presence of the Germans was avoided: one Allied spokesman was appointed for each subject. Disarmament came first on the agenda; but the German Ministers, newly installed in office, were not well informed. The Conference marked time for the arrival of German military advisers; then on 7th July an outspoken statement by Von Seekt made painfully apparent the delay in the execution of the military clauses. Next the coal problem was taken up: it produced an insolent outburst from Stinnes. Despite Millerand's conciliatory demeanour, Stinnes' influence showed itself in the increasingly refractory attitude of the German delegation. The Allies responded by a threat to occupy the Ruhr if their demands as regard coal deliveries and disarmament were not agreed to. In these circumstances, the Germans signed.[1] Nevertheless the French left the Conference with the conviction of having been cheated. The Coal Protocol provided for a loan to Germany to induce or enable her to continue the coal deliveries due under the Treaty—an arrangement which stuck in French throats, and was the less palatable in the knowledge that Great Britain had insisted at the same time on having ships delivered by Germany credited to her own reparation account at the knock-down prices paid by British buyers. Resentment at these transactions greatly contributed to the French revolt against the repetition of such conferences.

The original purpose of the Spa Conference was to consider the reparation offer which Germany had been invited to make. The German proposals were confined, however, to the discussion of general principles. The Government made no definite offer, for they justly feared that to mention the sum considered by the Germans to be within their capacity of payment would enrage opinion in France and England. The German memoranda were referred for examination to a committee, but the confusion which marked the opening stage of the Conference itself was repeated within this smaller body. The chairman demanded the statement of a minimum amount for reparation; the German members

[1] *The Times*, July 3–19, 1920; *The Nation*, July 10, 17, 24, 1920.

demurred, since they were not authorized to take this step. The meeting adjourned to allow the Germans to consult their Government. The following day they intimated their refusal to name a figure at the moment, and in consequence the committee did not reassemble. Lloyd George nevertheless proclaimed his satisfaction with the results and pronounced the German proposals 'a very satisfactory document' indicative of a real effort to face the problem.[1]

When, after long delay due to French obstruction, Allied and German representatives came together again, the meeting was between experts, not heads of Governments. Allied and German experts met at Brussels in December, and after a break continued their conversations informally in Paris in January. In the course of these discussions the French representative advanced the proposal that the determination of a total figure for reparation should be postponed, and that a provisional arrangement should be accepted for the payment by Germany of RM 3 milliard for five years.[2] The German Government reluctantly assented to this plan, in consequence of representations made in Berlin on behalf of the British and French Governments. But at the Allied Conference of Paris at the end of the month this idea of a provisional solution was rejected by Lloyd George, and a new Allied scheme, the Paris Proposals, was worked out without German participation. This new reparation plan provoked in Germany a furious outburst of protest, a background of ill-omen for the renewal of negotiation. Germany accepted the invitation to the succeeding London Conference on the understanding that German counter-proposals would be taken into consideration, but the German Government refused all prior consultation with regard to these counter-proposals. The Allied experts suggested in vain continued conversations with the German experts. Informal British requests for some inkling of German intentions evoked only the reply that the German proposals would be stretched 'to the extreme limit of what Germany could pay.'[3]

The consequences of this lack of contact were disastrous. The German counter-proposals to the Paris Plan were outlined by the German Foreign Minister, Dr. Simons, at the first session of the London Conference on 1st March 1921. They encountered an instantaneous rejection. Simons displayed an inexpedient ingenuity in scaling down the Paris demands, and his wisdom in reserving elbow-room for subsequent negotiation by keeping below what he was prepared to offer is open to question.[4] To Simons' request

[1] D'Abernon, i, pp. 65–66; U.S.A. Foreign Relations, 1920, ii, pp. 398–402; 132 H.C. Deb., July 21, 1920, col. 491; Kessler, H.: Walter Rathenau, pp. 284–291.
[2] D'Abernon, i, pp. 109–111.
[3] D'Abernon, i, pp. 113–125, 148; Bergman, C.: History of Reparation, pp. 55–59; The Times, February 9 and 19, 1921.
[4] Bergmann, C.: History of Reparation, pp. 63–64.

that the German proposals be read out in full Lloyd George, as President of the Conference, replied that it was useless to do so; the outline showed they did not merit examination. So the session was broken off. No discussion of the German proposals took place. The Allied Ministers turned instead to consider coercive measures to be applied against Germany. When on 3rd March the Germans were again summoned before the Allied Ministers, Lloyd George delivered a vigorous philippic against Germany for bad faith in the application of the Treaty terms, and concluded with the announcement that, unless by 7th March Germany either accepted the Paris decisions or submitted equivalent proposals, economic and military sanctions would be applied. With that threat this second session ended. Serious negotiation between the German and Allied Ministers commenced only on 5th March, and continued over the week-end. Lloyd George would now willingly have reverted to the provisional solution which the French had pressed in January. Unfortunately, the French delegation was no longer free to conclude an agreement on that basis, for their liberty of negotiation was now restricted by the understanding that no settlement should be accepted which failed to offer advantages equivalent to those of the Paris Resolutions. No complete understanding could be reached, and on 7th March Lloyd George reluctantly announced that sanctions would immediately be brought into force.

By 1st May 1921, the latest date set by the Treaty for the notification to the German Government of a schedule of payments, the policy of seeking a solution on the basis of a German offer was necessarily played out. The effort to reach a negotiated settlement of the reparation problem ended with a schedule of payments which, though issued in accordance with the procedure prescribed by the Treaty, had to be enforced by the menace of new measures of coercion.

Why, it may be asked, did Lloyd George's policy produce results so contrary to his hopes? Was it simply because the gap between German views of what could be paid, and French and British views, was too wide to be bridged? This clearly was the major element in the problem. But the conference procedure itself threw into the sharpest relief the gulf which separated German from British and French ideas of a reasonable settlement, and so tended to increase the prevailing tension. It was hardly possible for German statesmen, dependent for political support on party votes in the Reichstag, to take the responsibility of spontaneously offering to subject their people to a heavy burden of taxation to satisfy the claims of reparation. Lloyd George was yielding to the lure of a mirage in asking for a German offer as the starting-point of a conference. A preparatory exchange of views through the consultation of Allied with German experts would have made accessible all the necessary information about the financial and economic state of Germany, and would have revealed the improbability of bridging the gap between Allied and German views. Yet the Spa and the London Conferences met, as the German expert Bergmann expressed it, with the parties groping in the dark. The paradox may even be ventured, since experience demonstrated its truth, that the nature of these conferences precluded effective consultation between the participants. The contrariety of their approach tended to rule out preparatory consultation. The Allies set about working out what they proposed to demand, and the Germans what their financial position made it possible for them to offer. For these tasks neither side needed the help of the other. Consultation during the conferences was stifled by the coexistence of fully formulated antithetical schemes, which issued in one of two results. Either, as at Spa, the two sides maintained a discreet secrecy, and the silence remained unbroken; or, as in Paris and London, the two sides declared their proposals to the world, whereupon reason capsized in a tempest of protest. Reflecting, in 1924, on the Spa and London Conferences, Lord D'Abernon concluded that the presence of the German ministers 'did not do them much good, nor did it help the negotiations.' [1]

The later conferences do not lend themselves to the consecutive treatment possible in connexion with the first two conferences with Germany. They met intermittently; they have no continuous history. But it may be noted that the premature crystallization of views proved equally fatal to the Inter-Allied Conferences of 1921–1923. Thus the London Conference of August 1922 started off with two sessions at which first Poincaré and then Lloyd George made lengthy declarations on French and British policy respectively. The two Prime Ministers took up conflicting positions on the question of productive guarantees. A full report of these opening speeches appeared in the Press the following day. Thenceforward concession involved retraction in public, and the way towards agreement was made more difficult. A similar fate befell the Paris Conference of January 1923, immediately before the Ruhr occupation. Bonar Law arrived in Paris with a fully worked-out reparation plan which he presented on the first day. Poincaré countered with a similar French plan. The plans had been worked out by each of the two governments in isolation; both were immediately given full publicity. The British plan was condemned in the French Press, the French in the British Press. The Confer-

[1] *D'Abernon*, iii, pp. 78–79.

:nce stalled. It may well be that no mere modification of procedure :ould have promoted the reconciliation of policies so consciously)pposed as those of France and Great Britain in 1922–1923. In August 1922 Poincaré did jettison the larger part of the proposals 1e advanced at the outset; the Conference broke down when Lloyd George demanded that the French proposals should be :ntirely abandoned. In January 1923 Bonar Law and Poincaré 1ad become fully aware of their contradictory positions through :he discussions at the preceding Conference in London, and the :eport ran that they had arranged to meet in Paris to register their lisagreement rather than to renew the search for an understanding. But after three years of contention the British, French, and German Governments had at least come to realize the dangers of confronting)ne another with some elaborate plan. The course of events led Lord Curzon to reflect that 'Experience has shown that hard-and-fast schemes are apt to impede rather than promote a general agreement.' [1]

When reparation negotiations, which had been brought to a standstill by the Ruhr occupation, were resumed, towards the end of 1923, the governments concerned were well aware of the necessity of proceeding with the utmost circumspection. The successive attempts at working out a reparation settlement through the medium of conferences had tended only to exacerbate a naturally delicate situation. In 1924 a new procedure was tried— resort to settlement by the advice of independent experts. Between 14th January and 9th April 1924 the Dawes Committee worked out a plan which proved acceptable to all parties. Though the achievement of a solution must be primarily ascribed to favour-able circumstance, it is clear that the procedure exemplified by the Dawes Committee possessed merits which materially contributed to an abatement of tension.

Among the circumstances which conduced to a settlement, not the least important was the willingness of the United States to participate unofficially in the negotiations through this novel diplomatic device. Its employment was first recommended by the American Secretary of State Hughes in the last quarter of 1922. On several occasions he pressed the suggestion privately on the French Government. [2] Only when he found that the French Premier was not disposed to act on the suggestion did Hughes give public expression, in the well-known New Haven address of 29th December 1922, to his proposal.

'The first condition of a satisfactory settlement is that the question should be taken out of politics. . . . There ought to be a way for

[1] *Cmd.* 1943, p. 18. [2] *U.S.A. Foreign Relations,* 1922, ii, pp. 128, 175, 182.

statesmen to agree upon what Germany can pay, for, no matter what claims may be made against her, that is the limit of satisfaction. . . . Why should they not invite men of the highest authority in finance in their respective countries—men of such prestige, experience and honour that their agreement upon the amount to be paid, and upon a financial plan for working out the payments, would be accepted throughout the world as the most authoritative expression obtainable? Governments need not bind themselves in advance to accept the recommendations, but they can at least make possible such an inquiry with their approval and free the men who may represent their country in such a commission from any responsibility to Foreign Offices and from any duty to obey political instructions. In other words, they may invite an answer to this difficult and pressing question from men of such standing and in such circumstances of freedom as will ensure a reply prompted only by knowledge and conscience. I have no doubt that distinguished Americans would be willing to serve in such a commission.' [1]

The plan recommended in this Address was taken up again by the American Government after Germany had abandoned passive resistance. On 11th October 1923 President Coolidge intimated that the Hughes offer of 29th December 1922 still held good. Since Poincaré's policy seemed indicative of reluctance to come to any settlement with the German Government, Hughes warned the French Chargé d'Affaires on 22nd October that American opinion would turn against France if, having broken Germany's resistance, France was unwilling to aid in the working out of a financial plan. Thus the immense influence of the American Government was exerted towards securing French agreement to settlement by a procedure without precedent in international affairs.

It is desirable to dwell on the innovation which Hughes introduced into the idea of impartial investigation.[2] The German Government had from time to time proposed the submission of the reparation problem to an impartial commission whose findings they, and presumably other governments, would be required in advance to accept. Hughes believed that the value of the work of such a commission would depend on governments not being bound in advance to accept its recommendations. It was his conviction that only if governments retained their freedom in this respect would they be in a position to leave the experts to carry through an investigation without interference. The appointment of an independent expert committee offered, he felt, the only way of escape from the pressure of public opinion. His ideas are well

---

[1] *Toynbee, 1924*, p. 341.
[2] The credit belongs more probably to the American unofficial observer on the Reparation Commission, Roland Boyden, on whose suggestions, made during a vacation in the U.S.A. in the summer of 1922, Hughes was acting.

summed up in the memorandum of his conversation with the French Ambassador Jusserand on 7th November 1922. Hughes told Jusserand 'that he did not think that the statesmen of the countries concerned could solve the matter by meeting together directly or through delegates responsible to Foreign Offices. He said that the governments were committed; that they had the political situation in their countries to consider, and hence their freedom of action was restricted, and it was very difficult to have a financial plan developed which would fit the actual economic conditions. He hoped that in this emergency there might be found a way of enlisting authoritative financial opinion through a meeting of important financial men in the various countries, with the sympathy and approval of the governments but acting freely in the sense that they were to formulate without restriction by instructions from Foreign Offices their views as to what should be done. In this way a financial plan could be formulated which the governments could accept, because a plan thus formed would carry the highest weight and they could bow to it as inevitable. Such an arrangement would have the requisite financial backing in the various countries.' [1]

The Dawes Report, completed on 9th April 1924, was followed by the London Conference of 16th July–16th August 1924. The Conference was even more fortunate than the Committee in the circumstances in which it met, for the conciliatory Radical-Socialist Herriot had replaced the redoubtable Poincaré as Prime Minister. Yet some credit for its success may well be ascribed to the care in preparation and organization which distinguished the Conference from its predecessors.

Before the London Conference met, the governments concerned had notified their acceptance of the Dawes Plan. The Conference was not therefore required to discuss the contents of the Plan; its task was to consider the measures necessary to bring the Plan into force. The essentially political problems involved were elucidated in a series of ministerial conversations which culminated in the visit of the French Prime Minister to Chequers on 22nd June, and the visit of the British Prime Minister to Paris on 8th July. This last journey was necessitated in order to clear up a Franco-British misunderstanding which arose in part from the indeterminate character of the discussion between Herriot and MacDonald at Chequers. This final effort at elucidating Franco-British divergencies of policy greatly contributed to getting the Conference successfully off the stocks. For the British Government, as the Power qualified to issue invitations to the Conference, had in the original letters of invitation issued on 23rd–25th June proposed a

U.S.A. Foreign Relations, 1922, ii, p. 179.

form of agreement with Germany which provoked a revulsion of opinion in France because it appeared to involve the revision of the Treaty.[1] The outcome of MacDonald's visit to Paris was the Franco-British Memorandum of 9th July, which by setting out the main questions to be taken up at the Conference provided an agenda sponsored, not by the inviting Power alone, but by the two principal parties. It did not remove their differences of opinion, but stated the issues awaiting settlement in neutral terms.

When the Conference opened, MacDonald and Snowden proposed to commence with a general discussion in plenary session on the main political issues. Theunis, the Belgian Prime Minister, who had wisely initiated the preliminary conversations, objected that, if discussion commenced in plenary session on the most delicate issues, the danger might arise that positions would be strongly taken up and become so well known outside as to render compromise thereafter difficult of attainment.[2] He urged the immediate reference of all questions to committees of experts in order to prevent the assumption of definite positions by the leading delegates. The value of the preparatory work now became evident, for the Franco-British Memorandum provided an answer to Snowden's contention that only after the formulation of specific issues in general discussion would their reference to experts be feasible. The Memorandum listed the problems awaiting settlement; these therefore could be, and were, parcelled out among the committees. That the committees were composed of ministers as well as experts lent authority—indeed, finality—to their recommendations. Certain questions of special significance were reserved for consideration in informal private meetings of the principal delegates—the so-called Council of Seven. So successful was this procedure that when the German delegation arrived a similar course was followed. Throughout the Conference, debate in plenary session, with its danger of degenerating into a public wrangle, was avoided. Lest it be assumed that the Dawes Plan itself sufficed to rule out bitter contention, it may be recalled that at the outset Great Britain and France were divided by serious divergencies of policy, while if Stresemann had been called upon to open up with a broad declaration, it must needs have included the demand for the evacuation of the Ruhr. It may be doubted whether the Conference would have survived the immediate presentation of such a demand.

The London Conference differed also from the earlier conferences between the Allies and the Germans in the freedom of manœuvre accorded to the German delegation. The change resulted primarily from the general recognition that it was neither

---

[1] See *Cmd.* 2184.   [2] *Cmd.* 2270, p. 16.

permissible nor expedient to impose the Dawes Plan on Germany. The Plan could, as Stresemann insisted, be brought into force only as a result of 'discussion, deliberation, and free acceptance by Germany.'[1] Stresemann's main objective was to expand the Conference beyond its intended scope. The Dawes Report, while requiring the removal of all impediments to the fiscal and economic unity of Germany, did not stipulate that the military occupation of the Ruhr should be brought to an end. The evacuation of the Ruhr accordingly formed no part of the original agenda of the Conference. This limitation dismayed the German Government, for evacuation constituted a political condition of Germany's acceptance of the Plan. MacDonald's predilection for intimate personal discussion gave Stresemann the opportunity which he sought to push the question to the fore. In a private talk with Stresemann and Marx, on the very day of their arrival, MacDonald encouraged the German Ministers to approach Herriot. There ensued the Herriot-Stresemann conversations of 8th and 11th August, and the meetings of the Belgian, French, and German delegations on 12th–14th August—a veritable conference within the Conference.[2] MacDonald kept outside these discussions 'so as to be able finally to throw the weight of his opinion into the scale.' He personally was indeed in no position to press the French to withdraw completely from the Ruhr, for at Chequers he had intimated that he would raise no objection to the continuance of military occupation restricted to a few strategic points. The success of the Conference as a whole came to hinge on the outcome of these negotiations concerning the Ruhr, since agreement was reached with comparative ease on all points in the original agenda. Herriot, keenly sensitive of the isolation of France on this issue, shrank from jeopardizing the success of the Conference by insisting on the limitations of the agenda. He was driven to make extensive concessions, though less extensive than Stresemann had hoped to secure. The point was reached beyond which Herriot, despite his own good will, realized that he could not go; and at this point MacDonald and Kellogg, the American Ambassador, intervened with success, to the disgust of the Gallophobe Snowden, to procure German acceptance of Herriot's offer.[3]

That the formulation in advance of a common Franco-British programme tended to ossify the ensuing negotiations with the

---

[1] *D'Abernon*, iii, pp. 78–79. See p. 125.
[2] See p. 110.
[3] For these negotiations, see *D'Abernon*, iii, pp. 78–79; Bardoux, J.: *Le Socialisme au pouvoir*, pp. 248–261 (gives reports of General Desticker to Marshal Foch). Suarez, G.: *Une Nuit chez Cromwell*, pp. 49, 54, 60–61; *Stresemann*, i, pp. 360–362, 372–373, 381–403; Snowden, Viscount: *Autobiography*, ii, p. 675; *Toynbee, 1924*, pp. 500–501 (gives Notes exchanged on August 16); *The Times*, July 30, August 14, 15, 1924.

German Government was the lesson of the Conferences of 1920–1921. The London Conference on the Dawes Plan had remained free from the atmosphere of dictation, despite the large measure of Franco-British agreement arrived at as a result of the preceding discussions. The French Prime Minister had, however, been placed in an awkward situation when called upon to deal with a problem with which Great Britain was, professedly at least, not concerned; and his experience was calculated to intensify the French desire to co-ordinate French and British views, in advance of any further negotiations with Germany, not only with regard to the questions of interest to both countries, but also with regard to those deemed to concern France alone. The Locarno negotiations are of interest for their realization of that desire.

Six stages may be distinguished in the negotiation of the Locarno Agreements.[1] The first stage: a secret tentative approach by Germany. Stresemann communicated his offer of a Rhineland Pact to the British Government on 20th January 1925 under pledge of secrecy. Austen Chamberlain, suspecting an attempt to drive a wedge between Great Britain and France, loyally refused to respond without consulting Herriot. Accordingly, on 9th February, Stresemann communicated his offer to the French Government. The second stage: the preparation of a reply by France in concert with Great Britain. The difficulty to be surmounted in the formulation of a concerted reply arose from the determination of France to shoulder obligations towards Poland and Czechoslovakia which Great Britain would not assume. Briand's first draft foreshadowed a comprehensive security pact to contain, within a single framework, arrangements for both eastern and western Europe. This French draft proved too strong a potion for the British to stomach; Chamberlain proceeded to eliminate all the proposals which involved obligations beyond those which the British Government was prepared to accept. The French in turn could not abide this weaker British brew. Briand protested that to keep silence on the French resolve to protect the eastern European states would be 'to risk giving rise to wrong interpretations of the Rhineland Pact and encouraging dangerous aspirations.' His amendments resulted in the French Note to the German Government of 16th July, which was sent with the approval of the British Government. Whereas the British draft would have postponed the signature of Franco-Polish and Franco-Czech Treaties to the hazards of subsequent negotiation, this Note foreshadowed their conclusion simultaneously with that of the Western Security Pact. The third stage: the

---

[1] For a full review, see *Toynbee, 1925*, ii, pp. 25–66. The relevant documents are in *Cmd.* 2435 and *Cmd.* 2468. In addition to references below, see *D'Abernon*, iii, 121 et seq.

German reply. Stresemann deemed the Allied Note a distortion of his offer, 'extremely unsatisfactory . . . because it shows how far England has given way to France.' [1] The German reply of 20th July was indicative of German misgivings at the trend of the negotiations. The fourth stage: a draft pact was prepared by French and British jurists; outstanding questions were settled in conversations between Briand and Chamberlain in London on 11th–12th August. The fifth stage: the Jurists' Conference. German and Allied jurists met in London on 1st–4th September to examine the draft. Austen Chamberlain attached special importance to this preliminary step. The German jurist, he wrote, 'could be given a copy of the form in which we had put our ideas, and all the explanations which he might require could be furnished to him. He could then return to Berlin and discuss the general lines of our plan with Stresemann.' He 'will come here to get information, to make, if he desires, his suggestions; above all, to ascertain what are the real intentions of the Allies, and thus to avoid misunderstandings which might arise from the presentation of a text without any opportunity for exposition or explanation.' This course would 'enable Stresemann to know in advance the general character of the propositions we shall make, and to enable him to consult, if necessary, with his colleagues in Berlin before he sees us.' [2] The sixth stage: the Locarno Conference. During the Anglo-French conversations in London, in August, Briand himself, in anticipation of any expression of opinion on the question by Chamberlain, insisted on the necessity of 'a real discussion with the Germans so as to arrive at a mutual agreement and not another treaty imposed by the Allies upon Germany.' [3] At Locarno, Stresemann was able to secure extensive political concessions as the condition of agreement to the Locarno Treaties.

Thus at the outset of the negotiations France was assured of British support on the point to which she attached special importance, while Germany was enabled both to participate in the preparatory work and to enjoy complete liberty of negotiation in the concluding conference. That the Treaty of Locarno had been negotiated freely and without recrimination caused it to be hailed with especial satisfaction in Great Britain. The British people, said Lord Balfour, 'have always been anxious for appeasement'; the instinct of the people, he added, is not deceived when 'it regards the Treaty of Locarno as the symbol and the cause of a great amelioration in the public feeling of Europe.' [4] Locarno constituted the realization at last of that Utopian plan conceived

[1] *Stresemann*, ii, p. 95.
[2] Petrie, Sir C.: *Austen Chamberlain, Life and Letters*, iii, pp. 281–283.
[3] *Ibid.*
[4] 62 *Lords Deb.*, November 24, 1925, col. 838.

by Sir Edward Grey on the very eve of the war—an arrangement which should override the division of the European Powers into hostile groups and bring them together in relationships of mutual trust and confidence.[1]

The consequence of the signature of the Treaty of Locarno was the entry of Germany into the League, with permanent representation on the League Council. Briand and Chamberlain had from the outset of the negotiations insisted on German membership of the League as an 'absolutely essential condition of the conclusion of any pact.'[2] In part their insistence arose from the need to bring the Treaty between the western European states into conformity with their general obligations under the Covenant, and with the special ties which linked France with Poland and Czechoslovakia. The broader motive was the desire to bring German statesmen into constant personal contact with the representatives of the former Allied Governments. Thenceforward, it might be hoped, the Council would be able to function in the manner intended by its British creators—as the medium of regular conferences between the Great Powers.

The consequence, however, was not in fact to make the Council of the League itself the body within which the negotiations of the Locarno Powers were transacted in the course of the three ensuing years. The outcome is suggested by the caustic comment of an American scholar: 'During the successive sessions of that body Briand, Chamberlain, and Stresemann as Foreign Ministers sought earnestly to find a Rhineland compromise in Geneva hotel rooms while at the Council table they solemnly considered such weighty matters as the appointment of the governing body of the International Educational Cinematographic Institute at Rome.'[3] Alongside the Council proper there developed what, though traduced by the purists of the League as a cabal of Great Powers within the League Council, might with fair accuracy be described as a Supreme Council of the Locarno Powers, to the meetings of which Japan was admitted in virtue of her membership of the Conference of Ambassadors.

The explanation of this development lies partly in the special situation which arose in March 1926. When, on 8th March, the Special Assembly met for the purpose of admitting Germany to the League, the admission of Germany was first delayed and then temporarily blocked by the claims advanced by other states to a permanent seat on the Council. The entry of Germany into the League was in consequence delayed till 8th September 1926.

[1] On Sir Edward Grey's suggestion in 1914, see Zimmern, Sir A.: *The League of Nations and the Rule of Law*, pp. 80–81.
[2] Petrie, Sir C.: *Austen Chamberlain, Life and Letters*, pp. 272–274.
[3] Morley, F.: *The Society of Nations*, p. 385.

The details of this crisis—the claims advanced and the solutions proposed—need not be repeated here [1]; what is of interest is the manner in which the matter was handled. At the time, disapproval was widely expressed of the private conversations and intermittent meetings, in the course of which the Locarno Powers endeavoured to smooth a path through the tangle of rival claims. The matter ought, it was felt, to have been submitted from the first to the Special Assembly, the publicity of whose debates would have provided the surest means of pressure against the presentation of unjustifiable claims. Sir Austen Chamberlain feared that such a procedure might result in the embroilment of relations with Germany. To keep in touch with the German delegation was his primary anxiety. Germany was not yet a member of the League—not, therefore, a member of the Council nor of the Assembly. Arrangements had been made in accordance with Sir Austen's wish and that of the German Government for a meeting of the western Locarno Powers in advance of the meeting of the first Assembly in order that they might freely exchange their views 'in continuation of those free and friendly conversations which took place at Locarno itself.' [2] These private conversations were continued throughout the crisis. In this procedure Sir Austen Chamberlain saw the best promise of avoiding any action which would jeopardize good relations between Germany and the other Locarno Powers. 'A difference in the Council,' he reported to the Prime Minister, 'was a thing to be avoided at almost any cost, but a difference which split the Locarno Powers into two camps on the old lines would . . . be a disaster of unequalled magnitude.' [3]

The cleavage between the Locarno cabal and the League Council continued for quite other reasons than those which caused it to develop in the first instance with adventitious prominence. The Locarno cabal might be deemed to possess its sphere of competence distinct from that of the League Council. 'We have got special questions to settle among ourselves for which the League is not competent, since it is the ultimate Court of Appeal,' Stresemann commented. 'Regarding the questions that concern us solely as Locarno Powers, but do not involve the League, we do reach an arrangement.' [4] The meetings of the Locarno Powers were in effect concerned with the liquidation of the penal clauses of the Treaty of Versailles, in consequence of the understandings, some explicit and some implicit, which had been reached at Locarno. The 'special questions' which the Locarno Powers needed to 'settle

[1] For details, see *Toynbee, 1926*, pp. 161-171; Scelle, G.: *Une Crise de la Société des Nations*, pp. 1-48.
[2] 192 *H.C. Deb.*, March 4, 1926, col. 1664.
[3] Petrie, Sir C.: *Austen Chamberlain, Life and Letters*, ii, pp. 298-302.
[4] *Stresemann*, iii, p. 227.

among themselves' covered a large part of the field of European diplomacy; they ranged over such minor questions as that relating to the fortifications of eastern Germany and such major problems as the evacuation of the Rhineland and the conclusion of a definitive reparation settlement. Moreover, the Locarno Powers came necessarily to extend their private deliberations to questions which fell within the competence of the Council whenever these possessed a vital bearing on their own relationships. The investigation of the Szent-Gotthard incident—the discovery of a consignment of machine-gun parts in Hungary—was indisputably a matter for the League Council. Because, however, the decision with regard to an investigation in Hungary would establish a precedent with regard to investigations in Germany, the question as to the action to be taken was settled by the Locarno Powers before being brought before the League.[1] Inevitably, governments dependent for their authority on the support of the representative bodies of their own people preferred to settle between themselves, by a process of negotiation and compromise, the issues which vitally affected their interests. For such matters to be normally handled, not as the private affairs of the states immediately interested, but as the concern of the whole community of states, would almost certainly be conditional on the creation of a more closely integrated political organization than that provided by the Covenant of the League.

At the close of the Great War two specific remedies had been put forward for the defects of the 'old diplomacy.' The first—'open diplomacy'—was at once a reaction against the secret treaties and understandings by which the rulers of Europe, democratic and autocratic alike, had enmeshed their fellow-men in the toils of war, and an expression of faith in the pacifying influence of the good will and level-headed judgement of the citizens of democratic communities. Among Wilson's Fourteen Points, 'open diplomacy' came first: 'open covenants of peace, openly arrived at, after which there shall be no private international understandings of any kind, but diplomacy shall proceed always frankly and in the public view.' The second remedy was distilled from the experience of Inter-Allied negotiations in time of war. 'What the public opinion of the world demands is that the catastrophe of 1914 shall never be repeated. There is no panacea, but the best hope appears to lie in the judicious development of diplomacy by conference'—such was the conclusion which Sir Maurice Hankey drew from his survey of the work of the Supreme War Council.[2]

[1] See Ray, J.: *Commentaire du Pacte*, p. 186, and *Stresemann*, iii, pp. 361-363.
[2] Hankey, Sir M.: 'Diplomacy by Conference.' This address is most conveniently available in the *Round Table*, March 1921.

By 1929 the experience of a decade had demonstrated the limitations of 'open diplomacy' and 'diplomacy by conference.' President Wilson's faith in the beneficent influence of open diplomacy had sprung from his conviction of the existence of a comradeship of thought and purpose between the peoples of the world. But throughout the post-War years national feeling remained the predominant force in moulding the opinions of ordinary men and women, and the wider interest taken in problems of foreign policy almost certainly made it more, and not less, difficult for statesmen to follow conciliatory courses in their dealings with other countries. It would not be difficult to illustrate from the history of these twenty years the truth of Henri de Jouvenel's reflection: 'International peace is the principal victim of internal politics.' [1]

Experience served to illustrate, too, the wisdom of the emphasis laid by Sir Maurice Hankey on the '*judicious* development of diplomacy by conference.' The new diplomacy was found to require a technique no less skilful and subtle than the old diplomacy. Until that technique was developed and understood, the method of conference was productive of little else than mortification among the vanquished and vexation among the victors. Nor was the lesson once learnt always remembered. It may be of interest to summarize the conclusions drawn from the failure of the Geneva Naval Conference by one well versed in the negotiation of international agreements. [2] A conference, Sir Arthur Salter pointed out, should pass through certain phases. First a private exchange of views between the participants to see if their general principles are sufficiently in harmony to provide a framework of agreement; then the presentation at the outset of the conference of broad statements of policy, not of detailed plans; recourse thereafter to private discussions between the principal delegates simultaneously with deliberation in special committees on technical issues; and the holding of plenary meetings at suitable stages to report the interim results. Such a deliberate procedure both facilitates compromise and allows time for public opinion to take shape on the main issues under consideration.

That there are strict limitations to the value of what may properly be called diplomacy by conference is no less clear. Its chief value is rightly deemed to lie in the opportunity which it affords for personal intercourse between the principal statesmen of different countries. The Locarno interlude of 1925–1929 suffices to show how mistaken it would be to belittle the contribution to be made to the successful handling of delicate issues by confidence based on

---

[1] 'France et Allemagne,' *Revue de Paris*, July 1, 1935, p. 81.
[2] Salter, Sir A.: 'The Technique of Open Diplomacy,' *Political Quarterly*, January–March 1932.

personal acquaintance. But conferences of leading statesmen are necessarily hurried and of short duration. Attention may be drawn in this connexion to the excellent study by M. Bourquin which has unhappily escaped the attention it deserves.[1] 'The practice of conference,' comments M. Bourquin, 'ceases to be efficacious and even becomes dangerous when applied systematically to the settlement of political difficulties.' Statesmen are concerned to hasten back to their own countries; the feverish character of their deliberations has not seldom been responsible for the superficial nature of the solutions proposed. The tendency, as M. Bourquin points out, has often been to be content with a formula rather than patiently to elaborate a durable remedy. Diplomacy by conference necessarily fails to provide that continuous and thorough study by an international agency which is necessary for the elaboration of any detailed and workable solution which will stand the test of time. It is from this viewpoint that the handling of the reparation problem in the years immediately following the War is instructive.

CHAPTER VIII

THE HISTORY OF REPARATION

THE reparation clauses of the Treaty of Versailles owed the unenviable reputation which they acquired in England to a trio of shortcomings. Firstly, the Treaty did not state any total amount which Germany was to pay by way of reparation. It merely indicated the types of damage for which Germany was to pay. These were set out in Annex I to Part VIII, the Reparation Section, of the Treaty. Secondly, certain types of damage for which compensation was demanded, in particular the cost of pensions and separation allowances, could only by dint of sophistical argument be considered to lie within the scope of the obligation to make compensation for damage to civilian life and property which Germany had been required to accept in the Lansing Note of 5th November 1918. Thirdly, too little account had been taken—so at least it came to be felt in England—of German capacity to pay. The Treaty charged the Reparation Commission with the duty of assessing the damages; it was to complete its findings by 1st May 1921. At the same time it was to draw up a scheme prescribing the payment of the entire reparation debt within a period of thirty years from that date. Thereafter the Commission might sanction the postponement of payments or

[1] Bourquin, M.: *Dynamism and the Machinery of International Institutions.* (Geneva Research Centre, Geneva Studies, Vol. XI, No. 5, 1940.)

modify their form, but it might not, save with the specific authority
of the governments represented on the Commission, cancel any part
of Germany's liability.

An explanation of the controversy which the reparation clauses
engendered must start with a survey of the negotiations on reparation in 1919. An adequate account of those negotiations is to be
found in the chapters prefatory to Mr. Burnett's comprehensive
collection of documents.[1] Here the story must be told briefly.

Consideration of the reparation problem at the Peace Conference
was first confided to a Commission, set up on 25th January 1919,
composed of the representatives of Allied nations, great and small.
Since the deliberations of this unwieldy body threatened to be
endless, Lloyd George, Clemenceau, and Colonel House decided, on
10th March, each to appoint one member of a small secret committee
to report on the amount that Germany might be expected to pay.
The Committee of Three completed its work within five days;
its members recommended a definite figure, £6,000,000,000,
payable half in German currency, as the maximum that could
be expected. Estimates had hitherto appeared in bewildering
profusion, some mounting on the wings of hope to astronomical
heights. The report of the Committee of Three represented,
then, a triumph of moderation, the outcome of the successful
efforts of the American member, Norman Davis, to persuade his
French colleague, Louis Loucheur, to set down his real views,
uninfluenced by wishful thinking. Lloyd George, and even
Clemenceau, inclined at first towards acceptance of the Committee's
findings. But Lloyd George, before committing himself, desired
to secure 'for his own protection and justification' [2] the conversion
of Lords Sumner and Cunliffe, the advocates of a much larger
sum. The two Lords remained unregenerate; so the momentary
vision of agreement on £6,000,000,000 faded out.

Thereafter the influence of the moderates waned. On 26th
March Clemenceau commenced an action which drove the Conference into contrary courses.[3] From this time it was Klotz the
extremist rather than Loucheur the moderate who played the part
of first French advocate on financial questions in the Council of
Four. His persistence made its mark: 'we got Klotz on the
brain,' remarked President Wilson a few weeks later.[4] A few
days afterwards Lloyd George began to be made aware that the
way of moderation was beset by parliamentary dangers. The
whispering against him in the Commons was to culminate in the

---

[1] Burnett, P. M.: *Reparation at the Paris Peace Conference*, 2 vols. N.Y., 1940.
[2] *Baker*, iii, p. 383.
[3] Mordacq, Gen. J. J. H.: *Le Ministère Clemenceau*, iii, p. 184. Cf. Thompson,
C. T.: *The Peace Conference*, p. 277.
[4] *Baker*, iii, p. 480.

telegram of 8th April, whereby 233 M.P.s called on him 'to make Germany acknowledge the debt and then to discuss ways and means of obtaining payment.'

The new French drive was marked on 28th March by the presentation by Klotz of a complete draft for the reparation clauses. Lloyd George may well have gazed in dismay at this labyrinthine document. On 29th March he laid before his colleagues a brief memorandum of his own.[1] From this memorandum came the reparation clauses of the Treaty in direct line of descent. Disputed points were thrashed out in a series of bitter, even tempestuous, meetings between British, French, Italian, and American experts from 31st March to 3rd April [2]; yet at the close agreement seemed little nearer. The temperature dropped only when the Council of Four returned to the question on 5th and 7th April. Lloyd George aligned himself with the French, while owing to illness President Wilson was replaced at the council table by the more conciliatory House.[3] By 12th April the foundations of the reparation settlement had been laid—in so far as the Treaty itself provided a settlement.

From the very outset of these negotiations the omission from the Treaty of any definite monetary claim was urged insistently by the French and as vigorously combated by the Americans. It was Lloyd George's support, in his memorandum of 29th March, of this French demand that proved decisive. Even in the first days of June, when striving to revise the reparation clauses, he still refused to envisage the inclusion in the Treaty of a single total sum as the Americans desired. To fix a definite figure was, he said, 'like asking a man in the maelstrom of Niagara to fix the price of a horse.' [4] The outcome of Lloyd George's eleventh-hour effort for revision was an invitation to Germany to offer, within four months of the signature of the Treaty, a lump sum in settlement of her whole liability. On this invitation hinged the policy which he pursued with regard to reparation immediately after the signature of the Treaty.

The refusal to state any definite monetary claim in the Treaty itself was doubtless largely prompted by political considerations. The situation in Allied countries was unsettled. People had come to expect that the cost of the War would be laid upon the enemy, and politicians shrank from deflating popular illusions about the

[1] Klotz' draft in Klotz, L.: *De la Guerre à la paix*, pp. 215-249, reprinted in Burnett, P. M.: *Reparation*, i, pp. 726-754; Lloyd George's draft in *Miller*, xix, pp. 288-303, and in Burnett, P. M.: *Reparation*, i, pp. 754-756.
[2] For these meetings Burnett's documents should be supplemented by Crespi, S.: *Alla Difesa d'Italia*, pp. 374 et seq.
[3] See Mordacq, Gen. J. J. H.: *Le Ministère Clemenceau*, iii, p. 211.
[4] *Miller*, xix, p. 280.

amount the enemy was likely to pay. But this was not the sole motive. The French adduced quite other reasons. On the one hand they pleaded that it would be impossible to complete before the signature of the Treaty the monetary estimation of the damages charged to Germany's account. On the other hand they urged that if the sum expected of Germany was to be adapted to her capacity to pay, that capacity should not be judged by reference to her existing or even to her pre-War position. None could tell just how much Germany might be able to pay in the coming years. Her economy might undergo rapid growth. An estimate based on available information might release Germany from a liability which the future might show her to be fully capable of discharging. Hence, they insisted, Germany's liability should be expressed in elastic terms, to ensure the full utilization of her future capacity to make good the immense damage charged to her account. This view was shared by Lord Cunliffe. To this extent the refusal to fix immediately a definite figure was not just a political expedient, but a course dictated by the very nature of the problem. It may be added that, at a time when her own finances were deranged, France was the more disinclined to compound the German debt since all assurance of similar action with regard to her own debts had been denied.

Neither, indeed, was Lloyd George swayed solely by unwillingness to jeopardize his political position. He anticipated that, when a detailed survey had been made, a smaller sum might prove to suffice for the work of reparation than seemed possible at the time.[1] Events justified this expectation, for when, in April 1921, the Reparation Commission completed its valuation of the damages, the sum proved not greatly in excess of the amount which, in March 1919, the Committee of Three had reported as a reasonable estimate of German capacity to pay.

A cogent economic argument could, it is true, be presented against the refusal to state a definite sum in the Treaty. The case was well presented by Norman Davis in a memorandum to President Wilson on 1st June 1919.[2] Unless the demand was presented for some definite sum within the limits of what the Germans themselves felt able to pay, Germany would lack incentive to make the necessary effort; and as long as she staggered under the burden of a debt deemed impossible of discharge, financial assistance would be denied her, her economic recuperation would be impeded, her capacity to pay would continue to crumble. Such counsel com-

[1] *Miller*, xix, pp. 278–281.
[2] Burnett, P. M.: *Reparation*, i, p. 101. See also McFadyean, Sir A.: *Reparation Reviewed*, pp. 56–59. This work should be consulted for the whole reparation controversy from 1919–1929. It is without equal as a commentary upon the decade of which it treats.

manded attention neither among business men nor among politicians, until the onset of the financial crisis in the following winter. It then inspired Lloyd George to a new endeavour to speed up the determination of the German debt. The prolonged contention which ensued served only to bring home afresh the political expediency of a temporary solution.

When the American experts found themselves unable to secure the insertion in the Treaty of some total sum within Germany's capacity to pay, they strove to attain their objective by another method. They proposed that the permanent Reparation Commission should be instructed to call upon Germany to pay not a sum equivalent to the total valuation of the claims against her, but a lesser sum representing a reasonable estimate of what Germany could pay within a period of thirty years.

This proposal to pare down the bill of costs in accordance with a time-limit for payment was debated at length by the Allied experts in their meetings of 31st March–3rd April. The French rejected the proposal outright. The British representatives wavered between these opposed camps. Lloyd George, in his Fontainebleau Memorandum of 25th March, had proclaimed that reparation payments 'ought to disappear if possible with the generation which made the war.' He was ready then to agree to a time-limit. But he hesitated to authorize the Reparation Commission to demand, from the outset, only what it thought Germany could reasonably pay within a certain number of years. It was on this point that, on 5th April, he aligned himself with the French. The Council of Four decided to require Germany to do her utmost to pay for all the damage within thirty years. The essence of the American proposal was thus rejected.[1]

The decision to require payment in full made the list of damages the decisive factor in determining the financial burden to be laid on Germany. Criticism of this list has centred on the inclusion of the claim for the reimbursement of the cost of pensions and separation allowances. Lloyd George has explained that he fostered this claim because its inclusion assured Great Britain a larger proportion of the German payments than the country would otherwise have been entitled to. He did not, however, originate the claim—contrary to the general belief; the French had all along pressed a similar demand, though hoping to safeguard their special interest by securing priority for the reparation of the devastated areas. President Wilson, though doubtful at first, was brought to admit the legitimacy of the claim through the reasoning of General Smuts. Separation allowances paid to wives and children, and pensions

[1] Burnett, P. M.: *Reparation*, i, pp. 779–836; Klotz, L.: *De la Guerre à la Paix*, pp. 140–141.

payable to disabled soldiers after their discharge, to war widows and to orphans would constitute, Smuts insisted, payments for losses suffered in a civilian capacity. Smuts' memorandum convinced Wilson that the charges in question were—to quote from his statement to the American experts—'a proper subject of reparation under the agreed terms of peace.'[1] At the time—1st April— the American experts were the less inclined to protest, since the negotiations then appeared to be proceeding on the assumption that Germany's liability would be adjusted to her capacity to pay. Four days later the Council of Four deprived the Reparation Commission of the power to pare down the bill when presented.

Though insistent on the claim for pensions, Lloyd George otherwise exercised a real influence for moderation in the formulation of the list of damages. He secured, with the support of Clemenceau, the rejection of certain vague claims which the Americans proposed to include. 'I am opposed,' he said, 'to these small claims that can be so easily forced up to a big bill.'[2] In general these claims related to indirect loss to civilians through interference with their work, or through destruction of their property. It is not improbable that, of the two drafts of Annex I, the British and the American, the American would, if accepted, have imposed the heavier burden.

As a background to the following chapters, which are devoted to an analysis of British and French views on reparation, it may be well to sketch the main phases in the development of the problem in the later years.

Early in 1920 the British Prime Minister set out to fix with the least possible delay, and on the basis of a German offer, a definite sum for reparation. The period of four months within which, by the Allied Note of 16th June 1919, Germany was invited to propose a lump sum, had already expired; but in response to Lloyd George's insistence the Allies signified, in a Memorandum of 8th March 1920, their willingness to extend the time-limit of their invitation.[3] Lloyd George thereafter pursued his purpose through a series of conferences, now with the Allies alone, now with the Allies and Germany. The French followed reluctantly, and insisted that, since Lloyd George proposed to treat amicably with Germany if she was prepared to make a good offer, he must assent to use force against Germany if she showed no such intention. So conciliation and coercion marched side by side, to their mutual discomfort. Finally, coercion prevailed. On 8th March 1921

[1] Burnett, P. M.: *Reparation*, i, pp. 755–756. For another statement to the same effect at a later date: *Miller*, xix, p. 295.
[2] *Miller*, xix, p. 320.
[3] *The Times*, March 10, 1920.

sanctions were applied, in consequence of a German offer which provoked dissatisfaction in England and infuriated France.

The application of these coercive measures against Germany marked the breakdown of Lloyd George's efforts to secure an unconstrained agreement on reparation between Germany and the Allies. In the brief interval before 1st May 1921 the achievement of a reasonable settlement could be furthered only by a renewed effort to bring French views into line with the British. In this direction, at least, Lloyd George registered a measure of success. On 30th April 1921 the Supreme Council met in London. Three days earlier the Reparation Commission had announced that the damage which the Treaty required Germany to make good amounted in value to £6,600,000,000. Would Germany be called upon to pay amortization and interest on this sum in such manner as to ensure the discharge of the entire obligation within thirty years, as the Treaty required? The Supreme Council decided to make no such impossible demand. The Schedule of Payments, issued by the Reparation Commission on 5th May 1921, and accepted by Germany under the menace of an Allied occupation of the Ruhr, represented a virtual abatement of Allied demands.

The London Schedule of 5th May 1921 nominally maintained intact Germany's obligation to bear a reparation burden of £6,600,000,000. But this amount was divided into two parts. In respect of the larger part, the C bonds totalling £4,100,000,000, no immediate payment was required. On the other part, the A and B bonds totalling £2,500,000,000 interest and amortization payments were demanded as follows: Germany was required to pay in cash within twenty-five days the sum of £50,000,000: this amount was duly paid. Thereafter Germany was to pay a fixed annuity of £100,000,000 in quarterly instalments commencing on 15th January 1922, and in addition a variable annuity amounting to 26 per cent of the value of German exports, also payable quarterly, but commencing on 15th November 1921.

The Schedule broke down before the end of the year. The first instalment of the variable annuity was met by deliveries in kind. But on 14th December 1921 the German Government notified the Reparation Commission that it would be unable to pay more than £10,000,000 towards the two instalments due on 15th January and 15th February 1922. The grant of a partial moratorium was considered by the British and French Ministers, first at the Conference of London (18th–22nd December 1921) and subsequently in council with the other Allies at the Inter-Allied Conference at Cannes (6th–13th January 1922). The Allies were within an ace of agreement on a schedule of reduced payments for the year 1922 when the Conference broke up prematurely in consequence of the French political crisis. The dissolution of the Conference necessitated handing the matter to the Reparation Commission. After protracted negotiations between the Commission and the German Government, the Commission gave its approval on 21st March to the reduction of German payments, in cash and in kind, for the year 1922 to £108,500,000. The relief so provided speedily proved inadequate. On 12th July 1922 Germany requested the complete postponement of cash payments not only during the remainder of the current year, but for the next two years as well. At the London Conference (7th–14th August 1922) the Allies were unable to reach agreement about the conditions which should be attached to the grant of a longer moratorium. The menace of default was again staved off by a makeshift arrangement devised by the Reparation Commission. Six months' Treasury bills were accepted in lieu of the cash payments due for the remainder of the year 1922. The respite thus afforded was both brief and partial, for deliveries in kind were to continue, while if by January 1923 no more durable settlement were reached, Germany would then automatically become liable to meet the full London Schedule of Payments.

The failure to achieve any durable settlement in August made almost inevitable the advent of a yet graver crisis. On 14th November, in pursuance of the recommendations of a committee of international financial experts, Germany requested as conditions precedent to the stabilization of the mark a complete moratorium upon all payments in cash and deliveries in kind for three or four years, and the fixation of Germany's liabilities 'at an amount . . . which could be defrayed from the budget surplus.' When the Allied Governments met at the London Conference (8th–11th December 1922) and the succeeding Paris Conference (2nd–4th January 1923), to compare their views, the open confrontation of Anglo-French differences revealed a gulf which, as Bonar Law regretfully remarked, no bridge could span.

On 11th January 1923 French and Belgian troops entered the Ruhr. The professed object of Franco-Belgian policy was to enforce the payment of reparation by the direct control of German industries in the Ruhr. Such control was nullified till 27th September by German passive resistance, but from the cessation of passive resistance, on that date, control was effectively exercised till October 1924. The British Government, once its initial mood of confessed helplessness had passed, sought to intervene as mediator in the Franco-German struggle. The first British effort to bring about the resumption of reparation negotiations, of which Lord Curzon's speech in the House of Lords on 20th April was the prelude, stranded temporarily owing to the unconciliatory tone of the German Note of 2nd May. A renewed advance, facilitated by the more promising German Note of 7th June, broke against the adamant refusal of Poincaré to enter into any negotiations with Germany before the abandonment of passive resistance; and the British attempt at mediation terminated in the latent hostility of the Curzon Note of 11th August and Poincaré's reply of 20th August. After passive resistance had been dropped, a new and more diplomatic line of approach was opened up by the renewal, on 11th October, of the American suggestion, first made before the Ruhr occupation, for the reference of the reparation question to an independent committee of experts. Taken up by the British Government, and pressed by the American, this proposal proved the first milestone on the road out of the Ruhr. On 30th November the Reparation Commission decided to set up two Committees of Experts. The first Committee held its opening session, under the chairmanship of General Dawes, on 14th January 1924, and reported on 9th April. All the governments concerned, having first accepted the recommendations of the Committee, assembled at the London Conference of 16th July–16th August 1924, to consult together how to bring them into force. The Conference was successful in settling arrangements not only for the termination of economic control in the Ruhr, but also for its military evacuation.

The Dawes Plan remained in operation from October 1924 to May 1930. Throughout this period it worked without a hitch. Politically, the Dawes Plan has no history save for the gestation of its luckless successor, the Young Plan, conceived, it would appear, in a confusion of political and economic motives.[1]

Unlike the Dawes Plan—a temporary solution, though capable of indefinite prolongation—the Young Plan was designed to constitute a complete and final settlement of the reparation problem. The Committee of Experts charged with its preparation commenced their labours on 11th February and signed their Report on 7th June 1929. The first Hague Conference, which met from 6th to 31st August 1929, differed from the London Conference which followed the Dawes Committee in that the governments assembled had not previously committed themselves to the acceptance of the Experts' Report. The Conference assembled for the purpose of considering the Report itself in the first place, and thereafter the measures necessary for bringing it into force. The dispute precipitated by Snowden's determination to modify in Great Britain's favour the distribution of German payments proposed in the Report prevented the Conference from passing to the second part of its agenda, which was in consequence postponed to a second Conference at

[1] See p. 83.

The Hague, 3rd–20th January 1930. At this second Conference the question of sanctions in the event of future default was regulated. The Young Plan came into force on 9th May 1930.

The new Plan, the successful operation of which depended on the continued expansion of trade, fell a victim in its very infancy to the world economic depression. On 20th June 1931, confronted by the imminent collapse of German finance, President Hoover launched on a startled world his proposal for a moratorium of one year on all inter-governmental war debt and reparation payments. With the ensuing negotiations, interlinked with the development of the economic crisis, it is not proposed to deal.

CHAPTER IX

REPARATION: THE FACTORS OF DISCORD

IN the five years of disillusionment which followed the signature of the Treaty, reparation played a rôle in Anglo-French relations which far surpassed that of any other problem. In an enterprise the good conduct of which depended on their cordial collaboration, England and France found themselves unable to agree on a concerted policy capable of being carried out over a period of time. A series of false starts, to the accompaniment of increasingly bitter recrimination, ended in an atmosphere of suspicion, and even enmity. Not till 1924, when the Dawes Plan at last gave respite to Allied statesmen from their Sisyphean task, did reparation yield pride of place to other issues in Anglo-French relations. Then for another period of equal length—five halcyon years they appeared in retrospect—reparation was carried through quietly, and kept off the political scene. In 1929 it returned with new venom to the world of politics, and proceeded through circumstances which recalled those of its early years to a premature decease in 1932, which France lamented, while England sighed with relief.

In a study concerned not with the economic aspects, but with the political background of reparation, interest attaches mainly to the first years of controversy, 1920–1924. One major feature of this earlier period is singled out for consideration elsewhere. The British policy of seeking a direct understanding with Germany on reparation found its expression in a series of conferences, the story of which is told in Chapter VII. Here an attempt is made to elucidate the causes of the Anglo-French wrangle which started in the last days of the Peace Conference and terminated with the adoption of the Dawes Plan.

No factor contributed more to the inability of Great Britain and

France to formulate a common policy than the contrast between the forms assumed by the problem of reconstruction in the two countries. The enduring burden of war on Great Britain was the loss of foreign markets, which cumbered the land with a dead weight of unemployment. The revival of trade became the *summum bonum* of British policy towards Europe. But all roads towards this goal led through the jungle of reparation: here progress was blocked by the conflict of British and French plans. For economic recovery waited on the assuagement of war fever, which the French predilection for sanctions threatened to perpetuate. It was to lay the foundations of economic recovery that Lloyd George strove in 1920 to anticipate the reparation settlement. Since the French then consented to follow him in this course, the antagonism of French and British views became really acute only with the sharp depreciation of the mark in September–November 1921, and the ensuing breakdown of the London Schedule. Great Britain's first need was the stabilization of currencies, and of the mark above all. To this end a moratorium on reparation payments and—so it was widely believed—an amputation of the total liability were essential.

France, on the other hand, experienced in the early months of 1922 a brilliant economic revival. Her industrial population was fully employed, largely owing to the abnormal demand for labour on reconstruction works. What weighed on France was a financial burden which she deemed beyond endurance. Expenditure on pensions and on the reconstruction of the devastated areas was absorbing half the total annual expenditure of the Government.[1] This expenditure, termed 'recoverable' in view of the claim for its reimbursement by Germany, was met wholly by loan. In addition, war debts haunted the French, though they were not an immediate financial burden, for no repayments were being demanded for the moment. In consequence France demanded immediate German payments in the interests of her own financial stability, while Great Britain pleaded for the postponement of German payments in the interest of German, and hence European, economic recovery.

Yet in the last months of 1922 British statesmen could with reason claim that, if reparation was the cardinal claim of France, the economic postulates of their policy were as much in line with the French as with British interests. The stabilization of the mark was a condition of the receipt of reparation by France as of the recovery of British trade. The reduction of the capital debt to a sum within Germany's capacity to pay was in 1922, as the Report

[1] By the end of 1923, £1,140,000,000 had been spent on reconstruction, and £950,000,000 on pensions. It was estimated that £504,000,000 and £470,000,000 remained to be spent (Furst, G. A.: *De Versailles aux Experts*, p. 319).

of the Committee of Bankers demonstrated, an essential condition of the restoration of German credit; and without the restoration of German credit France could have no hope of reaping the proceeds of a loan to pay off the reparation debt. To the question: Why did the French Government refuse to agree with the British in the practical application of these simple economic truths?—an answer may be sought along three lines. In the first place, it may be suggested that the French mind continued to dwell in economic darkness. Secondly, attention may be drawn to the divergence of French and British views on the political issues which arose in connexion with proposals for the restoration of German financial stability. Thirdly, it may be held that France pursued a policy of security under the guise of demands for reparation. The first and second of these lines of inquiry are pursued in the sections which follow, while the third is held over till the end of the next chapter.

The hard core of the reparation problem was presented by French reluctance to scale down the capital debt. Nominally Germany owed RM 132 milliard; in fact there was no possibility that she would be able to pay half that sum. Economic adversity taught with impressive speed the once vengeful members of the House of Commons to temper the spirit of retributive justice with the cooling counsels of economic analysis; but the French *député*, under a different schoolmaster, continued for long to cherish the passions and the financial hopes which in 1919 his British counterpart had shared. So it was that even the most cordial of French statesmen saw a distasteful vision of political embarrassment when, supported by authoritative economic and financial opinion, his British colleague dwelt on the theme of Germany's capacity to pay.

From 1920 to 1924 British policy on reparation was based on the postulate that the economic recovery of Germany, and hence of Europe, would be possible only if Germany's total financial liability for reparation was first fixed once and for all within the limits of what Germany could pay. With this postulate was coupled the contention that this maximum sum payable by Germany could be precisely ascertained by objective investigation. To doubt or deny the truth of these doctrines was in British eyes to sin against the light. With an assurance of rectitude proper to the exponents of an incontrovertible faith, British statesmen stipulated, as the indispensable condition of a satisfactory settlement, the renunciation forthwith of all claims beyond the level of German capacity.

For this British gospel France proved stony soil. The French continued to profess an exasperating fidelity to that heresy which they had first propounded at the Paris Conference. They denied the practicability of stating a precise sum which should be taken finally to represent Germany's total liability. To this negative creed they adhered with an obstinacy as constant as their arguments were varied. In the early months of 1919 French experts had opposed the insertion of any fixed sum in the Treaty on the grounds that no monetary estimate of damage suffered could be worked out by the time of its signature. French statesmen, then and later, were further moved by the fear of a parliamentary revolt against any policy which pricked the bubble of popular hope. To this consideration of internal politics was added one of external politics when negotiations with Germany got under way; to postpone fixation of a total sum still seemed expedient, since no figure satisfactory to France could be acceptable to Germany. But in the end the French settled on an argument which, though present to their minds in 1919, gained more cogent form as the controversy proceeded. To the British contention that the assessment of Germany's capacity was 'a question of establishing a fact,' [1] the French replied that Germany's capacity would vary with the conditions of passing years, and could not be fixed once and for all. [2]

The historian, while forbearing to judge between these rival creeds, may observe that British policy acquired through unswerving adherence to its economic tenets a degree of rigidity which perhaps needlessly accentuated the conflict with France. In 1924 the Dawes experts found a way round the conflicting theses of France and Great Britain. The experts fixed the annual payments to be made by Germany, but not the capital debt. They circumvented the difficulty of squaring fixed annuities with variations in Germany's balance of foreign payments by the provision that Germany should pay in her own currency. They devolved on an Allied agency, the Transfer Committee, the responsibility for effecting such transfer of the annuities into foreign currency as would not endanger stability of the mark. The Dawes Plan was a provisional settlement capable of indefinite prolongation, which eluded the obstacle presented by French unwillingness to reduce the capital debt. Till 1924 the British Government was unwilling to consider any such compromise, from a conviction that no provisional settlement could suffice to restore German credit.

The question of choosing between a provisional and a permanent settlement was posed as early as the first days of 1921. The Allied Governments had convoked a meeting of Allied and German financial experts at Brussels, in December 1920, to examine together the problem of reparation. After a break, the conversations were continued informally in Paris in January 1921. On the initiative of the French representative, Seydoux, the Allied experts unanimously recommended that the determination of a total sum should

[1] Curzon's Note of August 11, 1923. *Cmd.* 1943, p. 50.
[2] Cf. Poincaré's Note of July 30, 1923. *Cmd.* 1943, p. 31.

>e postponed, and that a provisional arrangement should be
ccepted for the payment by Germany of RM 3 milliard for five
'ears. The acceptance of these recommendations was urged by
3riand at the Paris Conference (24th–30th January 1921). France,
ie declared, could not agree 'to imperil her future by making
what she would regard as a premature and unsatisfactory settlement
.t the present.' But, he added, France was ready to accept these
.nnuities for the time being and to investigate further the question
)f a lump sum. 'By adopting this policy the French people would
gradually get informed as to the true position, and perhaps learn
he necessity for accepting a lower figure than they would contem-
)late at present.' [1] Lloyd George, however, rejected out of hand
he experts' recommendations, and pressed forward the preparation
)f the Paris Proposals, designed to effect a permanent settlement.
Thereby he was drawn ineluctably into the vortex of the London
sanctions.

Lest it be assumed that the advocates of a provisional arrangement
were just floundering in the shallows of political expediency, it
may be noted that, from the time of the Spa Conference, Lord
D'Abernon enrolled himself in their ranks. 'Until the currency
s stabilized,' he wrote on 30th July 1920, 'no serious forecast can
)e made of the financial future of Germany.' And on 26th January
1921: 'They all take it as axiomatic that unless the total of the
German debt is fixed, Germany's recovery is rendered impossible.
This I believe to be a profound misconception.' [2] The acceptance
)f D'Abernon's view constituted an important factor in the *détente*
)f 1924.

The contention over the total to be paid by Germany derived
its virulence in large measure from dispute about the distribution
)f payments between the Allies. The ratios had been fixed at
Spa in July 1920—52 per cent to France, 22 per cent to the British
Empire. No recognition was accorded to the French claim to
receive compensation for the areas devastated by the war in
priority to the satisfaction of all other claims against Germany.
The French were unanimously convinced of the justice of this
demand. Millerand pressed it at Hythe in May 1920, but Lloyd
George refused all concession. Thereafter the cost of reconstruction, plus the sum necessary to meet French war debt payment,
constituted for France a minimum sum below which she refused
to reduce her own claims against Germany. Any proposal to
reduce the German debt gave rise to the question whether the
French share of the reduced sum would meet this minimum demand.

[1] Lloyd George: *The Truth about Reparations and War Debts*, p. 53. See also
Bergmann, C.: *History of Reparations*, p. 527; *D'Abernon*, i, pp. 109–122.
[2] *D'Abernon*, i, pp. 72, 118. Cf. also ii, pp. 128, 237.

Two inducements could thus be held out to France to agree to reduction: special consideration for the devastated areas, or an arrangement regarding war debts.

The expediency of meeting the French claim for special treatment in respect of the devastated areas received increasingly widespread recognition in Great Britain before the Ruhr occupation, as the legitimacy of the inclusion of pensions in Germany's bill came to be challenged. The claim for pensions had been the main factor in swelling the bill to a sum beyond German capacity to pay. There was force in the argument that a reduction of the total to be paid by Germany should be accompanied by revision of the ratios of distribution, in order to ensure that at least the cost of reconstruction should be met.[1] The refusal of the British Government to consent to any such arrangement struck the French as a close-fisted devotion to British claims of secondary rank which consorted ill with appeals to the French to consent to measures which would jeopardize the satisfaction of their own vital demands.

The refusal of the British Government to modify the Spa percentages had the effect of concentrating attention on the question of war debts. 'While the enemy owes me much money, I also owe money to some of my friends. As regards the arrangements to be made with the enemy, I have to take into account what is done by my friends': so Klotz had declared in the early days of the Peace Conference. But the American Treasury had sharply vetoed, in a note of 8th March 1919, any discussion directed towards the redistribution of the burden of debt; thereby the problem of war debts had—in politics at least—been effectively severed from the problem of reparation so far as the U.S.A. was concerned.[2] Nevertheless from 1920 till 1924 Anglo-French agreement on reparation seemed at all times contingent on a settlement of the French war debt to Great Britain. When Lloyd George pressed Millerand in 1920 to agree to a lump sum for reparation, Millerand seized the opportunity to resuscitate the French demand for the treatment of reparation and war debts as integral parts of a single

---

[1] Lord Curzon in August 1923 asserted that 'Great Britain's proportion of reparations would not in fact be seriously altered as a result of priority conceded to material damages' (*Cmd.* 1943, p. 52). The validity of this statement appears open to question. No authoritative figures of the composition of the total of 132 milliards have been published. Noel, P., *L'Allemagne et les réparations*, p. 25, gives the following as the valuation of damages by the Reparation Commission:

	Great Britain.	France.
	milliard marks gold.	
Dommages aux biens	5·5	35
Dommages aux personnes (G.B.) ⎱	22·2	30·5
Pensions et allocations (France) ⎰		

[2] *Lapradelle*, VII (*Commission financière*), pp. 348–350, 365–366; Nonu, J. M.: *Le Problème des dettes interalliées*, pp. 450–545.

problem.[1] He initiated the policy of refusing to agree to any reduction of the German liability below the Treaty level unless French war debts were simultaneously reduced. Proposals of this nature were advanced by Millerand's successors on each occasion when the menace of German default necessitated the revision of Germany's financial obligations. Thus Loucheur brought such plans for submission to Lloyd George at the London Conference of 18th–22nd December 1921 [2] ; and in the heyday of Cannes the belief was widespread, though perhaps not well founded, that an Anglo-French agreement would be reached on such lines. Some indication of the serious consideration given to the Loucheur plan is to be found in the suggestions brought forward by Sir Robert Horne as a modification of that plan at the Conference of Allied Finance Ministers in Paris during March 1922.[3] Poincaré himself adopted, in July 1922, the thesis of a simultaneous settlement of reparation and Inter-Allied debts, and a comprehensive scheme was approved by the French Cabinet on 28th July.[4] The Balfour Note of 1st August 1922 intervened to prevent the submission of this scheme at the London Conference. French hopes nevertheless continued to centre on the project of a new conference of all the Allied States, great and small, to deal with these two questions. It was in preparation for such a conference that the French, British, Italian, and Belgian Ministers met in London in December 1922 and in Paris in January 1923. Unfortunately, by the time these conferences met, French policy had turned irrevocably from the course mapped out in the summer, and Poincaré passed contemptuously over this last opportunity of a simultaneous Anglo-French settlement of reparation and war debts. When in 1924 the problem of reparation came back to the conference table, American participation had the result that for the first time, as Herriot realized to his dismay at Chequers, the discussion on reparation had to proceed without concurrent discussion on war debts.

No purpose would be served by a detailed exposition of the ingenious combinations which went to the making of this series of abortive projects in 1921–1922. All were based on the central idea of paying off war debts by the transfer to the creditor states of the debtor states' shares of the worthless German C bonds— an indirect means of effecting the cancellation of war debts. They were all variations on the French theme that, since France proposed to collect from Germany whatever sums she had to pay, the first step towards relieving Germany was to remit the French debt.

[1] Toynbee: *Survey, 1920–1923*, p. 117.
[2] *Eur. Nouv.*, February 18, 1922.
[3] *Eur. Nouv.*, March 18, 1922; *Economist*, March 18, 1922.
[4] Calmette, C.: *Les Dettes interalliées*, pp. 160–163; *The Times*, July 29, 1923.

But attention may be drawn to the contrast between the French proposals of July 1922 and those of six months later. In July 1922 the Poincaré Cabinet adopted a plan the leading features of which were as follows. The complete elimination of the C bonds was to be conditional on the cancellation of Inter-Allied debts and of the European debts to the U.S.A. The British share in the RM 50 milliards of German debt that would remain was to be reduced to 10 per cent. A moratorium was to be granted Germany in order to facilitate the raising of loans for the payment of reparation. By comparison with this plan, Poincaré's proposals before the Ruhr occupation demonstrate that he had lost interest in any solution along these lines. He was prepared to cancel the C bonds only to a nominal amount, corresponding to the French debt to Great Britain and the debt of the smaller Allies to France, which were to be cancelled simultaneously.

The British Government hesitated to conclude an exclusive Franco-British arrangement on war debts such as the French envisaged. Though the British Government favoured the general cancellation of war debts, it judged that the British financial position was too weak to permit the remission of the French debt save as one element in an all-round settlement which would include the British debt to America. An approach by Lloyd George to President Wilson in August 1920 met with a decided rebuff. So was built up a fatal concatenation. The United States refused to forgo the debt due from Great Britain; thus burdened, Great Britain refused to forgo the debt due from France ; denied relief in this direction, France refused to lighten the load on Germany. This vicious chain, though weakened as time passed, was never broken until in the world economic crisis all its links successively snapped. British policy crystallized in the Balfour Note of 1st August 1922, which intimated that Great Britain proposed to collect from Germany and the Allied countries together enough to pay the amounts due from Great Britain to the United States. Perhaps no other diplomatic declaration has been the subject of such diverse appreciation. Ostensibly it constituted a generous gesture, for, read in conjunction with the total figures of British credits and debts, the Note signified the cancellation of three-quarters of the British claims against Continental nations. Yet from the viewpoint of Anglo-French relations it creates the impression of an unfortunate manœuvre. The immediate effect of the Balfour Note was to warn Poincaré off the road he was preparing to tread. The London Conference, which a correspondent thought might prove 'the most important since the signature of the Treaty of Versailles,' degenerated into a miserable dispute over Poincaré's now barren programme of productive pledges. Though, in January 1923, Bonar Law offered the practical remission of the pre-armistice European debts to Great Britain, as an element in a definitive reparation settlement, Poincaré had by then set his mind on the occupation of the Ruhr. Anglo-French relations with regard to reparation and war debts, viewed as a single problem, were to some degree analogous to their relations on security problems. Standing between Europe and the U.S.A., Great Britain shrank from aligning herself with European countries in any manner which might jeopardize her relations with the U.S.A. The broad financial settlement which represented the British ideal was made dependent on American co-operation, which was unlikely to be forthcoming. The American Government was tied by the injunction of Congress to permit no connexion between the negotiation of reparation and war-debt settlements. For this restriction was adduced the plausible justification that 'Germany cannot pay one mark more or less because of what France may owe, and France cannot collect what Germany is unable to pay.'[1] The refusal to couple reparation and war debts created for a time a political impasse. French statesmen asked why France should shoulder the responsibility of applying the principle of capacity to pay to the German debt without some assurance that it would be applied to their own debts; neither from England nor America had they any such assurance.[2] As the French saw it, British policy was condemned to hobble unless Great Britain decided to proceed regardless of American co-operation.[3] No remission of war debts, no reparation settlement; no reparation settlement, no economic recovery; this proved a chant whose potency for evil was not broken till 1924.

[1] Hughes to Herrick, October 17, 1922. *U.S.A. Foreign Relations*, 1922, ii, p. 169.

[2] Boyden wrote to Hughes, October 14, 1922, that he thought there was a great chance of France agreeing to a discussion of reparation based on the general principle of capacity to pay 'if it could be applied to a general settlement including Inter-Allied debt' (*U.S.A. Foreign Relations*, 1922, ii, p. 168).

[3] At the outset of 1922 plans for the simultaneous remission of war debts and the revision of Germany's liability were abandoned, it would seem, because the participation of the U.S.A. could not be procured, and without the U.S.A. Great Britain refused to move. The consequent elimination of war debts from the potential agenda of the Genoa Conference contributed to the French determination to exclude from its discussions the problem of reparation, and so to belittle its utility, and cloud its prospects of success. The British Government, wrote Philippe Millet, 'before agreeing to offset the European debts, awaits the co-operation of America. It has a right to do so. But in that case let it cease to believe that the Genoa Conference can alleviate in the least the economic crisis from which Great Britain is suffering' (*Eur. Nouv.*, February 18, 1922). Cf. the article by 'Un Européen' (William Martin) in *Revue de Genève*, May 1923: 'Les Responsabilités du monde anglo-saxon,' which concludes: 'The secret of the Ruhr must be sought in the Mississippi plain.'

CHAPTER X

REPARATION: THE PROBLEM OF GUARANTEES

THE compensation of war debts and the reduction of the capital reparation debt formed two themes in a trilogy of problems which, burked in 1919, came up for discussion at each reparation crisis from 1920 to 1923. The third was the problem of guarantees and sanctions, which owed its prominence to the contention incessantly advanced by the French that Germany would carry out no engagements save under constraint. Between guarantees and sanctions it is possible to draw in conception a clear line of differentiation. Guarantees are measures normal in their application, to ensure the regular execution of obligations. Sanctions are penal measures, exceptional in their application, brought into force in the event of failure to execute obligations. In the actual history of reparation the distinction is less precise. Measures taken by way of sanction were retained in operation as guarantees, and guarantees were on occasion indistinguishable from sanctions. In spite of this overlapping, the distinction has sufficient practical validity to justify separate treatment of these two aspects of French policy. Sanctions in connexion with reparation have been discussed in an earlier chapter, in which the question is treated as one aspect of the wider problem of the enforcement of Treaty obligations.[1]

In no respect was the continuity of French policy before and after the Treaty more marked than in the demand for guarantees. Throughout the negotiation of the Treaty the French delegation envisaged two types of guarantee for the payment of reparation. The first followed the time-honoured method of stationing an army of occupation on enemy soil. There resulted the ill-contrived scheme of occupation, inept both from the viewpoint of reparation and of security, which formed Part XIV of the Treaty.[2] Detailed treatment is called for here of the second type of guarantee envisaged by the French, which is not inaptly described as a system of 'Ottomanization'—the application to Germany, though in much modified form, of the methods of foreign financial control once pursued to safeguard the service of foreign loans in Greece, Turkey, and Egypt.[3]

---

[1] See Chapter VI.   [2] See pp. 80–83 and 186–188.

[3] It may be desirable to emphasize the difference in meaning between the English word 'control' and the French word '*le contrôle.*' Control implies the power to issue orders, and hence administrative intervention; '*le contrôle*' is a milder word, signifying inspection or supervision. Anglo-French misunderstanding was at times probably intensified by the impression that when the French spoke of '*le contrôle*' they meant 'control.'

The prototype of French proposals regarding guarantees is to be found in the ambitious scheme advocated in vain by the French Finance Minister, Klotz, at the Peace Conference. That scheme looked forward to the appropriation to the payment of reparation of a wide range of German revenues—excise duties, customs duties, direct taxes, an export tax of 20 per cent, and the yield of economic enterprises such as mines and railways. It provided, too, for the creation of an Inter-Allied Financial Commission to control these revenues and at the same time to act, in conjunction with a Financial Section of the League of Nations, as the main-spring in a mechanism of sanctions. The scheme had been formulated even before the start of the Conference.[1] It was submitted on 12th March 1919 to the Third sub-Commission on Reparation, which had been set up at Klotz's behest to inquire into 'the guarantees that should be obtained for payment.' Finally it was included by Klotz in his reparation plan presented to the Council of Four on 28th March. But all his efforts were in vain. The fundamental problem even then was seen to be the problem of transfer; the appropriation of revenues would not help solve it. When, on 5th April, Klotz proposed that the Allies should establish 'a charge on the income of the railroads, ports and customs,' Lloyd George replied, 'I do not see any gain in this. What would we get if we took the customs?'[2]

The most eloquent testimony to Klotz's defeat in 1919 is provided by the inchoate state of the financial guarantees stipulated by the Treaty.[3] Of these, Article 248 alone demands consideration. It provided that reparation should be a first charge on all assets and revenues of the German Empire and its constituent states. The Reparation Commission was empowered to approve exemptions from this rule of priority. Literally interpreted, Article 248 might presumably have been construed to debar the German Government from taking any decision on questions of finance without first securing the approval of the Commission. But the clause had one meaning to an English lawyer and another to a French lawyer, though neither could be quite clear what it meant even in the light of his own legal training. The Reparation Commission had no authority to interpret this article, since it was inserted in the financial, not the reparation, section of the Treaty. Act 248 proved, indeed, a misbegotten provision.[4]

The failure to demand precise guarantees of payment gave rise

---

[1] See Cambon's Memorandum of November 26, 1918 ; *Miller*, ii, pp. 206–214.
[2] Burnett, P. M.: *Reparation*, i, p. 835.
[3] Articles 234, 241, 248, with para. 12*b* of Annex II of Part VIII.
[4] See Fischer Williams, Sir J.: 'A Legal Footnote to the Story of German Reparations,' *British Year Book of International Law, 1932*, pp. 24–26; Noel, P.: *L'Allemagne et les réparations*, pp. 137–139.

to criticism in France as soon as the conditions of peace became known. On all occasions when the reparation problem came back on the stocks in 1920–1924 French policy recurred to proposals akin to those first presented by Klotz in 1919. The post-War history of reparation turns round the scaling down of payments and the scaling up of guarantees in order to bring these two aspects of the problem into due relationship.

After the signature of the Treaty the French demand for the clarification of guarantees and sanctions acquired a new urgency from the conviction that Germany was seeking to escape the payment of reparation by wilful financial mismanagement. This accusation provides one of the many examples of the difference of French and British appraisal of developments in Germany. The true situation appears to have been that, while the governments of the newly-born Republic possessed all too little authority to impose the measures of financial reorganization which would in any event have been indispensable, their task was rendered quite hopeless by the remorseless pressure of Allied demands. Nevertheless, what infuriated the French was their belief, which was far from groundless, that leading German industrialists were loth to see the process of inflation arrested and were exerting their influence to sabotage the payment of reparation. While it is fantastic to impute a deliberate policy of financial disruption to the German Government, it seems reasonable to believe that no policy of fulfilment could have been carried through without a change of attitude on the part of obstructionist elements in German industry and finance. Poincaré's occupation of the Ruhr at least achieved this object. When the Dawes Committee visited Berlin, Stresemann asked Owen Young to try 'bringing the Industrialists into line, because if Germany was to make an honest effort' they were in a position 'to block him.' On meeting Stinnes and his fellow-industrialists Young brought them round by bluntly explaining that they had only to choose between an economic settlement such as the Committee would recommend or the continuance of French occupation.[1]

In the elaboration of guarantees supplementary to the Treaty four stages may be distinguished. The first was marked by the London Schedule of Payments of 5th May 1921; the second by the intensification of supervision exacted in return for the grant of a partial moratorium early in 1922; the third by the interlude of productive pledges, initiated by Poincaré at the London Conference in August 1922, and which opened out into the Ruhr occupation

[1] Dawes, C.: *Journal*, p. 77. Cf. Bonn, M.: *Der neue Plan*, pp. 8–10; *Department of Overseas Trade: Report on the Economic and Financial Conditions in Germany to March 1922*, by Thelwall, J. W. F., pp. 9–23; *D'Abernon*, ii, p. 120.

of 1923–1924; and the fourth stage by the system in operation from 1924–1929, which formed part of the Dawes Plan. While the experiment of productive pledges must be reserved for separate treatment, the common character of the guarantees instituted at other stages justifies their discussion *en bloc*.

The London Schedule of Payments supplemented the Treaty of Versailles, not only in defining the payments to be made by Germany, but in stipulating the appropriation of German revenues to the payment of reparation and in providing for the institution of a rudimentary supervision of German finance. Germany was required to earmark for reparation payments the yield of all import and export duties, together with the proceeds of a levy of 25 per cent on the value of all German exports.[1] To supervise the appropriation of these revenues a Committee of Guarantees was set up. The Committee was charged also to secure the application of Articles 241 and 248 of the Treaty—i.e. to safeguard the priority of reparation as a charge upon German revenues and to watch over German legislation designed to give effect to the reparation provisions of the Treaty. To the disgust of the French, this Committee remained centred in Paris, and paid only occasional visits to Berlin in order to enter into closer contact with the German Government when problems of special gravity demanded attention.[2]

In May 1922 this limited oversight of German finance was extended from the appropriated revenues to the whole German budget. The extension of scope was exacted by the Reparation Commission as a condition of granting the partial moratorium which Germany had requested on 14th December 1921. The German Government was required to impose new taxation and to attempt the reduction of expenditure, to put into force effective measures for preventing the flight of capital, and to resume the publication of adequate economic and financial statistics. The Committee of Guarantees was to be granted the necessary facilities for gaining a full insight into the application of these reforms.[3]

These measures of supervision were introduced on French instigation and were accepted by the British somewhat reluctantly. 'The question of guarantees,' Loucheur insisted at the London Conference (May 1921), 'is a *sine qua non* for France.'[4] The Committee of Guarantees gave real satisfaction to the French, but not

---

[1] Mitigations of these stipulations were granted subsequently. See *Rep. Comm. Report, 1920–1922*, pp. 152–153, and *Rep. Comm. Official Documents*, iii, pp. 42–43, 48.
[2] *Rep. Comm. Official Documents*, i, pp. 22–24; *Rep. Comm. Report, 1920–1922*, pp. 149–150.
[3] *Rep. Comm. Report, 1920–1922*, pp. 154–156, 267–277; *Rep. Comm. Official Documents*, i, pp. 118–144.
[4] Barnich, G.: *Comment faire payer l'Allemagne*, p. 25.

for long. Seydoux hailed it as the application to Germany of the system 'which saved Egypt, Turkey, and Greece from insolvency.' A month sufficed for his disillusionment; by June he was protesting, 'this is not our idea of the Committee of Guarantees; this is not what France expected.' [1] In December 1921 Briand and Loucheur promptly countered the German application for a moratorium by the presentation of plans for the reinforcement of control; these were agreed to by the British Ministers at the London Conference and formed the basis of resolutions which the premature dissolution of the Cannes Conference alone prevented from becoming operative.[2] The more stringent supervision imposed by the Reparation Commission in May 1922 derived from proposals presented by the French Delegation to the Commission on 15th March at Poincaré's behest. The contribution of other delegations was to tone down the French demands. In 1922 the experience of 1921 was quickly repeated. Hardly had the new measures entered into force before French opinion again commenced to fume at the inability of the Committee of Guarantees to check the process of financial disintegration in Germany. As the mark plunged downwards, measures for the supervision of German finance went to a heavy discount in the French political market, and the French Government turned to consider the attractions of 'specific and productive pledges.'

The French policy of 'Ottomanization' was indeed bound to break against two obstacles, the one legal, the other practical. In Egypt, Turkey, and Greece, well-ordered systems of financial administration had been introduced under the direction of foreign administrators. It was not possible to do the same with Germany. The Treaty gave neither the Allied Governments nor the Reparation Commission any right to intervene in German financial administrations; in consequence the Committee of Guarantees was entitled to the melancholy satisfaction of an insight into the methods of German finance, but it could neither give orders to nor supersede German officials. The British questioned the legality of the more far-reaching intervention desired by the French. In 1924 the correctness of the British interpretation of the legal position was established by the Report of the Committee of Jurists at the London Conference. It read as follows:—

1. The Treaty of Peace contains no provision allowing the Allied Governments to intervene in the exercise of Germany's sovereign rights as regards the methods by which the German Government is to procure the sums required for the payment of reparation. . . .

---

[1] Seydoux, J.: *De Versailles*, pp. 55, 60.   Cf. Millet in *Eur. Nouv.*, July 22, 1922.
[2] Text in *D.D. Documents relatifs aux Réparations*, i, pp. 178–179; also *Eur. Nouv.*, January 21 and February 4, 1922.

3. The Reparation Commission has no power to exact from the German Government the application of such or such sources of revenue or the adoption of such or such means for the purpose of raising the sums required for the payment of its debt. The treaty gives the Commission no power to dictate to Germany its internal legislation, to prescribe the establishment or collection of taxes or to dictate the character of the German budget (Allied reply of the 16th June 1919, p. 33).

4. Subject to the provisions of the Treaty, which provide for the surrender of particular assets . . . Germany retains a free hand as to the means of procuring the sums which she requires in order to satisfy her obligations.[1]

The political consequence of this finding was that, whereas in 1921 and 1922 guarantees had been imposed on Germany on legal grounds which need not be discussed here, the acceptance of the Dawes system of control was the subject of free negotiation with Germany.

Apart from this legal obstacle, the utility of direct intervention in German financial administration was open to question. Foreign administrative control might rapidly be stultified unless the creditor states were prepared to enforce their edicts by ubiquitous armed forces and to proceed to a complete replacement of administrative personnel. British hesitancy to agree to measures of control arose, therefore, not only from legal considerations, but also from forebodings that the Allies might find themselves involved in direct responsibility for the conduct of German internal affairs, with no likelihood of compensation by way of increased payments. The British held firmly to the conviction that regular payment could be assured only by the loyal collaboration of Germany in the making of reparation payments, and that such co-operation could be brought about only when the burden of reparation had been adjusted to Germany's capacity.

This British line of thought did not, however, issue in the conclusion that measures of control were necessarily otiose in all circumstances. Though at the outset control was repugnant to the British mind, its necessity was slowly but, in the end, fully recognized. It was acknowledged that control might have practical value as a symbol of Allied determination to resort to punitive measures if Germany failed to show a spirit of collaboration when faced with obligations capable of execution. Such considerations inspired the plan of control which Bonar Law presented at the Paris Conference in January 1923. It provided for the creation of a Foreign Finance Council empowered to dictate the broad lines of German financial policy without meddling in the details of administration, and for coercion if Germany wilfully impeded the

[1] *Cmd.* 2270, p. 132.

stabilization of the currency, or wilfully defaulted in the making of reasonable payments after a four years' holiday to allow for recovery.

The prolonged discussion, in 1921–1923, on the supervision of German finance found its consummation in the network of supervisory agencies which, as an element in the Dawes Plan, operated in Germany from 1924 to 1930. Under the Dawes Plan specified revenues were assigned for the payment of reparation. They consisted of the 'controlled revenues' diverted from the German budget—customs and the excise duties on alcohol, tobacco, beer, and sugar—of a transport tax not hitherto levied, and of the interest and amortization of RM 16 milliards of railway bonds and industrial debentures. The system of control was designed to watch over the periodic payment of reparation from these sources. To safeguard the stability of the currency, the Reichsbank was reorganized as a private corporation independent of the Reich, with the exclusive privilege of issuing bank notes. The administration of the Bank remained entirely in German hands, subject, however, to the oversight of a General Council half-composed of foreign members. To promote the profitable operation of the German railways, their management was transferred from the Government to a newly constituted joint stock company. Of the members of its Board of Directors, seven were foreigners, of whom one, the Commissioner for German Railways, was given special responsibility for watching over the management. A Trustee for Railway Bonds and a Trustee for Industrial Debentures were appointed to supervise the regular payment of the sums due from these sources. Another Commissioner exercised a general oversight over the yield of the controlled revenues. The purchase of foreign exchange for reparation payments ceased to be the responsibility of the German Government; it was entrusted to a Transfer Committee, which assumed thereby a large measure of responsibility for maintaining the stability of the German exchange. The co-ordination of this organization of control was entrusted to the Agent-General for Reparation Payments.

This outline of the control set up under the Dawes Plan may easily convey an exaggerated impression of interference in German administration. It is necessary, therefore, to stress its limitations. In budgetary matters intervention did not go beyond the assignment of certain revenues for the payment of reparation. In all other respects Germany was left a free hand in taxation and expenditure. Moreover, as long as reparation payments were punctually made, control meant supervision only in the sense of keeping a watch on the appropriate fields of German administration and economic life, and not supervision in the sense of giving orders. The powers of the Commissioners were to be extended beyond this restricted scope only if reparation payments became deficient. The varied nationality of the officials, and especially the appointment of an American citizen as Agent-General, ensured that control would not be distorted in the political interests of any country. It is well to add that, in the view of those best qualified to judge, these measures constituted, from the financial viewpoint, no more than an impressive façade. 'Control could have made things unpleasant and even unworkable for the German Government and for the German people,' Sir Andrew McFadyean comments, but 'it could not have produced money.' [1]

The revival of control by the Dawes Committee was greeted by the French as a vindication of their attitude. The Committee's recommendations in this respect may be ascribed to a compound of political and economic considerations. In the first place, they were a response to the problem how to induce France to abandon the stranglehold over German economic life which the Ruhr occupation enabled her to exercise. Not the least valuable of General Dawes' qualities was his sense of political realities and his regard for French susceptibilities. His diary records his own solution of this problem: 'Clearly we have got to recognize the principle of guarantees if we are to get a settlement of the Ruhr question in the interest of a restoration of economic Germany.' [2] A second political advantage of control was stressed in the Report itself: that Germany would be relieved of a main source of German internal political controversy if the payment of reparations ceased to depend on the constant maintenance or renewal of governmental decisions. Thirdly, control made it possible to evade the issue how to determine a sum within Germany's capacity, which should be high enough for France and satisfactory to Great Britain. Experts gave this dilemma up, but advanced as a practical solution the device of placing the responsibility for the transfer of German payments into foreign currencies on an Allied agency as an element in the control organization.

If the Dawes Report vindicated the conception of control, it none the less condemned the particular form of guarantee on which Poincaré had set his mind since July 1922, a form far removed from the idea of supervision of German finance. At the London Conference, in August 1922, Poincaré refused to grant Germany a partial moratorium on reparation payments unless as a condition the Allies took up 'specific and productive guarantees.' At the later conferences in London and Paris, when the Allies were confronted with a German demand for a complete moratorium, Poincaré refused to deviate from this policy. Its prosecution led

[1] McFadyean, Sir A.: *Reparation Reviewed*, p. 79.
[2] Dawes, C.: *Journal*, p. 82 (February 8, 1924).

France into the wilderness of the Ruhr. Only after the cessation
of passive resistance could the operation of 'productive pledges'
commence. Two questions will be singled out for discussion
here. First, what did Poincaré mean by 'productive pledges'?
Secondly, why did he demand them?

Productive pledges implied Allied control of specific German
enterprises and administrative services with a view to the diversion
of their produce for the payment of reparation. In August 1922
Poincaré's minimum demand was that state mines in the Ruhr
and state forests in the occupied territories should be placed under
Allied officials, empowered to direct the disposal of coal and
timber produced and to dismiss the personnel of the management.
At the Paris Conference (2nd–4th January 1923) Poincaré's minimum
was less modest; he proposed in addition to impose a levy on
German exports, and to confiscate customs and coal tax revenues
in the Rhineland and the Ruhr. Without British assent, a Franco-
Belgian Commission of Engineers, the M.I.C.U.M.,[1] was sent into
the Ruhr on 11th January 1923 with instructions to supervise
the coal syndicate and 'to take all measures required to secure the
payment of reparation.' The accompaniment of 10,000 troops
made this action indistinguishable from military occupation.

The General Strike, alike of employers and employed, against
the Commission killed the blossom of productive pledges. The
occupying authority sought consolation in the seizure of industrial
stocks and of the customs and excise revenue. Unoccupied
Germany was divided from the occupied territories by a customs
frontier, and a Franco-Belgian Régie took over, as best it could,
the railways of the Rhineland and the Rhur. These, however, were
hardly more than punitive measures, save for the railway administration, which was treasured as a means of assuring the security of
France.[2]

Only after the cessation of passive resistance, on 27th September
1923, did the organization of productive pledges become possible.
Agreements were signed with various branches of German industry
in the Rhineland and the Ruhr whereby they undertook to make
deliveries without repayment. The coal agreements provide the
outstanding example. The collieries agreed to supply coal and
coke in conformity with reparation demands, to pay retrospective
coal tax assessed at 15 million dollars, and to pay a coal tax in
the future of not more than two and two-thirds gold marks per ton.
The workers bore the brunt of this burden, through the imposition
of longer hours and a reduction of wages. The general effect of
such agreements was to turn the Rhineland and the Ruhr 'into

[1] *Mission interalliée de contrôle des usines et des mines.*
[2] See p. 189.

a "Reparations Province" in which France and Belgium extracted a local tribute from private German industry in lieu of the payments due to them by the Government of the German Reich.'[1] It was with an eye to the termination of such agreements, and the removal of the customs barrier between occupied and unoccupied Germany, that the Dawes experts stipulated as a condition of their Plan the restoration of German economic unity. Productive pledges were in consequence abandoned in the autumn of 1924.[2]

No single motive suffices to explain Poincaré's insistence on productive pledges. The historian must tentatively assess the varied reasons advanced by Poincaré at different times. In August 1922 he pointed in justification to the necessity of guarantees for the continuance of coal and timber deliveries; but the excellent security for their continuance offered by the German Government —the provision of 50 million gold marks in foreign securities to cover any deficiency—he nevertheless rejected. At the end of the year, when a total moratorium, including deliveries in kind, was under consideration, Poincaré's response was to demand more extensive pledges. Bonar Law justly objected that the French proposals would render a moratorium nugatory and would con- stitute an insurmountable obstacle to the restoration of German credit.

The conclusion is inescapable that if, on the eve of the Ruhr occupation, British and French policy could not be harmonized it was due to a conflict of aim that was fundamental. To Great Britain, currency stabilization and German economic recovery were cardinal objectives, and the essential condition of their attain- ment was a long moratorium. Against this there rose the French fear that at the end of a moratorium France, weakened through having exhausted her borrowing powers for the restoration of the devastated areas, might find herself faced with a Germany prosperous and aggressive, less inclined than ever to pay. Poincaré's insistence on productive pledges is probably best interpreted as a determina- tion to hold bail for the resumption of reparation payments when Germany should again be in a position to make them; bail in the first place against the conspiracy of German industrialists—so Poincaré, with most Frenchmen, saw it—to defraud France of her just claims, but bail also against the danger that, at the end of a moratorium, England might endeavour to hinder France from demanding her due if Germany showed then no inclination to yield save at the point of the sword.

---

[1] Toynbee: *Survey, 1924*, p. 300.
[2] For the M.I.C.U.M. agreements, see *Department of Overseas Trade ; Report on Economic Conditions in Germany to April 1924*, pp. 118–129; Toynbee: *Survey, 1924*, p. 287–300; *Stresemann*, i, pp. 135–136, 152, 173–175, 196–197, 258–259, 273.

Moreover, there is little reason to doubt that Poincaré, despite protestations to the contrary, desired to defer rather than hasten the economic recovery of Germany, from a conviction that Germany's recovery would constitute a menace to his own country. England, he wrote, 'takes no thought for the future; she recks not the truly terrifying danger which threatens, not France and Belgium alone, but England and the whole of Europe: an economic hegemony which will suddenly be revealed, and which will give Germany all the results which she expected from the War had she been victorious. It is impossible to enter into the views of the British Government without risking our independence.'[1]

It has seemed worth while entering into this somewhat lengthy disquisition on the subject of guarantee for two reasons. In the first place, insufficient attention has hitherto been paid to this question as a factor in the long-drawn-out reparation controversy. That controversy becomes more intelligible and less arid if proper stress is laid on guarantees as one of the vital issues on which Great Britain and France were divided and with regard to which they slowly felt their way towards agreement. And in the second place, the successive experiments with different forms of guarantee, and the discussion to which they gave rise, afford some indication of the problems attendant upon foreign intervention in the financial administration and economic life of a modern state.

CHAPTER XI

THE PURSUIT OF DISARMAMENT

I. *How the Disarmament Clauses were drawn up*

THE disarmament of Germany was one of the first questions dealt with at the Peace Conference. It was Lloyd George who brought the question to the fore. To the British Prime Minister the speedy disarmament of Germany presented itself in January 1919 as a pressing political problem. Its urgency was a penalty which he paid for his acceptance of the armistice terms proposed by Foch. For Foch had not seen fit to insist on the disarmament and demobilization of the German army as General

---

[1] Poincaré to St. Aulaire: *D.D.*: *Documents relatifs aux notes allemandes des 2 mai et 5 juin sur les réparations* (Paris, 1923), p. 52. Cf. *Economist*, January 6, 1923 (French Correspondent): 'To the British plea that Germany must be allowed to get on her feet again, the French man in the street retorts with the argument that there is no reason why she should be allowed to do so, when there is every ground for believing that she will make use of her recovered strength only to make herself a military and economic nuisance to the rest of the world. The suggestion is, perhaps, not one the bishops would generally support . . .'

liss and the military advisers of the Supreme War Council had desired. In the first two months of 1919 the Allied leaders came to feel that the German army was still a force to be reckoned with. Yet Lloyd George, probably anticipating the conclusion of a preliminary peace within a few weeks, had raised in the mind of the British public the expectation of the speedy demobilization of the British forces. To proceed with British demobilization while the forces of Germany remained strong enough to resume the struggle was to court disaster. So, to make British demobilization possible, Lloyd George insisted that the disarmament of Germany must be proceeded with immediately.

The only immediate result was to make clear the real difficulties in the way of disarming Germany. Two committees were appointed, one after the other, to go into the question. The first, presided over by Louis Loucheur, reported on 7th February; the second, composed of Lansing, Milner, and Tardieu, on 8th February. The difficulty was that the Allies had no precise knowledge of the amount of war material in the possession of the enemy. For this reason they could not state how much material Germany would have to surrender to bring down her armaments to the level fixed. They could only demand that Germany hand over all material in excess of certain permitted quantities. But Wilson insisted that the demand presented to Germany should be for the surrender of a specific quantity of material. Then, when Germany had complied, food could be sent in. Wilson feared that a vague demand for the surrender of all material in excess of a stated amount would lead to interminable disputes as to whether Germany still retained more material than she ought to possess. There was another difficulty. How could the Allies prevent the replenishment of stocks by the continued manufacture of armaments in Germany? The Loucheur Committee put forward two suggestions: either the control of important munitions factories by Allied missions, or the military occupation of the Ruhr. Either course meant imposing new and more stringent armistice terms, a step which Wilson considered unjustifiable. The Germans, he felt, might refuse the new terms: then the fighting would start again. In the end it was decided that, in advance of the coming renewal of the armistice, Germany should be asked for information about the quantity of war material in her possession. The request was duly presented, but no reply appears to have been received.[1]

A few days later the idea of immediately disarming Germany came up again in a different way. On 10th February Klotz and Balfour complained of the failure of the Germans to carry out the

[1] *Miller*, xiv, pp. 236–273, 279–285; Nudant, Gen.: 'A Spa: L'Armistice, 1918–19,' *Revue de France*, March–April 1925, p. 293.

financial and naval terms of armistice.   A committee was appointed
to consider methods of enforcing German compliance.   Its report
on 12th February was not very helpful.   The economic advisers
showed how the blockade could be used, but deprecated such
action except in the event of 'deliberate infringement of the armistice
on points of substance and importance.'   The military experts
recommended that the Allies should, as a condition of renewing the
armistice, impose a limitation of Germany's armed forces.   If the
Germans refused, military operations would recommence.   So the
threat of renewed warfare to impose stiffer armistice terms again
presented itself.

The Committee suggested, however, one way of escape from
this impasse.   They proposed that naval and military terms of
peace should be drawn up immediately and imposed on the enemy.
The naval authorities, especially Admiral Wemyss, the First Sea
Lord, had been urging this proposal for some little time;   they
were anxious to free the navy from the onerous task of maintaining
the blockade.   Recommendations about the naval peace terms
had already been presented to the Council of Ten on 8th February.
'The Admirals know exactly what they want and what they can
get,' Wemyss had then told the Council, and had added: 'The
Allied Admirals have come to the conclusion that they can now
fix what should be the state of the German fleet in time of peace.'
That day neither Wilson nor Balfour had welcomed the suggestion.
'It is not possible,' Wilson interposed, 'to anticipate the conditions
of peace in the renewal of an armistice.'   But on the 12th Wilson
greeted with enthusiasm the same proposal made by the Committee
on enforcing armistice terms, for it offered a way out of the
difficulty facing him.   He could not, he said, agree to the renewal
of hostilities because the Germans refused to comply with some
small item of the armistice terms, but to enforce the final military
and naval terms he was ready to employ the whole strength of the
American army.   Balfour agreed readily.   Clemenceau, at first
reluctant, fell into line.   So it was decided on 12th February to
appoint a new committee to draft the final naval, military, and air
terms of peace.[1]

The committee appointed to draft the military terms comprised
a distinguished personnel, including Foch and Sir Henry Wilson,
the British C.I.G.S.   Their recommendations were submitted to
the Council of Ten on 3rd March, but discussion was postponed
until 6th March, by which time Lloyd George had arrived back
from England.   He immediately found the recommendations of
the Foch Committee highly objectionable in one respect.   They

[1] *Miller*, xiv, pp. 285–287, 301–310, 334–343, 352–355, 374–381; Wemyss: *Life
and Letters*, pp. 416–418.

allowed the continuance of conscription in Germany; Lloyd George insisted on its abolition. A bitter controversy arose between Foch and the British Prime Minister over the method of recruiting the German army. Clemenceau closed the discussion with the comment that it was 'the duty of the Heads of Government finally to decide the whole question.' The matter was, in fact, settled at a private meeting between Lloyd George, Clemenceau, and House the following morning. In the afternoon the military experts were instructed to draw up a scheme for recruiting the German army by voluntary enlistment. The revised draft was brought before the Council of Ten on 10th March. Although Foch secured the reduction of the German army to 100,000 men, he and the French generals present were beside themselves with rage. Clemenceau in the chair cut off further talk with the remark that he could only give the generals the satisfaction of having their protest recorded in the minutes. Thereupon he adjourned the meeting.[1]

By 12th March the military, naval, and air terms had all been referred to a drafting committee. So when Wilson returned from America on Friday, 14th March, he found that work on the disarmament terms had been brought almost to completion in his absence. This accorded with the desire which he had expressed before leaving Europe. The Council of Ten had arranged to go over the disarmament terms finally on Saturday afternoon. The Council met, with military and naval experts in full force, at 3 P.M. To the vexation of his colleagues, Wilson stayed away, but sent a message requesting postponement of the discussion as he had not had time to go through the draft. So the meeting was not held till 17th March. Wilson is said to have intimated before the meeting his intention of challenging the principle of the abolition of conscription. It is more probable that, inspired by General Bliss, he was gravely concerned about the smallness of the proposed German army, for that was the only question of substance raised by him in the discussion, most of which turned on minor details. 'All the articles presenting any difficulty are reserved, so that we haven't done much after three hours' discussion. Everyone is tired out,' commented Jules Cambon.[2]

In truth, the formulation of the military, naval, and air terms was ceasing to be a matter of urgency. Foch, it is true, still pressed for their immediate presentation to the Germans. The military arrangements concluded between the Allies in January

---

[1] *Miller*, xv, pp. 134–144, 177–184, 244–248, 287–300; Lloyd George: *Peace Treaties*, i, p. 285; *House*, iv, p. 369; Palmer, F.: *Bliss*, pp. 374–375; Callwell, Sir C. E.: *Sir Henry Wilson*, ii, p. 173.

[2] *Miller*, xv, pp. 299, 340–361, 367–401; Callwell, Sir C. E.: *Sir Henry Wilson*, ii, p. 174; Riddell, Lord: *Intimate Diary*, p. 32; Cambon, J.: 'La Paix,' *Revue de Paris*, November 1937, p. 21.

seemed to him to safeguard the superior strength of the armies under his command until 1st April, but not beyond. He desired a definitive settlement with Germany on major issues before that date.[1] But to Lloyd George and Wilson a speedy conclusion in the matter of German disarmament seemed no longer so vital. By the Balfour Resolution of 24th February clauses dealing with reparation and German frontiers were to join company with the military, naval, and air terms in the preliminary treaty with Germany. As yet, progress towards a settlement on reparation and Germany's western frontier was hardly perceptible. In any event, Wilson had come to doubt whether the project of concluding a preliminary treaty was compatible with American constitutional requirements. Ratification by the Senate would be necessary, and the Senate could not be hurried.[2] For Lloyd George, too, the position had changed. A bill to prolong conscription till April 1920 was making its way through the House of Commons in the face of bitter opposition. Conscription was not to disappear immediately from the political life of England. English military strength would be assured; the less need then to force through the immediate reduction of the German army.

The military, naval, and air terms were, however, substantially completed by 17th March. The most fateful addition thereafter was the preamble. For at the last moment the Fourteen Points were again remembered. Owing to the manner in which this section of the Treaty had been pushed forward, in response to pressing armistice problems, its relation to the Wilsonian basis of settlement had been somewhat overlooked. On 26th April President Wilson suggested to his colleagues that the disarmament terms would be 'more acceptable to the enemy if they were presented as preparing the way for a general limitation of armaments for all nations.' Lloyd George's assent was doubtless readily given; he had made a similar proposal a month earlier. In the Fontainebleau Memorandum he had urged that only the universal limitation of armaments would secure lasting peace or the permanent observance of the limitation of German armaments. Clemenceau cautiously replied to Wilson that he would like to see the formula before he agreed. Before they broke up, the Council of Four agreed on the preamble to be adopted:

'In order to render possible the initiation of general limitation of the armaments of all nations Germany undertakes strictly to observe the military, naval, and air clauses which follow.'[3]

[1] Statement in Council of Four on March 3 (*Miller*, xv, pp. 138–139). Cf. his advocacy of the immediate conclusion of a preliminary treaty in his Memorandum of February 18; Lloyd George: *Peace Treaties*, i, p. 389.
[2] Cf. statement in Council of Ten on March 17 (*Miller*, xv, pp. 394–395).
[3] *Miller*, xix, p. 208; *Baker*, i, p. 375.

It was an afterthought, and on the whole an unhappy afterthought. This verbal homage to Wilsonian aims advanced the cause of general disarmament by hardly an iota, at the cost of incorporating within the Treaty yet another imprecision, the fruitful source of dispute in coming years.

No object would be served by stating here in any great detail the content of the military, naval, and air clauses which form Part V of the Treaty of Versailles. Analyses of them have frequently been published,[1] and for full understanding the Treaty itself must be referred to. Only the briefest possible statement will be made here. Not only was the strength of the German army fixed at 100,000 men, but its organization was prescribed in minute detail. Its arms and ammunition were restricted in both quality and quantity. The use or possession of certain of the more dangerous modern weapons of warfare—tanks, armoured cars, poisonous gas—was prohibited outright. On the western frontier Germany was obliged to create a demilitarized zone. The naval clauses limited the German navy to six battleships, six light cruisers, twelve destroyers, and twelve torpedo-boats. All other fighting ships were to be surrendered to the Allies. Submarines were prohibited to Germany. The air clauses provided for the abolition of Germany's air forces. Time-limits were set within which Germany was to bring down her armed forces to the prescribed levels, and Inter-Allied Commissions of Control were to supervise the process of reduction.

II. *How German Disarmament was carried through*

After the Great War the disarmament of Germany was the sole question on which British and French policy remained substantially in unison. Despite initial misgivings whether the German army was really strong enough, the British Government rallied to the support of the French in demanding the strict execution of the military terms. German efforts to secure modifications of substance in the military provisions of the Treaty provoked a sharp rejoinder in the Boulogne Note of 22nd June 1920: 'The Allied Governments have unanimously decided to maintain in their entirety the clauses of the treaty signed by Germany concerning her disarmament. . . .' They 'likewise expect that the German Government will submit to them no further requests for derogation from the military clauses of the Treaty, as such requests can only receive a negative reply and consequently lead uselessly to further delay.'[2] Allied stipulations concerning the execution of the

---

[1] E.g. Temperley, H. V. W.: *History of the Paris Peace Conference*, ii, pp. 131–136, 149–152; Chaput, R. C.: *Disarmament in British Policy*, pp. 56–64, 258–265.
[2] *Cmd.* 1325, p. 150.

military terms were embodied in the Spa Protocol of 9th July 1920 and the Paris Resolutions of 29th January 1921.[1]

Throughout the summer, autumn, and winter of 1921 German disarmament proceeded apace, and by the spring of 1922 was nearing completion. The Aeronautic Commission of Control had finished its work; it was disbanded on 5th May 1922. The Allies were ready to withdraw the Naval Commission in the summer, though in the outcome it was not dissolved till 30th September 1924. On 14th April 1922, and again on 29th September 1922, the Allied Governments intimated their willingness to withdraw the Military Commission as soon as the definitive settlement of five outstanding questions was in sight. Since the German replies gave no promise of satisfaction as regards these five points, the Allies informed the German Government on 17th November 1922 that the Military Commission would continue to function until a settlement on them had been reached.[2]

Then the Ruhr occupation intervened. While passive resistance lasted, no progress could be made with the settlement of the outstanding military questions. Indeed, the clock moved backwards. Throughout 1923 the German Government obstructed visits of inspection to the army corps, and only permitted visits to factories by British and Italian officers. The Council of the Commission refused to sanction visits by officers of these two nationalities alone, and insisted on the resumption of control operations in their full amplitude. Their decision was upheld by the Conference of Ambassadors. At length, on 11th November 1923, the German Government replied that the resumption of control would aggravate the internal situation; they requested the Conference of Ambassadors 'to put off its demands under the pressure of circumstances.' The request met with a refusal, and the German Government reluctantly agreed to visits of inspection, which took place on 10th–12th January 1924. These, thought Stresemann, must be the last.[3]

Stresemann's hope was not fulfilled. For in a note of 6th March 1924 the Allied Governments insisted on a final general inspection; if satisfaction was received, control might thereafter be restricted to the five points set out in the note of 29th September 1922. Germany, it was suspected, had strengthened her army in 1923. The German Government contested the Allied claim to proceed to a general inspection, and refused its agreement until 30th June 1924. The inspection did not commence until 8th September, and did not finish till 25th January 1925. So a whole

[1] Text of Spa Protocol in *Cmd.* 1325, p. 171; Paris Resolutions in Honnorat, A.: *Le Désarmement de l'Allemagne*, pp. 46–51.
[2] Honnorat, A.: *Le Désarmement de l'Allemagne*, pp. 68–74.
[3] Nollet, Gen. C. N. E.: *Une Expérience de désarmement*, pp. 146–153; Honnorat, A.; *Le Désarmement de l'Allemagne*, pp. 75–80; *Stresemann*, i, pp. 257, 294.

year had slipped by. On 18th December 1924 Lord Curzon announced that the work of the Commission had been delayed 'by constant and persistent obstruction from German hands.' Ten days later the Conference of Ambassadors decided to postpone the evacuation of the Cologne zone.

The Report of the Control Commission was at length handed in on 17th February 1925. It was not until 4th June that the Allied note on the results of the inspection was presented to Germany. It contained a formidable indictment. The note contained a detailed list of the measures to be taken by Germany on the points in regard to which Germany had so far failed to give satisfaction. The Allies gave the assurance that, when these enumerated breaches of the Treaty had been made good in the manner required, the Cologne zone would be evacuated and the Military Commission withdrawn. No reply was received from the German Government until 23rd October, a week after the close of the Locarno Conference (5th–16th October 1925). The German note intimated the extent to which the Allied demands had been, or would shortly be, fulfilled. Five questions were singled out as presenting special difficulty and necessitating further discussion. They were:

1. The organization of the police.
2. The High Command.
3. Prohibition of training with certain weapons.
4. Artillery arming of the fortress of Königsberg.
5. Military associations.

The Allied reply was sent with unusual rapidity. On 6th November the Conference of Ambassadors requested the German Government to submit proposals for the settlement of these specially difficult questions. The Allied Governments would be happy, the Ambassadors added, if the German response was of a nature such as would enable them to fix 1st December as the date for the commencement of the evacuation of the Cologne zone. In truth the form of the German note of 23rd October and of the Allied reply of 6th November had been agreed between Stresemann, Briand, and Chamberlain at Locarno.[1] Though the German response was little more than a reiteration of the German viewpoint on the five outstanding questions, the Conference of Ambassadors was able to declare on 16th November that complete agreement had been reached with Germany on the points still in dispute, and that evacuation of the Cologne zone would commence on 1st December 1925. On 1st January 1926 it was further announced that the Military Commission would be reduced in

[1] *Stresemann*, ii, p. 187.

personnel and that its district organizations, except at Munich and Königsberg, would be discontinued.

Despite this progress the Military Commission survived another year. At the end of January 1926 the Commission reported that no progress had been made towards the settlement of the five points of special difficulty indicated in the German note of 23rd October 1925. Through summer and autumn negotiations dragged on between the Commission and the German military experts. On 24th November 1926 Stresemann impressed on the British Ambassador that 'Germany's whole policy of understanding would be at stake if the question of Military Control was not put out of the way.' The Ambassador assured him that the British Foreign Secretary had already recommended the withdrawal of the Commission to France and Italy.[1] Briand, indeed, set little store by the outstanding points except one—the problem of the Military Associations. The basis of a settlement was laid in conversations between the Locarno Powers from 5th–11th December at Geneva, and the Military Commission was withdrawn on 31st January 1927.

III. *General Limitation of Armaments*

The history of the negotiations for the general limitation of armaments has been told too often, both in detail and in outline, to necessitate its repetition here. It may, however, be well to recall to mind the conferences and commissions set up to deal with the question, and to which reference will be made in the following chapters.

The examination of the problem was first entrusted by the Council of the League to two bodies:

(i) The Permanent Advisory Commission set up on 17th May 1920, and composed of military, naval, and air experts. In 1926, with the addition of representatives of Germany and the U.S.A., it worked under the guise of Sub-Commission A of the Preparatory Commission for the Disarmament Conference. Its *chef-d'œuvre* was the Report of Sub-Commission A, which presents a comprehensive survey of expert opinion on general disarmament.

(ii) The Temporary Mixed Commission, set up on 25th February 1921, composed of both civil and military personnel. From its discussions, which were diverted to the problem of security, emerged, in September 1923, the Draft Treaty of Mutual Assistance.

The concentration on the problem of security caused the question of general disarmament to recede into the background during the years 1924–1925.

[1] *Stresemann*, iii, pp. 59, 69.

The resumption of discussion was marked by the establishment of a new body, the Preparatory Commission for the Disarmament Conference, on 12th December 1925. The Commission held six sessions. At its final session, 6th November–9th December 1930, it completed its task, which was to draw up a draft convention embodying appropriate methods for the limitation of armaments. The World Disarmament Conference opened on 2nd February 1932. Anglo-French negotiations within and on the marge of this Conference will come under review in the following two chapters.

CHAPTER XII

PROBLEMS OF GERMAN DISARMAMENT

THE disarmament of Germany in 1919 was supposedly based on the principle, stated in Article 160 of the Treaty, that the German army should be devoted exclusively to 'the maintenance of order within the territory and to the control of the frontiers.' This principle was of Wilsonian origin. The Fourteen Points had called for the reduction of national armaments to 'the lowest point consistent with domestic safety.' President Wilson readily agreed, on arriving in Europe, that the intricate problems of general disarmament could not be settled at the Peace Conference itself, and that Germany would have to be disarmed first. In the Council of Ten on 12th February 1919 he pointed out that, since Germany was not for the present expected to make any contribution to the general force of the League of Nations, account need be taken only of 'the amount of armed force required by Germany to maintain internal order and to keep down Bolshevism.' Accordingly the Foch Committee based their recommendations on the assumption that the German army should have 'no other duty than the maintenance of internal order, and, in cases of necessity, the police control of the frontiers.' [1] What 'police control of the frontiers' implied was not defined.

But though a guiding principle was thus established, the character of the German army was in fact dictated by quite other considerations—its form by British prejudice against conscription, and its size by French fears of a standing German army.

Foch proposed that the German army should consist of 200,000 men. The period of service was to be one year. Soldiers might

[1] Lloyd George: *Peace Treaties*, i, p. 187; Borden, H.: *Robert Laird Borden*, ii, p. 889; *Miller*, xiv, p. 375; xv, p. 199.

be recruited by conscription. Foch is sometimes accused of having
sought to maintain conscription in Germany from the fear that
its abolition there would provide a precedent for its abolition in
France. This is almost certainly misrepresentation. Short-term
service necessitated conscription in some form, for Germany could
not recruit 200,000 soldiers annually by voluntary enlistment.
Foch was prepared to let Germany raise her army by any system
she chose, provided the men served only one year. He advocated
the short-term period of service because he feared that the long-
service army, the corollary of voluntary enlistment, would create
cadres which could easily be expanded to form a large force.

Lloyd George's opposition to the Foch Plan arose primarily
from antipathy against conscription. In election speeches he had
pledged himself to bring about its abolition in all countries. To
the British mind, conscription was the mainspring of militarism.
It was abhorred as an invasion of individual rights, and condemned
as a menace to peace through its creation of the nation in arms.
Nor did it meet the requirements of British imperial defence;
Great Britain needed an army ready for service overseas, and hence
a professional army. It is hardly necessary to emphasize the very
different attitude to conscription which has prevailed in France.
A legacy from the Revolution, conscription has for long received
approval as a democratic institution. Jaurès, the great Socialist
leader, whose assassination in 1914 was perhaps an even greater
loss to Europe than to France, had advocated as the most suitable
form of military organization for France a citizen army, modelled
after the Swiss militia system, and providing periodic military
training for all citizens from boyhood to middle age. The more
France moved to the Left, the more tenaciously she would cling
to such a form of army organization. Between the British and the
French outlook the English Channel made all the difference. As
the Belgian Socialist Louis de Brouckère remarked in the Preparatory Commission in 1927, 'History shows us quite clearly that
those democracies which have been exposed to invasion have always
had conscription, and that those which have been more happily
situated, and have thus had no need of armies except to defend
distant interests, have never had conscription.' [1]

But Lloyd George contested Foch's proposals not only on
political but also on military grounds. The annual recruitment of
200,000 men would give Germany, he insisted, a formidable array
of reserves. Officers who had gained their experience in the war
would be available for twenty-five years. They would be ready to
come forward, thirsting for revenge, at the first opportunity. He
'would be very sorry to leave France after the signing of peace with

[1] P.C.D.C., iv, p. 50.

that threat facing her across the Rhine.' [1]   Lloyd George's argument was not indeed lacking in cogency on military grounds.

The decision to abolish conscription in Germany resulted in a considerable reduction in the size of the German army. Foch proposed an army of 200,000 men serving one year, with 9000 officers serving twenty-five years. Lloyd George, on the morning of 7th March, proposed 250,000 men of all ranks, serving twelve years, but agreed at Clemenceau's instance to a reduction to 200,000. The military experts three days later recommended a further reduction to 140,000. A standing army of this size, they advised, was the equivalent of 200,000 men serving one year, since in a short-term army a large proportion of the men would be undergoing training, whereas in a professional army all the men would be fully trained. Foch demanded a further reduction to 100,000. On this point Clemenceau supported him. Lloyd George and Lansing consented, despite opposition from Sir Henry Wilson and General Bliss. 'If France felt strongly about this question,' Lloyd George remarked, 'he did not think that the British or American delegates had a right to withstand her views.' [2] So 100,000 was agreed on.

Thereafter during the Peace Conference the feeling prevailed, except within the French delegation, that the German army would be too small. On 17th March Wilson asked to be assured that the exterior danger from Russia had been considered by the military experts in fixing the total number of effectives. Foch gave the required assurance. Others were less confident. The military terms, Sir Henry Wilson commented, are 'all much too drastic, but the French insisted on them, and the Frocks agreed.' [3]

Two months after the military terms for Germany had been settled, the question came up again in another connexion. On 15th May the military terms for Austria were being discussed. The military advisers recommended an army of 40,000 men as necessary for the maintenance of internal order and the control, but not the defence, of frontiers. Clemenceau protested. If Austria, with a population of six million, had an army of 40,000, he asked, how could the reduction to 100,000 be justified for Germany? Wilson interjected, 'Perhaps Marshal Foch was right in recommending an army of 200,000 men for Germany.' 'I absolutely refuse to reopen the question,' Clemenceau retorted. Eight days later General Bliss pleaded, in a long and eloquent speech before the Council of Four, that inadequate provision would exist for the maintenance of order in eastern and south-eastern Europe if reductions were effected in accordance with the standard adopted for Germany. 'It seems

---

[1] *Miller*, xv, pp. 180–181.   [2] *Miller*, xv, p. 291.
[3] Callwell, Sir C. E.: *Sir Henry Wilson*, ii, p. 174.

useless to repeat,' he commented, 'that the figure fixed for Germany was not based on military opinion. . . . I have never heard an argument which could convince me that the figure of 100,000 was sound from the military point of view.' Lloyd George indicated his agreement with General Bliss. 'In my opinion,' he commented, 'the Germans will never accept such a figure.' [1]

Despite. these misgivings, the German delegation made no protest when the terms of peace were presented. But on 20th April 1920 the German Government requested Allied consent to the permanent retention of an army of 200,000 men, under the veil of which General von Seeckt planned to retain the framework of the old army, with all its organization for expansion and mobilization. The request was peremptorily rejected by the Allies in the Boulogne Note of 22nd June 1920. [2]

These discussions turned round both a political and military problem. A political problem—how to prevent the growth of military influence in the political life of Germany. A military problem—which type of army was the less dangerous to neighbouring states: one based on short-term or one based on long-term service. The Allies succeeded in resolving neither problem satisfactorily. The opponents of conscription overlooked the danger of confirming in Germany, through the creation of a professional army, the authority of that military hierarchy which, so Lord Haldane had impressed on the Cabinet in 1915, must 'be dethroned' to ensure that Germany should never again bid for armed supremacy. [3] Further, the form of military organization imposed on Germany provoked consternation in France. 'This army—Germany will make it a real jewel,' declared André Lefèvre. [4] It is unnecessary to dwell on the fulfilment of that prophecy through the labours of von Seeckt. During the Disarmament Conference it became apparent that the very foundation of any Franco-German agreement on military armaments must be the reversal of the British-inspired decision of March 1919. Just fourteen years later the British Prime Minister of the day proposed to replace the German army of Versailles by a militia of 200,000 men. [5]

To go into the technical difficulties encountered in the execution of the military terms lies beyond the scope of this study. Only those political questions which affected Anglo-French relations call for attention. Three questions may be so distinguished : first,

---

[1] Aldrovandi, L.: *Guerra Diplomatica*, pp. 343–352, 395–399. On June 4 it was agreed that Austria should have an army of 30,000 men. For this session, and subsequent discussion of the small states, see Aldrovandi, L.: 'Le ultime sedute dei Quattro' in *Nuova Antologia*, May 1, 1937, pp. 95 et seq. See also *Baker*, i, pp. 400–407.
[2] *Cmd.* 1325, pp. 89–93, 150–151; Morgan, J. H.: 'The Disarmament of Germany,' *Quarterly Review*, October 1924.
[3] Maurice, Sir F.: *Haldane*, ii, p. 15.
[4] *Chambre: Débats*, December 24, 1920, p. 708.   [5] See p. 151.

the concessions made to safeguard the maintenance of internal order in Germany; secondly, the problem of control; thirdly, the duration of the unilateral disarmament of Germany.

Repeatedly, in 1920 and in later years, the German Government complained that the Treaty left insufficient forces at the disposal of the Government for the suppression of revolutionary movements. This plea was advanced in March 1920 to justify the organization of civic guards, the Einwohnerwehr; in April 1920 to justify the retention of an army of 200,000 men, equipped with heavy artillery and, temporarily, with military aircraft; and in later years to justify the maintenance of special police forces quartered in barracks under centralized control. Concessions were made by the Allies only as regards the police.

The Treaty provided that the German police should exceed the number engaged in 1913 only in proportion to the increase of population. But in 1919 the German Government established, in addition to the old police force, the Ordnungspolizei, which was organized on a local basis, a new force, the Sicherheitspolizei, under state control. The Sicherheitspolizei, 60,000 in number, was well armed, and constituted in effect a military formation. In July 1920 the Allies demanded its dissolution. Recognizing, however, 'the need for leaving sufficient police forces at the disposal of the German Government to ensure the maintenance of internal order,' they agreed to an increase in the Ordnungspolizei from 92,000 to 150,000 men. This force was permitted to maintain armaments which it did not possess in 1914: in particular, heavy machine-guns and machine-pistols. But the Allied Governments insisted on several occasions, from 1920 to 1925, that the German police should be organized, as in 1914, under local, not state, control. The German Government, while welcoming the increase in the Ordnungspolizei, evaded the demand for the suppression of the Sicherheitspolizei by transforming it into the Schutzpolizei, a force which possessed a military character, was grouped in units, quartered in barracks, provided with special staffs, and carried out collective military training. In June 1925 the Allies dropped the demand for the complete suppression of this powerful force, while insisting on certain modifications in its organization. The German Government was authorized to maintain, in a certain number of important towns, state police such as had been hitherto prohibited. Certain detachments of the state police might be quartered in barracks in the larger towns. In 1925 the dispute between the Military Commission and the German Government as far as the police was concerned turned principally round the number of such police to be quartered in barracks. The German Government demanded 35,000; the Military Commission would sanction only

20,000. In November 1925 the Conference of Ambassadors agreed to 32,000 men, enlisted for twelve years.[1]

An even more serious cause of anxiety than the German police was the problem of irregular military formations. These had as their forerunner the Einwohnerwehr, a civic guard, locally organized and armed with rifles and machine-guns, which was formed 'by the order-loving section of the population' in the later months of 1919. The Allied Governments demanded the dissolution of this force also. But its work of military instruction was continued by the numerous associations which sprang up all over Germany—the Stahlhelm, the Wehrwolf, the Jung Deutscher Orden. In a Note of 24th June 1924 MacDonald and Herriot expressed their concern at the 'most disquieting reports . . . of continued and increasing activities of nationalist and militarist associations, which are more or less openly organizing military forces to precipitate further armed conflict in Europe.' At Thoiry, Briand's complaints provoked the reply from Stresemann: 'The Republic in Germany has taken no account of the psychological needs of the masses. It is getting hidebound in the dull black jacket of everyday life. Men want colour, joy, and movement—hence the success of the Stahlhelm on the one side and the Reichsbanner on the other.' 'These organizations are perhaps a danger in domestic politics . . . but from the military point of view they mean nothing.' [2] In consequence of Allied remonstrance the German Government issued, in February 1926, decrees for the prevention of military training by such organizations, and one or two minor associations were broken up. But it had neither the desire nor the power to effect their general suppression.

These problems caused no rift between France and Great Britain, but it can hardly be said that the two countries saw eye to eye with regard to them. The French viewed with grave concern the enlargement of the German police force and the formation of the military associations because, as Briand told Stresemann, 'they were regarded as constituting an army of millions that would supplement the Reichswehr when the moment came.' The French tended to magnify this military danger and to dismiss Bolshevism in Germany as a bogy. Some Englishmen, probably only a few, took the danger of Bolshevism in Germany seriously and favoured concessions to facilitate the repression of Communism. The British General Staff were at first inclined to accede to the German request for an army of 200,000 effectives. So, too, British representatives in Germany opposed the complete suppression of the

[1] See *Cmd.* 1325, p. 153; *Cmd.* 2429, pp. 17–21, 43; *Toynbee, 1920–1923*, pp. 104–110; ibid., 1925, ii, p. 190; Roques, P.: *Le Contrôle militaire*, p. 60.
[2] *Stresemann*, iii, p. 21.

Einwohnerwehr. 'I consider the French demand for the total disarmament of all Einwohnerwehr and similar organizations almost insane,' wrote Lord D'Abernon in November 1920. 'It is like cutting the branch of the tree on which you are sitting. The French do not appear to understand that the military danger-point is past and that the real danger in Germany is communist disorder.' There is no reason to labour these aberrations; but they explain the feeling, widespread in France, that British representatives in Germany after the war had little understanding of French interests and that Englishmen in general underestimated the danger of the secret organization of a national army of reserves.[1]

The second perennial problem of German disarmament, seen from the viewpoint of Anglo-French relations, arose from the insistence of the French on the establishment of some permanent organization to watch over German armaments. *Le Temps* expressed in 1919 a widely accepted French view when it wrote: 'We shall have only a temporary guarantee if we do not exercise permanent control.' [2]

In the Military Committee which drew up the military terms of peace in 1919 Marshal Foch pressed for the establishment of a permanent military commission in Germany. Almost nothing is known of the discussion which resulted, for the records of this Committee have not been published. That Foch's proposal was dropped owing to American opposition is clear from a letter of General Bliss. 'It would mean,' Bliss wrote on 26th February, 'that the United States might be dragged into war over any trivial dispute ten years from now. I told the Marshal that it was silly for him to expect me to agree to it when it would do no good if the Senate rejected it. . . . To-day he has receded and we have agreed on a draft.' [3] In consequence the draft military terms presented by Foch on 3rd March contained two mild provisions relating to control.

Of these two provisions, the more important provided for the establishment of a temporary Commission of Control. It was to last only so long as was required to effect the reduction of the German army and its equipment to the prescribed levels. Similar commissions were proposed for the naval and air terms. But when the text came back from the Drafting Committee, on 17th March, it no longer emphasized the temporary character of the commissions, though no modification had been authorized. In

[1] Morgan, J. H.: 'Disarmament of Germany,' *Quarterly Review*, October 1924, p. 438; *D'Abernon*, i, p. 287; Benedict: 'Comment l'Allemagne peut désarmer,' *Eur. Nouv.*, January 9, 1921. Cf. *Stresemann*, ii, p. 185.
[2] *Temps*, March 19, 1919. Quoted Noble, G. B.: *Policies and Opinions at Paris*, p. 180.
[3] Palmer, F.: *Bliss*, p. 372.

the Council of Ten, Balfour expressed the view that the commissions would have to remain in existence at least some time after the process of reduction had been completed. Wilson objected. To meet American objections the article was amended to read: 'All military, naval, and air clauses . . . *for which a time-limit is fixed* shall be executed by Germany under the control of Inter-Allied Commissions. . . .' This became Article 203. It was an unhappy improvisation. No time-limit was prescribed for the execution of many provisions, e.g. the abolition of compulsory military service. Naturally the German Government claimed that such provisions were exempt from control. And the commissions, which Foch had suggested might last three months, lasted for varying periods up to seven years. This was certainly not intended in 1919.[1]

But was there no desire in 1919 to set up a control more permanent than that of these commissions, whose life was then reckoned in months? Foch wanted it, and Lloyd George and Balfour were in favour of it. On 10th March Lloyd George deplored that 'no certain means' had been provided for continuing control 'for ten, twenty or thirty years. He thought the supervision should be organized and maintained by the Allied and Associated Powers.' And on 17th March Balfour questioned 'whether it would not be necessary to continue to exercise supervision over the German army and its armaments in order to ensure their maintenance in the status stipulated.' Supervision might, he suggested, have to last for an indefinite, but not an eternal, period. Orlando expressed the same view more forcibly. It was necessary, he said, to determine what guarantees the Allies would have for the continuance of the disarmed condition of Germany. 'Commissions could not be charged with this duty, as Germany would, as a result, always remain under the control of such commissions. He personally would not object to such a proposal, but he did not think it would be accepted. . . . Some Inter-Allied agency would, thereafter, have to be constituted.' The opposition came from President Wilson. 'Supervision of that nature,' he commented, 'would become endless.' For the moment the idea of permanent control was dropped.[2]

Almost immediately, however, Clemenceau and Tardieu took up the question again in connexion with negotiations that were going on regarding the Anglo-American Treaty of Guarantee, which was being offered in substitution for the Rhineland Occupation. To begin with, Clemenceau and Tardieu requested the establishment of a Franco-Anglo-American Commission of Inspection in the demilitarized zone. They proposed that it should be empowered to report not only on violations of the demilitarized zone, but also

---

[1] *Miller*, xv, p. 397; xix, p. 243; Roques, P.: *Le Contrôle militaire*, pp. 10–11.
[2] *Miller*, xv, pp. 287–300, 395–397.

of the military, naval, and air clauses generally. Should the Commission report any infringement, France should be entitled to occupy the line of the Rhine and the bridgeheads. The proposal only broke against 'Anglo-Saxon' reluctance to sanction provisions which savoured of interference with German rights of sovereignty. So the form of the French demand was then changed. At least, pleaded Tardieu, on 22nd March, let us write into the Treaty a clause to empower the League of Nations to set up, if necessity arises, a commission to inquire into the observance by Germany of her disarmament obligations. To fail to do so, he urged, would impart an air of impermanency to German disarmament. Only so would the Allies ensure in the future a unison of view concerning the state of Germany's armaments. Still consent was withheld.

At last, in mid-April, Wilson gave way in this as in other matters. On 17th April he offered a formula:

'So long as the present Treaty remains in force, Germany undertakes to respond to any inquiry that the Council of the League of Nations may deem necessary.'

This was accepted. On 28th April it was agreed, at Clemenceau's request, that for this purpose the Council's decision should be taken by majority vote. With this modification, the formula went into the Treaty as Article 213.[1]

The omission from the Treaty of any provision for permanent control provoked lively dissatisfaction in France as soon as the Treaty became public. In default of more solid assurance, hope centred on this Article 213—'the fundamental article of the Treaty': so Henri Paté, the Chamber of Deputies rapporteur on the military terms, described it. Article 213 proved a broken reed. Its history is soon told. In September–December 1924 and in March 1925 the Council adopted, in pursuance of Article 213, a scheme for the organization of League investigations into German armaments. On 11th December 1926 the Council completed this scheme by the adoption of additional explanatory paragraphs.[2] Thereafter the scheme remained a dead letter.

From 1922 to 1929 successive French governments endeavoured in vain to bring about the establishment of some permanent control. At first their efforts had some measure of British support. 'I am apprehensive about the period when the Military Commission is withdrawn,' wrote Lord D'Abernon on 7th February 1923. From April 1922 to March 1924 each Allied offer to withdraw the Control Commission was made conditional on German agreement to the setting up of a Committee of Guarantee which would continue to

---

[1] *Miller*, xix, p. 246; *Anglo-French Negotiations*, pp. 75–76; Tardieu, A.: *La Paix*, pp. 151–156.
[2] Text in *League Documents*, 1926 (C. 729), ix, 17.

watch over certain aspects of German disarmament. This insistence on a Committee of Guarantee was dropped by MacDonald and Herriot in June 1924. Thereafter the French demanded the establishment of a permanent Commission of Investigation in the Rhineland. They based this demand on a provision in the League scheme for the application of Article 213. But in the German view, as also in the British, this article provided no justification for such a demand. Stresemann explained his objections to the League scheme at Locarno, and again in a letter to the Secretary-General of the League in January 1926. In December, Briand was induced to accept the British and German interpretation of Article 213, and accordingly the League Council, on 11th December 1926, included in the 'explanations' of its scheme of investigation a paragraph to the effect that the scheme did not provide in the demilitarized zone for 'any special control by local standing and permanent groups.' For the next three years Briand endeavoured to secure voluntary German agreement to a Rhineland Commission. He appears to have entertained the idea of a 'Committee of Verification and Conciliation,' which should carry out investigations immediately in the event of any threat of violation of the demilitarized zone, which should operate on both sides of the frontier and should include a German representative. Stresemann was at first ready to consider the project, but only as counterpart to the evacuation of the Rhineland and on condition that the Commission lasted only until 1935. But at The Hague Conference in August 1929 Stresemann secured the evacuation of the Rhineland while finally rejecting this French proposal.

Thus after January 1927, when the Military Commission of Control was withdrawn, there existed no permanent organization to watch over the disarmament of Germany, while even the institution of any special investigation under Article 213 was virtually ruled out after the first months of 1928 by the failure to apply that article in connexion with the Szent–Gotthard incident.[1] In any event, such special investigations would at best have been of doubtful efficacy, for the task of inspection baffled at times even the Control Commission, despite its experience and its branch organizations throughout Germany. It was not, however, the lack of permanent machinery of inspection which permitted the rearmament of Germany, essential though such machinery be to the continued enforcement of military restrictions. The failure to provide such machinery was itself the result of that division of purpose on the part of the victorious Powers which, already present in 1919, was accentuated by the passage of time and sapped their will to keep Germany disarmed.

[1] See *Toynbee, 1928*, pp. 161–168.

Indeed, the question how long the unilateral disarmament of
Germany was to last received no answer in the Treaty of Versailles,
for the Treaty-makers stilled their own discordant voices only by
the conspiracy of silence.   When the matter was raised by Balfour,
on 3rd March 1919, Clemenceau protested that 'he himself was not
prepared to sign an invitation to Germany to prepare for another
attack by land after an interval of three, ten, or even forty years.' [1]
The question was put aside and not again considered, save when
Wilson objected to the drafting of certain clauses which provided
that the German army should 'never' exceed the limits stipulated.
The word 'never,' he commented, would cover all future time, and
if that were the intention, 'some permanent machinery would have
to be set up to ensure the execution of the conditions therein set
forth.'   So the word 'not' was substituted.[2]   Doubtless an im-
provement, for the Treaty-makers could not legislate for all eternity.
But the underlying problem, thus glossed over in 1919, became
the critical issue of the World Disarmament Conference.

The Treaty gave Germany the assurance that the restrictions
imposed were intended as the first step in 'a general limitation of
the armaments of all nations'—an assurance repeated in the Allied
Note of 16th June 1919.   But the Allied Governments entered
into no engagement that the conclusion of a general limitation of
armaments should involve the abrogation of the military, naval,
and air clauses of the Treaty.   Sir Austen Chamberlain has recorded
that no member of the British Government in 1919 contemplated
'that the limitation of armaments would be of such a character as
to reduce the victor Powers to the level of disarmament which was
imposed upon the vanquished.' [3]   It was then a legally correct
viewpoint which the French Government expressed in its Memorandum of 21st July 1931—that there was no obligation to adopt
in a general convention either the methods or the figures laid
down for Germany in the Peace Treaties.   The French Government
concluded that the general limitation of armaments would become
impracticable were an attempt made, 'in the name of a theoretical
principle of equality, to modify the relative situation created by
the provisions of Part V of the Treaty.'

Yet by 1932 a position legally correct had become politically
untenable.   The German delegation to the Disarmament Conference explicitly demanded, at the very outset, the termination of all
discriminatory restrictions.   This German claim was supported by
British journals of all shades of opinion, from *The Times*, which
called for 'the timely redress of inequality,' to *The New Statesman*,
which proclaimed the need 'for unqualified recognition of the

---

[1] *Miller*, xv, pp. 133–144.   [2] *Miller*, xv, p. 370.
[3] 281 *H.C. Deb.*, November 7, 1933, col. 91.

principle of equality of status.'[1]   The more cautious attitude of the British Government provoked widespread impatience, and when, in a statement issued on 18th September 1932, the British Government enunciated the legal position with almost unbecoming clarity, there was general agreement in blaming the addiction of the Foreign Secretary to legal niceties.   Under the pressure of public opinion the British Government a month later announced its readiness to meet the German claim.   In December French inhibitions were overcome by the formula that Germany should be granted 'equality of rights in a system which would provide security for all nations.'   This formula, inserted in the declaration of the British, French, and Italian Governments of 11th December 1932, brought Germany back into the Disarmament Conference, which it had quitted in July because the Conference had then failed to ratify the German claim.

The later history of the Disarmament Conference turns round the series of abortive efforts to find some practical application of this formula equally acceptable to France and Germany.   This objective could be attained only along a double line of advance; on the one hand with political understandings to satisfy the French desire for security; on the other hand with an armaments programme to meet the German demand for equality.   Only the second aspect is relevant to the subject of this chapter.

The statements issued by the British, French, and German Governments preceding the Declaration of 11th December 1932 envisaged not equality of military strength for Germany, but only 'equality of status.'   As for Germany, both Brüning and von Papen, though insistent on the principle of equality, had declared their willingness to moderate the practical application of the principle.   Their specific demands were the reduction of the Reichswehr period of service, the formation of a volunteer reserve of 100,000 men, and the immediate possession only of samples of all weapons whose abolition was not agreed upon.   The setting within which the French Government were prepared to envisage 'the progressive equalization of the military status' of Germany with that of other countries was exemplified by the Herriot Plan of 14th November 1932.   It combined within the embrace of one 'indivisible' scheme security proposals universal in their scope with military arrangements, the central feature of which was the reconstitution of all European home-defence forces as national short-service armies with limited effectives.   British views were set out in a declaration issued on 17th November 1932.[2]   To the principle that 'the kinds of arms permitted to other countries ought

---

[1] *The New Statesman*, January 30, 1932; *The Times*, February 11, 1932.
[2] *Cmd.* 4189.

not to be prohibited' to Germany was added the rider, on which British opinion was equally insistent, that the Disarmament Conference should not 'authorize in the name of equality the increase of armed strength.' The 'reorganization of the German forces must not involve increase of Germany's powers of military aggression,' and German naval construction must 'not increase the total tonnage in any category to which her navy is at present restricted.' As regards air armaments, the British Government concluded that it was not unreasonable to expect Germany to make no claim to military or naval aircraft pending the examination of proposals for their complete abolition.

Doubtless once 'equality of status' had been conceded, the transition to 'equality of strength,' at least on land, was inevitable. It was effected by the MacDonald Plan of 16th March 1932. The British Government adopted the French proposal for short-service armies throughout Continental Europe, but added precise figures for the troops of each country. For Germany, as for France, 200,000 was proposed—about the maximum that France could raise on the basis of the proposed eight-month period of service. As regards military material, mobile land guns were in future to be limited to a maximum calibre of 105 mm.—the limit prescribed for Germany by the Treaty—and tanks to a maximum weight of 16 tons. All material in excess of these limits was to be destroyed within three years, with the exception of guns up to 155 mm., which might be retained but not replaced. The restrictions on German naval armaments were to remain unchanged until 1935. Military aircraft was to remain prohibited to Germany for the duration of the convention, while each of the other Great Powers was to reduce its air force to 500 planes. Such, in outline, was the MacDonald Plan.

After the presentation of this plan the question of the date at which Germany should be allowed to attain practical equality emerged as the critical issue of the negotiations. The French Government refused to contemplate the destruction of their heavy war material until after a delay of four years, during which the reduction of the Reichswehr and of the French army to a militia level would be effected, and the efficacy of the proposed system of supervision over armaments fully tested. During this period no increase in German armaments would be permitted, save for a numerical increase proportionate to the increased number of effectives in the transformed Reichswehr. The British Government acquiesced in this viewpoint, while insisting that the reduction of armaments to be effected by France at the end of the four years' period should be specified in an agreement for immediate signature. To this the French agreed.

On 14th October 1933 Sir John Simon reported these tentative proposals to the Bureau of the Disarmament Conference. Forthwith the German Government gave notice of its withdrawal from the Conference and from the League.

The French programme was indeed irreconcilable with the demand presented by Germany for the attainment of actual equality within five years. The German Government had declared its willingness to renounce all 'aggressive' weapons which other Powers were prepared to destroy within five years, but had demanded the right to proceed immediately to equip its forces with all weapons which other Powers intended to retain. The diplomatic negotiations of December 1933–April 1934 were directed towards finding a basis of Franco-German agreement. The French Government, though prepared to cut the French air force by 50 per cent within the next four years, otherwise refused to combine the immediate disarmament of France with the immediate rearmament of Germany. The German Government was prepared to consent to the postponement of French disarmament for five years, on condition that Germany was allowed to reconstitute the Reichswehr as a force of 300,000 men engaged for one year, equipped with guns up to 155 mm. in calibre, with anti-aircraft guns, with tanks up to 6 tons, and with fighting planes equal in number to 30 per cent of the combined air forces of Germany's neighbours or 50 per cent of the military aircraft possessed by France, whichever was the less.

British opinion inclined to the view that these German proposals were not unreasonable. The British Government early abandoned the formula of 14th October: no German rearmament. Since Germany was in fact steadily rearming, it appeared the wiser course to set a limit to the process by the conclusion of a convention, even if achieved at the cost of legalizing a measure of rearmament by Germany. Thereby a race in armaments might be avoided. The British and German Governments had reached, indeed, substantial agreement when negotiations were abruptly broken off by the French on 17th April 1934, owing to the revelation of the scale of German rearmament in the budget estimates which had just been published.

For the remainder of 1934 the negotiations remained in abeyance. The Anglo-French *communiqué* of 3rd February 1935 envisaged their resumption on the basis of the replacement of the disarmament clauses of the Treaty by a general agreement regarding armaments, simultaneously with the conclusion of security agreements for eastern and central Europe. Hitler, however, seized the opportunity provided by the issue of the British White Paper of 4th March 1935, and by the prolongation of the period of military service in France, to restore conscription in Germany. The

British Government joined the French and Italian Governments in securing the adoption by the League Council, on 17th April 1935, of the resolution condemning Germany's unilateral repudiation of Treaty obligations; but forthwith opened the negotiations for a naval agreement which resulted in the Anglo-German naval agreement of 18th June 1935. The incoherence of British policy, and the signature of the agreement after little more than a pretence at consultation with France, provoked sharp resentment across the Channel. The French feared that this realistic policy of accepting the fact of German rearmament, and of attempting to circumscribe its development by the conclusion of a separate bilateral agreement, might be followed in respect of air as of naval forces, and that Great Britain would then disinterest herself in the negotiation of security agreements and the limitation of land forces. Through Mr. Eden the British Government is understood to have given assurances disclaiming any such intention. Thereafter the emphasis in negotiations with Germany shifted from the sphere of armaments limitation to that of arrangements for European security.

The eventual fiasco of German disarmament may in some measure be attributed to the confusion of motives which inspired the action of the Allies in 1919. The disarmament of the enemy is in the first place a problem of armistice; the victors must assure their military predominance during the ensuing negotiations. In November 1918 Foch refrained from demanding radical disarmament and demobilization; in consequence, this essential problem of armistice presented itself with renewed urgency at the Peace Conference. It then became the subject of thorough consideration only in its military aspects; the political received little attention. Methods of disarmament demand adaptation to the purpose in view. Thus the military conditions of an armistice agreement are unlikely to be appropriate for the long years of peace. The military conditions of peace have their own, quite different *raison d'être*. They may on the one hand be conceived as promoting a process of moral and political regeneration within the defeated country. So President Wilson claimed for the Allies the right to subject Germany to 'a generation of thoughtfulness.' The experience of twenty years is conducive of a certain scepticism about the realization of such an aim; at least it is clear that little is gained if military activities, hemmed in as regards the armed forces of the state, are allowed to flood the spheres of civilian life; and all is endangered if the limited army, preserving the personnel and the traditions of the old, fails to reflect the qualities of the new political régime. German disarmament may be regarded further as necessary for the redress of the balance of power, as an arbitrary arrangement designed in the interests of political equilibrium and corresponding to the territorial safeguards taken in past centuries. Finally, German disarmament may be envisaged, as Wilson and Lloyd George envisaged it, as the precursor of general disarmament. The problems raised thereby await examination in the next chapter, but it is well to note how the interconnexion between German disarmament and general disarmament proved fatal to the maintenance of the Treaty provisions. The aspiration inserted by way of preamble to the military, naval, and air clauses was added in order to make them more palatable to the vanquished, but its fulfilment came to be taken as a condition of their continued observance.

CHAPTER XIII

ARMAMENTS AND NATIONAL DEFENCE

A CONTRAST used to be drawn between the British and French theses on disarmament. The British inclined to the view that armaments provoked fear and suspicion, and so were themselves a cause of war. Nations should first disarm, and security would then ensue. Accordingly the British called for a direct approach to the problem of disarmament. They proposed to inquire straightway how armaments might be reduced and to conclude agreements forthwith. The French looked at the matter in a different way. The fear of war, they said, makes nations arm for their defence. Remove the fear of attack and armaments will wither away. Accordingly they called for an indirect approach to the problem of disarmament. Let us, they urged, build up the apparatus of security; then nations will be able to disarm.

This, maybe, is too simplified a report of the Anglo-French debate. Yet it is not difficult to cull from the speeches of leaders of opinion in the two countries illustrations of these national viewpoints. At the Washington Conference, in November 1921, Briand quashed all discussion of land disarmament by refusing to envisage any reduction of the period of military service in France below a year and a half save in return for pledges of assistance against attack. 'If anybody asks us to go further,' he said, 'I should have to answer clearly and definitely that it would be impossible for us to do it without exposing ourselves to a most serious danger. You might possibly come and tell us: "We are going to . . . put all means at your disposal in order to secure your safety!" Immediately, if we heard those words, of course we would strike upon another plan. . . . If France is to remain alone . . . you must not deny her what she wants in order to ensure her security.'[1]   Successive French governments were adamant in their refusal to budge from this attitude.   It was taken up with regard to naval armaments as well.   In 1930 the London Naval Conference failed of its main purpose largely through the insistence of France on some agreement of mutual assistance, preferably a Mediterreanean Naval Pact, as the necessary condition of an agreement for limiting the number of auxiliary vessels.   On no issue were the French people so united as on the priority of security over disarmament.

Though, as the years passed by, the French attitude received increasingly sympathetic understanding in Great Britain, in the British mind there lurked the suspicion that the French were seeking to impale the cause of disarmament on the barbed entanglements of security.   In Liberal and Labour circles, and to a lesser extent among Conservatives, a belief born of the experience of pre-war years had taken deep root.   It was the conviction expressed in Lord Grey's oft-quoted warning: 'Great armaments lead inevitably to war. . . . The enormous growth of armaments in Europe . . . made war inevitable.'[2]   British yearning for peace found expression in a deep aversion against whatever savoured of preparation for war.   In January 1922 Lloyd George appealed for French co-operation 'in building up a great system of European accord, which will put the maintenance of peace between nations and the reduction of national armaments in the forefront of its aims.'[3] 'Security for all fundamentally depends on armament reduction,'[4] echoed the British Foreign Secretary in his opening speech at the Disarmament Conference.   His terse phrase epitomized the British doctrine.

British statesmen could claim, too, that British practice accorded with British precept.   The British army, on the whole the strongest in the world at the armistice, was by the end of 1920 weaker than the Belgian.   Its regular strength fell to 170,000 by the spring of 1922, and till 1934 each year brought some further reduction.   The British air force experienced a similar curtailment.   In November 1918 Great Britain topped the list for air strength, with 14,000 serviceable machines.   Four years later the R.A.F. in Europe comprised 15 squadrons of 12 planes each, while France held in Europe 100 squadrons of 8–10 planes each.   A programme of expansion in the air announced in 1922 was slowed up after the signature of the Locarno Treaties.[5]   The British navy, too, was cut down.   By the Washington Agreement of 6th February 1922.

[1] *U.S.A. Foreign Relations*, 1922, i, p. 315.
[2] Lord Grey: *Twenty-Five Years*, i, pp. 91–92.
[3] *Anglo-French Negotiations*, p. 120.
[4] *The Times*, February 9, 1932.
[5] 125 *H.C. Deb.*, February 23, 1920, col. 1339; 135 *H.C. Deb.*, November 30, 1920, col. 1092; Chaput, R. A.: *Disarmament in British Policy*, pp. 273–276, 325–344.

Great Britain consented to the scrapping of 40 per cent of her existing strength in capital ships, and accepted the standard of parity with the battle fleet of the U.S.A. With the conclusion of the London Naval Treaty of 22nd April 1930 the whole strength of the British navy was subjected to limitation by international agreement. 'We have,' claimed MacDonald in June 1931, 'gone pretty nearly to the limit of example.' [1]

It is, however, well to distinguish between disarmament as an issue in internal politics and disarmament as an aspect of British foreign policy. Admittedly the two interacted, and the distinction is to that extent unreal. But disarmament became in Great Britain a popular faith, uncritical, unquestioning, and unrealistic.[2] Popular pressure, the urgent need for economy, and the general sense of security—reflected in the official assumption of no war for ten years—combined to produce the 'unilateral disarmament' of Great Britain. It was largely the outcome of internal political considerations. Disarmament as an aspect of British foreign policy is a more enigmatic phenomenon. It is hardly necessary to insist on the inexactitude of the term; but its magic must not drive from the mind its mundane sense as a policy directed towards securing international agreements for the reduction and limitation of armaments. It is necessary to inquire what blessings were expected from disarmament so interpreted, and why the French discounted them so heavily.

Such an inquiry must begin by a consideration of the criteria by which each country decided the level of armaments it needed to maintain. The British Government stood by the principle that the size of the British army was not dependent on the size of other armies, nor the cruiser strength of the British navy on the number of auxiliary vessels in other navies. The needs of overseas garrisons determined the size of the British army. Calculation of the number of cruisers required 'to keep the highway of the seas open for trade and communication' fixed the cruiser strength of the navy. These were rock-bottom requirements, which would not be affected by any reduction in the military or naval forces of other countries. This doctrine of absolute needs was put forward on several occasions, notably at the first session of the Preparatory Commission in May 1926, at the Geneva Naval Conference in 1927, and in reply to the Hoover Proposals in 1932.[3]

It has been the well-founded contention of the British Govern-

---

[1] 254 *H.C. Deb.*, June 29, 1931, col. 916.
[2] See Zimmern, Sir A.: *The League of Nations and the Rule of Law*, pp. 330–332.
[3] See *P.C.D.C.*, ii, pp. 14–15; *C.R.L.A.*: *Docs.* i, p. 266. See also Richmond, Sir H. W.: *Sea Power in the Modern World*, pp. 58, 140; and Richmond, Sir H. W.: *The Navy*, pp. 47–51. In 1927 the minimum number of cruisers was fixed at 70; in 1929 the Labour Government lowered the number to 50.

ment that, in normal times, the armed forces of other countries determine British strength only in military aircraft and in battleships. For these weapons relative standards were established. In June 1923 the Prime Minister announced the Government's decision to build up a Home Defence Air Force 'of sufficient strength adequately to protect us against air attack by the strongest air force within distance of this country.' [1] But thereafter—to quote the White Paper of 11th March 1935—'the attainment of the minimum air strength regarded as necessary to our security in face of air developments on the Continent' was postponed from time to time 'in pursuit of the aim of permanent peace.' [2] The battle fleet was maintained at a more effective level. Naval supremacy was sacrificed on the altar of friendship with the U.S.A., but British mastery in home waters and in the Mediterannean was safeguarded as far as possible by keeping the British fleet on something higher than a two-Power standard in relation to European fleets. To sum up the British claim for armaments. For the army, an absolute minimum for imperial defence; for the air force, a 'one-Power standard' as compared with the strongest air force within striking distance; for the navy, battleships on the basis of parity with the U.S.A. and a 'two-Power standard' as regards Europe, with an absolute minimum number of cruisers for trade defence.

It is perhaps comprehensible that the example of Great Britain should have failed to impress the French. For they claimed that they, too, had disarmed as far as existing political circumstances would permit. If reminded that German armaments had been cut down, and that the victors were under at least a moral obligation to reduce their own armaments, they were liable to retort that they had taken this factor into account. Had they not on three occasions reduced the period of service for conscripts—in 1922 to two years, in 1923 to eighteen months, and in 1928 to one year?

But comparison is pointless. It is the premises of French armaments policy that require consideration.

For the army, the French General Staff appears to have worked, like the British Admiralty, on a well-founded theory of minimum needs. The reorganization of the French army, effected by the military laws of 1927–1928, represented the adaptation of military needs to popular pressure—the demand for the reduction of the period of military service to one year. Each annual contingent numbered, in normal years, roughly 240,000. Of these only half would at any time be fully trained. If allowance be made for other services, only about 107,000 would be available from the annual contingent for the defence of the frontier. But in the view

[1] See Chaput, R. A.: *Disarmament in British Policy*, pp. 331 et seq.
[2] *Cmd.* 4827, p. 4.

of the French General Staff 300,000 men had to be immediately available for frontier defence should hostilities threaten. They were required as a covering force behind which mobilization could proceed unimpeded by enemy incursions. The crucial problem of military reorganization was to reconcile one-year service with the requirements of this covering force. A partial solution was sought in an increase in the number of professional soldiers. Their number was raised from 72,000 to 106,000. But a large proportion of these were assigned to duties other than frontier defence— service in the overseas army, instruction of the annual contingent, conduct of the mobilization centres. Only some 50,000 men could be available for co-operation with the 107,000 men of the annual contingent. So the necessary covering force was only half provided by the peace-time army: 143,000 men were required for its completion. They would be drawn from the contingents of the three preceding years, who were to be held *en disponibilité*— i.e. subject to immediate recall to the colours. It seemed very doubtful whether, confronted by the Reichswehr, France could further reduce the effectives of her peace-time army without gravely jeopardizing the defence of the frontier in the event of sudden attack. The reductions effected by the laws of 1927-1928 were made possible only by the construction of extensive frontier fortifications —the so-called Maginot Line.[1]

The exigencies of war with Germany determined also the trend of French naval policy. The French army overseas numbered, in 1931, some 237,000 men. It might be reinforced by part or all of a mobile force of 66,000 trained men which was normally stationed in the home country, but which acted as a reservoir for the relief of overseas forces and as a reserve in the event of colonial disturbances. The first objective of French naval policy was to safeguard the transport of these troops, of trained reserves, and of war supplies across the Mediterranean in the event of war. 'The Mediterranean,' exclaimed André Géraud; 'there lies the centre of the French military system.' [2] To ensure unimpeded transport, the British and Italian navies must be held at bay. Presumably the British navy provoked little anxiety, though doubtless the French Government desired to maintain sufficient naval strength to warn off British interference. But the deeper cause of apprehension was the Italian navy. Italy claimed naval parity with France; France was determined not to concede the claim, since it implied Italian superiority in the Mediterranean. Competitive Franco-Italian

[1] See Brindel, Gen.: 'La nouvelle Organisation militaire,' *Revue des Deux Mondes*, June 1, 1929; Debeney, Gen.: *Sur la Sécurité militaire de la France*; Rocque, Col. de la: 'Le Malaise militaire,' *Revue de Paris*, November 1, 1929.
[2] Géraud, A.: 'The London Naval Conference,' *Foreign Affairs*, July 1930.

naval construction would draw in Great Britain through British determination to maintain the two-Power standard.

The French naval programme reflected this Mediterranean preoccupation. France accepted the Washington ratios, though they rankled.[1] But Briand rejected their extension to cruisers and submarines because 'a nation which, like France, has a large extent of coasts and numerous distant colonies' could not agree to restriction 'in the means essential to its communications and security.' [2] Coastal defence and the protection of the Mediterranean routes called for the construction of submarines and cruisers. At Washington the French delegation stood out for the right to build up to 90,000 tons of submarines. In December 1924 a naval programme—the Statut Naval—was presented to the Chamber of Deputies, providing for the gradual construction of 96,000 tons of ocean-going submarines, 30,000 tons of coastal submarines, and 210,000 tons of cruisers. It was this programme which the French delegation at the London Conference refused to curtail save in return for guarantees of security.[3]

Inevitably this French naval programme provoked misgivings in England. Was it not apparent, asked Balfour at Washington, on 24th December 1921, that from a strategic and tactical standpoint France was proposing to build against Great Britain? At Cannes, a few days later, Lloyd George warned Briand that 'Britain's sea communications are to Britain what France's eastern frontier is to France.' If the French submarine programme were carried out, British opinion would insist on a heavy programme of anti-submarine craft. 'The two countries would thus be launched on a course of competitive naval construction. . . . Naval competition in any form between Great Britain and France would corrode good will.' [4] From the Paris Conference to the Disarmament Conference Great Britain consistently advocated the abolition of the submarine; the lesser naval Powers as consistently demanded its retention. Short of abolition, a solution was sought through a general naval agreement. The negotiations ran up against the obstacle of Franco-British dissension on methods of naval limitation—a dissension which focused the contrast of interest between the greater and the smaller naval Powers. Great Britain demanded that naval units be standardized and the tonnage of each class of vessel limited. Then each navy would know what types of vessel were to be encountered and how many each Power possessed. The element of surprise would be eliminated. And by this crystal-

[1] See Buell, R.: *The Washington Conference*, pp. 213 et seq.
[2] *U.S.A. Foreign Relations*, 1922, i, p. 135.
[3] Engely, G.: *The Politics of Naval Disarmament*, p. 107.
[4] *Anglo-French Negotiations*, p. 118.

lization of naval forces the superiority of the strongest would be enhanced and confirmed. France demanded that only the total tonnage of each navy should be limited. Each country should be free to build as many vessels of any type as it chose, provided it kept within the permitted total tonnage. Then, each country could build in accordance with the peculiar requirements of its national defence. The lesser naval Powers could construct warships of varied character—could, in short, keep the greater naval Powers on tenterhooks.

This Franco-British dissension on methods of naval limitation marked the third session of the Preparatory Commission (21st March–26th April 1927). Thereafter several compromise proposals were put forward. The most significant was the so-called Anglo-French Compromise of July 1928. The French and British Governments tentatively agreed to advocate the limitation only of battleships, aircraft carriers, large 10,000-ton or 8-inch-gun cruisers, and ocean-going submarines over 600 tons. This arrangement suited France because it would leave unshackled the construction of small submarines to operate in the Mediterranean and off the French coasts, and it suited Great Britain because she would be free to build the cruisers of the light type she required. The agreement evoked protests both in Great Britain and the U.S.A. Did the Anglo-French agreement mean that the British Admiralty was more apprehensive of powerful American cruisers on the high seas than of French submarines in the Channel? In the outcome, the Anglo-French proposal was dropped. Not until the London Conference was a comprehensive method of naval limitation agreed upon by Great Britain, France, and the U.S.A., together with Japan and Italy.[1]

An odious record, this Anglo-French naval discord. Though in the later years French naval construction was pointed against Italy, at the outset it appeared rather a thrust at Great Britain. Why should France have turned to a policy of naval assurance against her former ally? The explanation must be sought in the exigencies of power politics. Armaments are the ultimate support of policy, the final determinant of the degree of pressure which a state can exercise to make its will prevail. Till 1925 French policy towards Germany clashed with that of Great Britain; and even Locarno failed to resolve, though it did indeed mitigate, the conflict of British and French policy in eastern Europe. The impairment of French naval defence would jeopardize the capacity of France to follow her European policy. It would relegate her to a position of dependence on Great Britain and deprive her of

[1] For their recommendation to the Preparatory Commission, see *P.C.D.C.*, x, p. 462.

'the freedom . . . to follow her own diplomacy.'[1] In the same spirit Sir Austen Chamberlain, deploring in 1931 the weakening of British armed strength compared with that of France, warned his fellow-members that 'the less our strength, the more our policy depends upon other nations and the less it is within our own control.'[2]

That an agreement on armaments can develop only within a framework of political understanding, whether tacit or explicit, is now a truism that calls for no elaboration. The armaments that France deemed necessary for the implementation of her European policy were, to the British mind, a potential menace to Great Britain and a factor of European unrest. Wherein lay the solution? It could not be found in a closer political understanding with France. Such understanding involved commitments in eastern Europe and in the Mediterranean which Great Britain—so it then seemed—would never assume. Could a solution be found instead in a 'direct approach'—by the conclusion of a general disarmament agreement?

It would seem that the British thesis that disarmament would promote peace was capable of three interpretations. It could be held that no system of collective security could operate as long as nations remained highly armed. Common action against an aggressor would be possible only in a world in which armaments had been reduced to the lowest practicable level. Such was the context within which the Covenant contemplated disarmament. Had the British Government displayed any willingness to extend its commitments within the framework of an agreement for the reduction of armaments, this argument would not indeed have lacked force. But of such a development in British policy there was no sign until the timid proposals of 1933–1934, gestures of despair designed to revive the fast-vanishing hopes of agreement.

The place of disarmament in British foreign policy must be attributed rather to faith in its efficacy as a solvent of national rivalries. An agreement about armaments 'would be the most effective and significant proof of international appeasement and an encouragement of the mutual confidence which springs from good and neighbourly relations'[3]—so the British Memorandum of 29th January 1934. Great Britain had good reason to seek a naval agreement with the U.S.A., the country with which a friendly understanding was above all desired, and the one which could outbuild Great Britain on the sea. So, too, a disarmament agreement for Europe was in line with the general trend of British

---

[1] See Kerguezec, G. de: 'French Naval Aims,' *Foreign Affairs*, April 1926.
[2] 254 *H.C. Deb.*, June 29, 1931, col. 1015.
[3] *Cmd.* 4498, p. 3.

policy. It was welcomed as a milestone on the road by which Germany would return to her place of influence in the Concert of European Powers. But to France disarmament turned a less pleasing countenance. Her interest in disarmament was allayed by the agreement concluded on 28th June 1919. As long as Germany remained relatively disarmed, the European settlement was secured against violent overthrow. The French saw no reason why this situation should not continue indefinitely. They recoiled against the reduction of their own armaments without compensatory pledges of external assistance, because they feared it might lead to the substitution of a real German for an alleged French hegemony in Europe. In England such fears were counted craven, or were dismissed as the unlovely legacy of an outworn militarism. It was a lone voice which declared in the Commons in 1931 that 'the French army at the present moment is a stabilizing factor. . . . The sudden weakening of that factor of stability, the unquestioned superiority of French military power, might open floodgates of measureless consequences in Europe at the present time, might break the dyke and

> 'Let the boundless deep
> Down upon far off cities while they dance—
> Or dream.' [1]

Clearly the British feeling that the French army was bigger than the political situation in Europe justified had its origin in the difference between the French and British outlook on European politics. Great Britain claimed maritime supremacy in European waters as an essential condition of British security. The French claimed military preponderance over Germany as an essential condition of French security and as the essential factor of peace in Europe. Why then, asked the French, should not Great Britain recognize the French military position in Europe as France recognized the British naval position? The agreement tentatively reached in July 1928 seemed, to the French delight, symbolic of such an understanding. It foundered in the face of fierce opposition from all circles of British opinion. The agreement was condemned largely, it is true, because the naval provisions gave offence to the U.S.A. But it was condemned also because, as *The Spectator* expressed it, 'British public opinion . . . will never be a party to a policy . . . which in practice will give support to a French hegemony of Europe.' [2] To the British mind the French 'hegemony' could not be durable; Germany would not in the end be satisfied with anything less than military parity with France;

[1] Churchill, Winston: 254 *H.C. Deb.*, June 29, 1931, col. 963.
[2] *Spectator*, October 13, 1928. Cf. *The Round Table*, December 1928: 'A Plea for an Independent Foreign Policy.'

better then to let parity come about by agreement through the reduction of French armaments within the framework of a general convention than wait till Germany should proceed to rearm.

Not unnaturally the French were at a loss to understand why the British claim to naval supremacy in European waters was right and proper while their own claim to military preponderance was a dangerous pretension.[1] Is the inconsistency resolved by the claim that British sea power is no menace to the security of any nation, since it is incapable of dealing a sudden knock-out blow? The most reasonable of Frenchmen dismissed the theory as the mere rationalization .of British interests. Disarmament—as conceived by British opinion—was, they felt, a nostrum for use on land but not at sea. This suspicion goes far to explain French insistence on the interdependence of military and naval forces. To discuss them separately would 'be favourable to those who aim at the reduction of land armaments but who intend to keep their maritime supremacy.' [2]

It is then comprehensible that Frenchmen approached the Disarmament Conference 'avec scepticisme et méfiance' while in England it called forth 'une espérance de caractère religieux.' [3] The illusion of a 'direct approach' to the problem of disarmament continued to permeate British opinion. It faded only after the failure of the last essay by President Hoover. The Hoover Proposals of 22nd June 1932 for an all-round reduction of one-third in armaments was enthusiastically greeted by Italy, Germany, and Russia. Had the U.S.A. continued to work for the adoption of the integral plan, it would have become the leader of the revisionist bloc in Europe. 'When the true position was realized by responsible American officials in Washington and Geneva they saw that the real choice was either to assist an agitation which pointed to the disorderly overthrow of the existing European system, or to participate in the organization of a system of security under which political grievances might be gradually and peaceably settled and armaments voluntarily reduced.' [4] Thereafter it was more widely realized that—to quote again the White Paper of 29th January 1934—'protracted debates on disarmament in its limited and purely technical aspect can lead to no conclusion, unless wider considerations touching the equality and the security of nations are borne in mind and provided for.'

[1] Cf. 'L'Angleterre garde la supériorité navale; elle est juste et nécessaire. La France perd la supériorité militaire; elle n'est ni juste ni nécessaire. Pourquoi? Sir John Simon ne le dit pas' (Bardoux, J.: L'Ile et l'Europe, p. 460).
[2] 'La première session de la commission préparatoire,' L'Europe Nouvelle, July 3, 1926.
[3] De Traz, Robert: 'Les Débuts de la conférence,' Revue de Paris, March 1, 1932.
[4] Lippmann, W.: The United States in World Affairs, 1932, pp. 242–245.

There remains for examination the third way in which, to the British mind, disarmament might promote peace. 'I have never contended,' wrote Lord Esher to Cecil in August 1922, 'that to limit armaments was to end the possibility of war. But I do contend that it brings within narrow limits the possibility of sudden attack by one nation upon another.' [1] That—to quote again from Sir John Simon's speech on 8th February 1932—disarmament should be directed towards 'limiting the risks and suffering of sudden and devastating wars' lay at the back of British proposals both in the Preparatory Commission and the Disarmament Conference. If sudden attack was made more difficult, time would be available for recourse to procedures of peaceful settlement. The outbreak of war, if postponed, would be averted; such was the conviction. It found its logical culmination in the emphasis on qualitative disarmament—the abolition of offensive weapons—by the British Foreign Secretary during the first phase of the Disarmament Conference. The technical British objective throughout the disarmament discussions was to increase the efficacy of defence by decreasing the power of attack.

It is clear that, though occasionally paying lip-service, the French were at heart opposed to the British idea of reducing the power of attack. The reason is not far to seek. The great source of French anxiety was the superiority of Germany in industrial resources and population. 'Who would care to maintain,' demanded Briand at the Ninth Assembly, 'that a great country, so powerfully equipped for peace—that is to say, for industrial development—would be at a loss to supply an army with war material?' The fear that, given equality, Germany would rapidly advance to the possession of overwhelming force, and that France would be doomed to fall behind in an armaments race, was responsible for the acuity of the debate on war potential in the first sessions of the Preparatory Commission. It was not that France proposed to include, within any scheme of disarmament, limitations on the productive capacity of industries capable of diversion to war purposes. What France sought was to establish the principle that, in the determination of a just level of armaments for each country, a comparative deficiency in war potential should be compensated by a correspondingly higher level of armaments. After the fourth session of the Preparatory Commission, in March-April 1927, this debate on war potential was dropped; but the problem of German superiority in man-power and industrial resources remained a dominating element in the later discussions. It lay behind the French opposition to British proposals for reducing the power of attack.

[1] Esher, Lord: *Journals and Letters*, iv, pp. 281-282.

After the Great War French strategists came to the conclusion that their only hope of victory in any future struggle would lie in a crushing attack on Germany at the very outset. In a long war, enabling Germany to mobilize her man-power and industrial resources, Germany would crush France by the sheer weight of superior armaments. Only at the start would France enjoy, thanks to German disarmament, a real military superiority. She must therefore maintain an army sufficiently powerful to exploit this initial advantage by a strategic offensive.[1] 'In order to ward off the danger which menaces her,' wrote an acute French publicist in 1922, 'France may be brought to anticipate aggression. The object of her policy must be to make a long war—or war itself—impossible. We can discern in process of development the conception of an active, independent, and mobile army, always ready to penetrate into enemy territory and capable of assuring by itself the maintenance of the European *status quo.*'[2]

Even the most cursory study of French military development reveals, however, that French trust in salvation by a strategic offensive died long before the twenties drew to a close. Sudden attack to nip German rearmament in the bud was ruled out by the obligations assumed at Locarno. The French army was not reorganized in 1927–1928 as a mobile instrument capable of 'driving home an offensive punch,' since the professional soldiers were not grouped together in a regular army distinct from the national army of conscripts. Instead they were distributed among all the units and services of the national army, in such a manner as to form 'a large and powerful, but slow-moving steam-roller of fire designed to push back gradually, as in 1918, any similar army . . . aligned against it.'[3] So constituted, the French army could not be that 'ever-ready instrument of intervention' for the creation of which Captain de Gaulle called in 1934.

Yet though a profoundly defensive spirit came to dominate in French military circles, French opposition to the abolition of the more powerful weapons of war remained unabated. French military superiority rested on the possession of large stocks of heavy war material. Their unwillingness to agree to its destruction largely arose from the knowledge that Germany was in a position to manufacture new stocks with far greater rapidity than France. Once the 'aggressive' weapons of France had been destroyed, Germany would have an interest in violating the agreement for

---

[1] *Temporary Mixed Commission: Report,* September 1922, pp. 47–50.

[2] Fabre Luce, A.: *La Crise des Alliances,* p. 391. See also Fabry, J.: 'La France de 1921 et la nation armée,' *Revue de Paris,* January 1, 1921; Reynaud, P.: 'Avons-nous l'armée de nos besoins?'—*Revue hebdomadaire,* July 1924.

[3] Hart, B. L.: *The Remaking of Modern Armies,* pp. 240–270, Cf. Fabry, J.: 'Ou va notre armée?'—*Revue de Paris,* September 1925.

their abolition; France could have none, for she would soon fall behind in an armaments race. Hence the insistence on supervision and guarantees of execution. The war-potential problem continued to hover over the debates long after the problem itself had ceased to be discussed.

The determination of France to retain a large reserve of powerful war material was evident throughout the disarmament discussions. In the Preparatory Disarmament Commission the French had little difficulty in safeguarding their interest in this respect. The limitation of material by the tablification of permitted stocks—the direct method which had been applied to Germany—was rejected as a method for general application, on the grounds that its enforcement would entail a stricter system of supervision than states were prepared to accept. Hence the draft Convention adopted in December 1930 provided only for the limitation of the annual expenditure of each state on land armaments—a method of indirect limitation which the French had advocated from the outset and to which the British, though initially hostile, had been converted by the construction of the German pocket-battleships. The views of the British Delegation were succinctly stated in the final report of the Preparatory Commission in December 1930. The Delegation was 'ready to admit that direct limitation may, in theory, be the most effective and the most obvious system, but feared that this method of limitation would, in practice, prove unsatisfactory. Even if adequate definitions and categories could be established, it would be impossible to impose on all countries such a system of verification and control as to give the assurance that the limitation would be properly observed. The British Delegation had hoped that it might be possible to limit directly the larger weapons, such as big guns and tanks, but here again similar difficulties would be encountered. They would be prepared to accept any practical scheme for direct limitation of the more important weapons that would offer any prospect of general acceptance and reasonable effectiveness. It may be that the governments at the Disarmament Conference will be able to find such a scheme.' [1]

What measures should be taken with regard to powerful war material proved indeed the most critical of the technical problems before the Disarmament Conference. Widespread support was evident for the abolition of weapons specially suitable for offensive warfare. The British Government proposed the abolition, among land armaments, of heavy mobile guns and of tanks over twenty tons. The French Government, on the other hand, advocated not the abolition, but the internationalization, of powerful war material under the control of the League of Nations. This

[1] *P.C.D.C.*, x, p. 573.

principle, enunciated by the conservative Tardieu Ministry, was upheld with equal tenacity by the Radical Socialists under Herriot. The Herriot Plan of 14th November 1932 provided that the national armies of Europe, reduced to a militia level, should be deprived of bombing aircraft and of powerful mobile land material, especially heavy artillery and tanks such as were necessary for delivering attacks on permanent fortifications. But a restricted amount of powerful mobile material was to be retained by specialized contingents of long-term soldiers, who were to be maintained by each state and held at the disposal of the League for common action against an aggressor. Moreover, material in excess was not to be destroyed, but stored in each state under international supervision. If engaged in a war of legitimate self-defence, a state was to regain full use of its League contingent of troops and of the stocks of material within its territory. This military organization was to be crowned by the constitution of 'an organically international air force.'[1]

Behind these French proposals for the internationalization of offensive weapons lay the conviction that the alternative course of abolition would mean, as M. Aubert insisted in the Land Commission, 'upsetting the existing situation in regard to security. The prohibition of certain categories of weapons would be to the advantage of states which did not at present possess them.'[2] The French feared that, despite an agreement for the abolition of heavy guns and heavy tanks, Germany might secretly equip its forces with such material, and successfully invade the territory of an ill-equipped neighbour. In order to dislodge the enemy from the occupied area it would then be necessary to employ the weapons of offensive warfare. Their abolition, the French protested, would serve the turn of the faithless aggressor, against whose assault protection must be sought not by the destruction of vital material, but by plans for assuring the defender of a full complement of arms within 'the organization of peace by concerted action against aggression.'[3] After the presentation of the MacDonald Plan, however, the French Government dropped their insistence on internationalization as opposed to abolition, and the last stages of the negotiations were concerned not with the question whether the French Government would abandon 'offensive weapons,' but at what stage they would do so.

Just as they were loth to deplete the stock of war material on which they could draw in the event of German attack, so the

[1] Tardieu Plan in *C.R.L.A.* : *Docs.*, i, pp. 113–116; Herriot Plan in ibid., ii, pp. 435–440.
[2] *C.R.L.A.* : *Land Commission*, pp. 40–41, May 19, 1932.
[3] Cf. ibid., pp. 47, 67; Tardieu, April 12, 1932, in *C.R.L.A.*: *Gen. Comm.*, i, p. 51; Paul Boncour, May 23, 1933, ibid., ii, p. 493.

French were equally unwilling to give up training the whole male population in national defence. Their freedom to do so was at first threatened by the support given by the British delegation in the Preparatory Commission to proposals for the limitation of trained reserves. 'What we ought to seek to do,' Lord Cecil urged, 'is to limit the forces that can be used for sudden aggression, and the most direct and certain way of doing it is by actually cutting down the number of men you can put into the fighting line.' [1] Since the substitution of a professional for a conscript army in France was out of the question, the proposal meant, in practice, training only part of the annual contingent. The French military representatives protested that the limitation of trained reserves, like the limitation of material in reserve, 'would have the effect in case of conflict of giving the *certainty* of victory to the state with the greatest war potential.' The weaker countries must organize completely their national defence in time of peace, in order to bring the whole of their resources to bear upon an enemy as rapidly as possible. Otherwise 'security would no longer exist except for states with a high war potential, and these would have all the others at their mercy. This cannot be the aim of disarmament.' [2] The British Government had too little direct interest in the question to insist on its viewpoint, and in 1928 it agreed to cease pressing for the limitation of trained reserves in return for French concessions regarding methods of naval disarmament.

The problem of army recruitment remained thereafter at a standstill until the presentation of the Herriot Plan. The Plan provided that the military forces for the home defence of all European states, with the exception of Great Britain, should be reduced to a uniform general type, that of the national short-service army with limited effectives. In discussion a period of eight to nine months' service was suggested. The French Government claimed that this reorganization would lessen the danger of aggression more effectively than would the abolition of offensive weapons. 'It is much less important to inquire whether a particular type of material can facilitate aggression than to determine the form of military organization which in a given area and in given political conditions would make a policy of aggression more difficult.' [3] The professional army was always ready for action; it was highly trained and designed for manœuvres; while the smallness of its numbers made it 'unsuitable for the defensive, for placing along the whole length of a frontier, for that network

---

[1] March 26, 1927. *P.C.D.C.*, iv, p. 46.
[2] *P.C.D.C.*: *Report of Sub-Commission A*, pp. 35–36.
[3] *C.R.L.A.*: *Docs.*, ii, p. 435.

of continuous fire which was, so to speak, the very armour of the defensive.' By contrast the short-term service army must be mobilized before going into action; its movements could be neither rapid nor secret; ill-adapted for offensive operations, it was eminently suitable for the defensive.   An exception was made with regard to the British army on the grounds that it 'was un-suitable for aggression because Great Britain was separated from the Continent by the sea.' [1] Herriot's proposal for the formation of national militia throughout Continental Europe was incorporated in the MacDonald Plan of 16th March 1933.

French reluctance to agree to the limitation of war material and of trained reserves is eloquent of the reserve with which France approached the idea of disarmament.   The French position may be briefly resumed. France was ready for disarmament within a system of 'collective security'; but of this there was no question. Disarmament as a method of appeasement was wholly contrary to the spirit of French policy.   Finally, the empiric British conception of disarmament as a method of reducing the danger of sudden aggression struck the French as a dangerous illusion.   When the French Radicals produced a scheme of their own, with this purpose in view, their proposals constituted a comprehensive plan involving the complete reorganization of the German and French armies on the one hand, and a world-embracing, though moderately conceived, system of security on the other.

A close examination of the disarmament negotiations reveals the somewhat deceptive nature of a contrast which used to be drawn between the British and French theses on disarmament—the one that disarmament would produce security, the other that security should precede disarmament. This difference· of view between the two countries served to veil a distinction of more fundamental character. The real cleavage between France and Great Britain centred rather on the question whether European peace should continue to rest on the sanction of preponderant force. In the circumstances which resulted from the Treaty of Versailles, dis-armament did not imply equal proportionate reduction in the armaments of all states; it implied the termination of the armed preponderance of France and her allies. For that preponderance, consecrated by the Treaty of Versailles, Great Britain sought to substitute a community of relatively disarmed states, the peace of which should be assured by the mutual confidence of each in the intentions of all.

[1] Pierre Cot, February 17, 1933, in *C.R.L.A.*: *Gen. Comm.*, ii, pp. 279–284.

CHAPTER XIV

THE RHINELAND IN ANGLO-FRENCH
RELATIONS, 1919

IN his classic presentation of the foreign policy of the French monarchy, the great historian Sorel sought to show how that policy was motivated by the desire for the expansion of France to her natural frontiers on the Rhine, the Alps, and the Pyrenees. There is a well-established tradition that Richelieu confirmed as the guiding line of French policy the objective of making the Rhine the frontier of France. 'Did you ever see Richelieu's testament?' wrote Lord Esher to Sir Maurice Hankey in October 1917. 'His methods have been steadily pursued ever since, both under Kings, Emperors, and Republics.' [1]

Yet this tradition has little foundation in fact, and Sorel's interpretation must, it seems, be consigned to the well-stocked limbo of historical legends. For it is more than doubtful whether, under the monarchy, French policy was ever directed towards the conquest of natural frontiers. The notion of pushing France out to her 'natural' frontiers was, before the Revolution, the chimera of a few solitary thinkers who exercised no influence on the direction of policy. The edition of Richelieu's famous Testament in which the doctrine of natural frontiers is proclaimed is an apocryphal production, the work of the Jesuit Pierre Labbé. The episodes in French frontier history which gave colour to Sorel's thesis were not the expression of a policy of expansion to the Rhine; save for Fleury's acquisition of Lorraine in 1733–1738 they were not the expression of any clearly formulated frontier policy at all. They were no more than a series of actions taken to meet the military exigencies of the moment. Sorel erred in attributing the design of well-thought-out policy to measures which were hasty responses to immediate problems. [2]

The doctrine of the natural frontier of France on the Rhine is a legacy not of monarchic policy, but of the French Revolution. Valmy was followed by the advance of the French armies to Mainz. Once this territory had been occupied, what was to be done with it? What guarantees could be found against the return of the old rulers, so hostile to the Revolution, save through annexation? But

[1] Esher, Viscount: *Journal and Letters*, iv, p. 212.
[2] For the reassessment of the foreign policy of the French Monarchy, see Zeller, G.: *La Réunion de Metz à la France, 1552–1648*, Paris, 1926; Mommsen, W.: *Kardinal Richelieu, Seine Politik im Elsass und im Lothringen*, Berlin, 1922; Battifol, L.: 'Richelieu et la question de l'Alsace,' *Revue historique*, vol. 138, 1921–1922, pp. 160–199; Picavet, C. G.: *La Diplomatie française au temps de Louis XIV*, pp. 175–180, Paris, 1930.

revolutionary France had forsworn conquest, and many of its leaders—Robespierre, Carnot, Desmoulins—warned against annexation. The conception of natural frontiers provided a welcome solution. These were the circumstances that called forth Danton's celebrated declaration: 'The frontiers of the Republic are marked by nature. We shall reach them all in the four corners of the horizon, in the direction of the Rhine, in the direction of the ocean, in the direction of the Alps. There the boundaries of our Republic must end, and no human power can stop us reaching them.' [1] A revolutionary tradition was thus born.

To trace the relations of France and the Rhine throughout the nineteenth century would involve too wide a digression. It must suffice to add that the Rhineland remained under French control for some twenty years, till in 1814 the first Treaty of Paris brought France back almost to the frontier of 1792. Prussia then gained where France lost, for in 1815 Prussia was placed astride the Rhine to provide a bulwark for the defence of Germany against France. But among the French the conviction survived that the Rhine was their natural frontier, and the hope of recovering the Rhineland was for long entertained.

When, therefore, the Great War brought to the fore the question how to ensure France protection against Germany in the future, the thoughts of French statesmen turned again to the Rhine. Their plans are indicated in two documents, both drawn up in the first months of 1917, the first a personal letter, dated 12th January, from the French Prime Minister Briand to Paul Cambon, Ambassador in London, and the second the Franco-Russian Agreement concluded on 14th February without the knowledge of the British Government. The two documents differ significantly in tone. Briand expressed his views in tentative and even equivocal language. What mattered to France, he insisted, was not to secure 'a glorious but precarious gain,' but to ensure a 'state of things which will be a guarantee for Europe as well as for ourselves, and serve as a rampart of our frontiers. In our view, Germany must henceforth have but one foot across the Rhine. The settlement of the future of these territories, their neutrality, their provisional occupation, must be discussed between the Allies, but it is meet that France, which is the most directly concerned in the territorial status of these regions, shall have the principal voice in the consideration of this serious problem.' The Franco-Russian agreement opened up no such vista of negotiation and compromise. It stipulated that the left bank of the Rhine should be freed from all political and economic dependence upon Germany. An autonomous and neutralized Rhineland state should be established, the territory of which would

[1] Danton: *Discours*, p. 268, Paris, 1920.

remain under French occupation until Germany had completely carried out all the terms and guarantees provided for in the Peace Treaty.[1]

Neither Briand's letter nor the Franco-Russian Agreement affected the later course of negotiations. Though Briand's letter originated in a request from Sir Edward Grey for some indication of the European war aims of France, it was not followed up, for it arrived after the fall of the Asquith Ministry. Six months passed before Cambon read the letter to Balfour; Balfour gave him no encouragement to pursue the subject. But in December the British Government was called upon to state openly its attitude to the French plan. On 12th December the text of the Franco-Russian Agreement, now a dead letter in consequence of the Bolshevik revolution, appeared in *The Manchester Guardian*. Balfour, in the Commons, affirmed that the British Government had no knowledge whatever of the agreement at the time, and bluntly expressed his views. 'Never did we desire, and never did we encourage the idea, that a bit of Germany should be cut off from the parent State, and erected into some kind of independent republic or independent government of some sort on the left bank of the Rhine, so as to make a new buffer state between France and Germany. That was never part of the policy of His Majesty's Government. His Majesty's Government were never aware that was seriously entertained by any French statesman.' In view of this emphatic repudiation of acquiescence with the French proposals, it is not surprising that the subject was not again raised by the French Government while the war continued.[2] Till the end of 1918 French plans in respect of the Rhineland remained wrapped in

[1] Text of Briand's letter in Barthou, L.: *Le Traité de Paix*, pp. 143–145. See also Mermeix: *Le Combat des Trois*, pp. 190–193. It may be noted that Briand's letter demands neither the annexation of the Rhineland nor even the establishment of an independent Rhineland state. The formula is: 'A nos yeux l'Allemagne ne doit plus avoir qu'un pied au délà du Rhin.' Tardieu: *La Paix*, p: 189, quotes this sentence differently: 'A nos yeux, l'Allemagne ne doit plus avoir un pied au délà du Rhin.' Barthou's quotation is the more likely to be correct. Tardieu's sentence, not Barthou's, has usually been quoted in German works. For the text of the Franco-Russian notes, see Paleologue, M.: *An Ambassador's Memoirs*, iii, pp. 178, 182–183, 192. Certain aspects of the Franco-Russian negotiations, especially Briand's rôle, remain obscure. The signature of the French note is said to have been authorized by the Quai d'Orsay in Briand's absence. See Suarez, G.: *Briand*, iv, pp. 128–135. To Briand's mind the Russian engagement constituted the counterpart of the Constantinople Agreements of 1915. On 15th February, however, Iswolski called on Briand with a request for French assent to freedom for Russia to fix her frontier with Austria and Germany. Briand was taken aback, but considered it difficult to refuse this further engagement. Owing to his hesitations this further agreement was not concluded until 12th March. For these negotiations, see Lafue, P.: *Doumergue*, pp. 102–103; Stieve, F.: *Iswolski im Weltkriege*, pp. 211–215; Pingaud, A.: 'La Mission de M. Doumergue en Russie en 1917,' *Revue d'histoire de la guerre mondiale*, vol. 15, October 1937, pp. 338–352; Ribot, A.: *Journal*, pp. 99–102, 136; Poincaré, R.: *Au Service de la France*, pp. 63–64, 146, 159.

[2] *Anglo-French Negotiations*, pp. 3–5.

obscurity, which the British Government presumably deemed it
unwise to attempt to penetrate.

Even at the Peace Conference Clemenceau appears to have
delayed the presentation of the French demands.   Possibly he did
not make up his mind until the middle of February 1919 to press
for the detachment of the Rhineland from Germany.   There is at
present, at least, no evidence that he had come to any decision
earlier.   Indeed, the memorandum on French policy communicated
by Paul Cambon to the British Government after the armistice
proposed for the Rhineland only 'military neutralization without
political interference,' and suggested military occupation 'as
guarantee for the execution of the preliminaries of peace,' so
implying a limited duration.[1]   The notes drawn up by Marshal
Foch, the first on 27th November 1918,[2] the second on 10th January
1919,[3] did not commit the French Government.   The Senate
Committee on Foreign Affairs first learned of Clemenceau's determination to demand the creation of an independent Rhineland
state on 16th February, and just a week later Clemenceau outlined
his ideas to Colonel House.[4]   The first official statement of French
Rhineland policy was the note of 25th February 1919, drawn up by
André Tardieu at Clemenceau's request.   Apart from justificatory
detail, the note went no further than the statement of two broad
principles:

1. The western frontier of Germany shall be fixed on the
   Rhine.
2. The bridges of the Rhine shall be occupied by an Inter-Allied
   force.

These demands, Tardieu asserted, constituted for France 'a vital
necessity on the principle of which she can admit no compromise.'[5]

While Wilson was away in America, Clemenceau and Tardieu
succeeded in making some headway with these demands.   Colonel
House was ready to agree to French occupation of the Rhine bridgeheads until Germany had fulfilled the obligations laid upon her
by the Treaty, and to accept the establishment of an independent
Rhineland republic for five years.   But Colonel House was disappointed in his expectation of an agreement with Clemenceau on
this basis, for Clemenceau insisted on the permanent separation
of the Rhineland from Germany.   Balfour may have shared the
views of Colonel House, but Lloyd George was more intransigeant:
he was more alarmed by the demand for an army of occupation than

[1] *Miller*, ii, pp. 206–214; *Anglo-French Negotiations*, p. 10.
[2] Text in Mermeix: *Le Combat des Trois*, pp. 205–210.
[3] Text in *Anglo-French Negotiations*, pp. 10–17.
[4] Ribot, A.: *Journal*, pp. 259–260; *House*, iv, p. 345.
[5] Text in *Anglo-French Negotiations*, pp. 55–57.

by the project of a Rhineland Republic, though he could not agree to the latter, he told House, upon the terms the French had in mind.[1] Nevertheless, on 10th March, Clemenceau, Lloyd George and House appointed a small committee instructed to 'definitely formulate the boundary lines of Germany.' The formation of the Committee was to be kept secret. Clemenceau nominated Tardieu; House his brother-in-law, Dr. Mezes; and Lloyd George his private secretary, Philip Kerr. But that very day a message from Wilson to House cut the ground from beneath the Committee's feet. The President cabled: 'I hope you will not even provisionally consent to the separation of the Rhenish provinces from Germany under any arrangement but will reserve the whole matter until my arrival.' Thereupon House countermanded his instructions to his brother-in-law. The Committee met on 11th and 12th March, but Mezes told his colleagues that House thought it inadvisable to reach any conclusions before the arrival of Wilson, since he was expected within forty-eight hours. Even if House had not retraced his steps, it is highly improbable that the Committee would have reached any agreed conclusions. The discussion between Kerr and Tardieu merely revealed the sharpness of the contrast between the British and French positions.[2]

After the President's return from America, on 14th March, the negotiations entered a new phase through the offer to France of an Anglo-American Treaty of Guarantee. Two days earlier Lloyd George had confided to House that to give France the security she desired 'he would be willing to say that, in the event of an invasion, the British would come at once to the rescue.' Perhaps to counterbalance his retraction of the concessions which House was willing to make, Wilson agreed precipitately to make a similar offer. On the afternoon of 14th March, Wilson, Lloyd George, and Clemenceau met in strict secrecy, without secretary or interpreter. Wilson and Lloyd George made it clear that they would agree only to a short occupation of the left bank of the Rhine, not as a measure of security but as a provisional guarantee for the payment of reparation. In compensation they formally offered an immediate military guarantee against unprovoked aggression on the part of Germany against France. Clemenceau expressed his appreciation, but asked for time to take counsel with his advisers before giving a reply.[3]

The French reply was handed to Lloyd George and Wilson on 17th March. In return for the Anglo-American offer the demand

[1] *House*, iv, pp. 356–357, 370, 399; Lloyd George: *Peace Treaties*, i, p. 287. See also Birdsall, P.: *Versailles Twenty Years After*, pp. 201–207, for hitherto unprinted extracts from the *House Papers*.

[2] *Miller*, vi, pp. 316–317; vii, pp. 57–59; Tardieu: *La Paix*, pp. 190–194; *Anglo-French Negotiations*, pp. 58–69; *House*, iv, p. 368.

[3] *House*, iv, p. 370; *Anglo-French Negotiations*, pp. 68–69.

for the political separation of the left bank of the Rhine from Germany was dropped. But the French Note affirmed that the Treaty of Guarantee could not alone provide a solid basis of security. Its terms would first require more careful elaboration; in addition, the Anglo-American guarantee would need to be supplemented by guarantees of a territorial character. A Joint Commission of Inspection should be stationed permanently in the demilitarized zone. The entry, or attempted entry, of German troops into the zone should be considered an act of aggression, bringing the military guarantee into operation. Allied troops should continue to occupy the left bank and the bridgeheads, not however indefinitely, as hitherto proposed, but for a specified period, 'as part of the guarantees to be required for the execution of the financial clauses.' After the withdrawal of the Allied troops France should be entitled to reoccupy the line of the Rhine if the Joint Commission of Inspection should report German violation of the demilitarized zone, or of the military, naval, or air clauses of the Treaty.[1]

The controversy over the Rhineland occupation continued for another month, eased only slightly by negotiations with regard to the Treaty of Guarantee. The American attitude was defined in a note of 28th March which—so House informed an American journalist two days earlier—'strongly appealed to the President, who believed it would be a basis of settlement.'[2] The note read:

(1) No fortifications west of a line drawn fifty kilometres east of the Rhine (as in the military terms already provisionally agreed upon).

(2) The maintenance or assembling of armed forces, either permanently or temporarily, forbidden within that area, as well as all manœuvres, and the maintenance of physical facilities for mobilization.

(3) Violations of these conditions to be regarded as hostile acts against the signatories to the Treaty and as calculated to disturb the peace of the world.

In a separate treaty with the United States:

(4) A pledge by the United States, subject to the approval of the Executive Council of the League of Nations, to come immediately to the assistance of France as soon as any unprovoked movement of aggression against her is made by Germany—the pledge to continue until it is agreed by the contracting Powers that the League itself affords sufficient protection.[3]

Thus the two principal demands which Clemenceau had advanced —an unqualified guarantee of the demilitarized zone, and a con-

[1] *Anglo-French Negotiations*, pp. 74–75.
[2] Thompson, C. T.: *The Peace Conference Day by Day*, p. 66.
[3] *Baker*, ii, p. 71. For the first draft of the Treaty of Guarantee prepared by Colonel House, see *Miller*, vi, Doc. 539, p. 474a; and another text in Palmer: *Bliss*, p. 386.

ditional right to occupy the line of the Rhine—were both rejected. This American Note, nevertheless, constituted one of the two elements in the eventual settlement of the Rhineland question; the first three paragraphs became Articles 42–44 of the Treaty.

Only, however, after two more weeks of not wholly unsuccessful insistence on the Rhineland occupation did Clemenceau accept the terms of this American Note of 28th March. On 31st March Marshal Foch was summoned, at the instance of Clemenceau, before the Council of Four. Foch submitted another Memorandum —his third—to demonstrate that only the presence of Allied forces on the Rhine could save France from invasion.[1] Lloyd George and Wilson just listened perfunctorily, and then declared it was useless to insist; they had already made up their minds. Four days later King Albert appeared before the Council of Four to press the Belgian claim for special treatment with regard to reparation. Clemenceau, in anticipation of the King's presence, put down the question of the left bank for discussion, but King Albert made it clear that he, too, would be content with a short period of military occupation. At length, impressed by the steady opposition of Wilson and Lloyd George, Clemenceau decided on a strategic retreat.[2]

On 6th April Clemenceau instructed his military *chef de cabinet*, General Mordacq, to report on the most advantageous method of ordering the evacuation of the Rhineland on the assumption that a section of the occupied territory should be evacuated at the end of five years, another section at the end of ten years, and the whole occupied area at the end of fifteen years. Mordacq recommended the evacuation of the northern area first, so as to retain control of Mainz to the very end. On the 14th Clemenceau told Colonel House that, if Wilson would accept this proposal for evacuation by stages, he would agree to the American terms regarding the demilitarized zone and the Treaty of Guarantee.[3] House broached the matter to Wilson the following day. 'The President made a wry face over some of it,' House wrote, 'particularly the three five-year periods of occupation, but he agreed to it all.' House went off immediately to see Clemenceau. 'I said to him, "I am the bearer of good news. The President has consented to all that you asked of me yesterday." He grasped both my hands and then embraced me.'[4]

When Wilson, on 15th April, consented to the fifteen years' occupation, Lloyd George had just left for England to defend his conduct of the negotiations before the House of Commons. The

[1] Text in *Anglo-French Negotiations*, pp. 85–88.
[2] Mordacq, Gen. J. J. H.: *Le Ministère Clemenceau*, iii, pp. 203, 210.
[3] See p. 175.
[4] Mordacq, Gen. J. J. H.: *Le Ministère Clemenceau*, iii, p. 214; *House*, iv, pp. 422–423.

previous day the decision to invite the Germans to Versailles had been announced. Probably this decision was taken in the firm belief, on Lloyd George's part, that prolonged occupation would form no part of the Treaty terms.[1] Lloyd George had left Paris with this impression. He returned on the 18th, well pleased with his success in the Commons, to find the situation greatly changed. Wilson and Clemenceau had agreed to occupation; the German delegation might soon arrive. In these circumstances Lloyd George, too, agreed to Clemenceau's proposal.

In the last days of April President Wilson and Clemenceau settled even the details of the Rhineland occupation between themselves, in advance of Lloyd George's approval. On 20th April they agreed on the main draft; Lloyd George accepted it on 22nd April. On the 25th Clemenceau brought forward in the Council of Four an additional article, which President Wilson had already approved; this was accepted by Lloyd George on the 30th.[2] One of these articles was revised a few days later, in consequence of Wilson's complaint that it did not reflect the intention he had in mind when he accepted it.[3] Therewith Part XIV of the Treaty, labelled 'Guarantees of Execution,' was brought to completion.

The circumstances which resulted in Lloyd George's acceptance of the occupation clauses explain his belated efforts in the first days of June to modify this part of the Treaty. It encountered severe criticism from British Ministers and Dominion Premiers when they were informed of the conditions of peace, and on 2nd June they authorized Lloyd George to insist on a shorter period of occupation and a reduction in the size of the army of occupation. Lloyd George started his campaign the same day in the Council of Four, and kept the question well to the front for a fortnight.[4] He failed to secure any change in the text of the Treaty, but he induced Clemenceau to sign, on 16th June, a joint declaration with Wilson and himself relating to the duration and cost of occupation.[5]

It may be desirable to recall again the occupation provisions, already summarized in an earlier chapter. The occupation was to last fifteen years, but, should the Treaty be faithfully carried

[1] See his statement on April 11 to the Dominion Prime Ministers: *Anglo-French Negotiations*, p. 92.
[2] *Anglo-French Negotiations*, pp. 95–96, 103; Tardieu: *La Paix*, p. 235; *Miller*, xix, pp. 485–487.
[3] See *Baker*, ii, p. 101; but cf. *Anglo-French Negotiations*, pp. 96, 105; *Miller*, xix, p. 487.
[4] See Lloyd George: *Peace Treaties*, i, pp. 692–718; *Anglo-French Negotiations*, p. 106; *Miller*, xix, pp. 488–489; Tardieu, A.: *Le Sleswig et la Paix*, pp. 248 et seq.
[5] *Declaration by Governments of the United States of America, Great Britain, and France in regard to the Occupation of the Rhine Provinces* (Cmd. 240). For the negotiations preceding this agreement, see also Mantoux, P.: 'L'Histoire à la conférence de la paix,' *L'Esprit international*, January 1929, pp. 39–50.

out by Germany, a part of the occupied area was to be evacuated a the end of each period of five years: first the area around Cologne then that around Coblenz, and finally, after fifteen years, the souther section, including Mainz. Provision was made for the reoccupa tion of evacuated territory in the event of German refusal t observe reparation obligations, and for the complete withdrawa of troops from the Rhineland in the event of complete fulfilmen of the Treaty by Germany in less than fifteen years. So fa Part XIV of the Treaty remained within the scope of its label 'Guarantees of Execution.' Only the final paragraph of Article 42 revealed the origin of these provisions in the preoccupation o France with the problem of security. This paragraph provided that, if at the end of fifteen years the guarantees against unprovoked aggression by Germany should not be considered sufficient by the Allied and Associated Governments, evacuation might be delayed to the extent regarded as necessary for the purpose of obtaining the required guarantees. This was the additional article pu forward by Clemenceau, with Wilson's approval, on 25th April.

The Declaration of 16th June which resulted from Lloyd George' agitation for revision provided that the Allied and Associated Powers would be ready to come to an agreement between them- selves to end the occupation as soon as Germany had given satis- factory guarantees for the fulfilment of her obligations. It consti- tuted a friendly understanding between Great Britain, France, and the U.S.A. for the termination of the occupation on less onerous conditions than those stipulated in the Treaty.

Lloyd George's abortive effort to secure the revision of the occupation clauses coincided with the equally abortive endeavour of General Mangin to present the Conference with the *fait accompli* of a Rhineland Republic. It may be noted, however, that the separatist movement in the Rhineland was not, at the outset, an artificially fostered movement. In the first weeks of the armistice there prevailed among Rhenish Catholic leaders and Rhenish industrialists a strong feeling in favour of autonomy. Primarily a reaction against the political and social disorders which threatened to overwhelm the rest of Germany, this feeling inevitably waned as the fear of revolutionary disturbances passed away. As the Prussian Government reaffirmed its authority, the more influential person- alities, like Adenauer, Burgomaster of Cologne, abandoned the cause of separatism. It was at this juncture, when others withdrew, that Dr. Dorten emerged into prominence as leader of the separatist movement. The French military authorities at first frowned on the Comité du Rhin, which he organized in the first days of March 1919. Not until the end of April was Dorten able to establish direct contact with General Mangin. Mangin himself aimed at the complete separation of the Rhineland from Germany, as a preliminary to its annexation by France. Dorten envisaged the inclusion of the Rhineland state within a federal German republic. An understanding between Mangin and Dorten's group was reached, after prolonged consultation, on 17th May 1919, as a result of which it was decided to proclaim the Rhineland Republic at Coblenz. The subsequent course of events is well known. Mangin, hoping to aid the separatists, communicated with General Liggett, Commander of the American troops at Coblenz; Liggett informed Pershing, and Pershing informed President Wilson; the President complained to Clemenceau, who thereupon ordered Mangin to observe an attitude of strict neutrality. On 1st June the Rhineland Republic was proclaimed at Wiesbaden; but, lacking Mangin's active support, it proved a fiasco.[1]

CHAPTER XV

SECURITY: THE MILITARY FRONTIER OF FRANCE

BETWEEN England and France stretches the English Channel, a mere nineteen miles wide at its narrow eastern end, yet wide enough for its waters to form an 'unplumb'd, salt, estranging sea.' To the sense of security which in the past it has induced in the British people may be ascribed in large measure the clash of British and French views on European questions. For centuries the navy, mounting guard in the North Sea and the Channel, has kept England free from invasion. Confidence in the navy's ability to keep the enemy in time of war confined to his own shores has made possible the restriction of British land forces in time of peace to a level derisory by continental standards. The navy has been counted on, should war come, to shelter the island throughout the initial period of military weakness, during which the country may proceed to rearm; and eventually it becomes the task of the navy to cover the transport of men and munitions to any part where attack seems possible and desirable.

Such immunity from invasion is denied to a Continental country; yet the ambition of France in 1919 was to procure for herself a

[1] Dorten, H. A.: 'The Rhineland Movement,' *Foreign Affairs*, April 1925; Dorten, H. A.: 'Le General Mangin en Rhénanie,' *Revue des Deux Mondes*, July 1, 1937; Traversay, G. de: 'La première Tentative de République rhénane,' *Revue de Paris*, November 15 and December 1, 1928; Mangin, Gen.: 'Lettres de Rhénanie,' *Revue de Paris*, April 1, 1936. See also Rathenau's comment in Allen, H. T.: *My Rhineland Journal*, p. 374, and Noyes' comment in *U.S.A. Foreign Relations*, 1920, ii, p. 296. Both Rathenau and Noyes agree that there existed at the outset a very substantial feeling in favour of the creation of a Rhenish state.

similar degree of protection. 'You forget,' Clemenceau exclaimed to Lloyd George, 'that in your isle, behind the rampart of the seas, you are sheltered; but as for us, we are on land with a vulnerable frontier. We must have a barrier behind which our people, who have few children, can work in security.'[1] The intractability of the problem of security resulted primarily from this French insistence on the provision of safeguards against actual invasion. For such safeguards could be found only in solid military guarantees, either of a geographical or of a political nature; either a military frontier beyond the eastern boundary of France, or political agreements capable of assuring immediate military assistance in the event of war. The very security enjoyed by the islanders disqualified them from understanding the apprehension of their neighbours. French preoccupation with the mobilization of force against an invader for long appeared an expression of unregenerate militarism to those who, more fortunately situated, were tempted to proclaim the all-sufficient potency of the mobilization of good-will.

The French demand for territorial arrangements to provide security against invasion across the north-eastern frontier was based upon the contention that the defence of France could not be effectively organized on the old political frontier which France had possessed before the loss of Alsace-Lorraine. That frontier, which was in fact restored by the Treaty of Versailles, may be divided into three main sections. The first section follows the line of the Rhine from the Swiss frontier north of Basle to the confluence of the Rhine and the Lauter. The second section extends in a direction roughly perpendicular to the Rhine from the Lauter to the Belgian frontier north-east of Longwy. The third section is the Franco-Belgian frontier which runs along the southern slope of the Ardennes, goes over the hills between the Meuse and the Sambre, and then crosses the plain to the coast east of Dunkirk.[2]

The danger which threatened France on the Franco-Belgian frontier had been amply demonstrated by the Schlieffen Plan, though it could hardly be forgotten that the French General Staff had left this frontier in 1914 in a singularly defenceless condition. Yet certainly Nature is begrudging of assistance to military defence

[1] Tardieu, A.: *Le Sleswig et la Paix*, p. 252.
[2] There appears to be no good modern military geography of the Franco-German frontier. See, however, Johnson, D. W.: *Topography and Strategy in the World War*. The essays by General Bourgeois in *Comité d'Etudes: Travaux*, 2 vols., Paris, 1918, would be of value, but no copy is available in England. For older writers, see Marga, A.: *Géographie militaire*, vol. i, Paris, 1885, and Niox, G.: *Géographie militaire*, vol. i, Paris, 1893. On the historical geography of the French frontiers, see Lavallée, T.: *Les Frontières de la France*, Paris, 1864, and Mirot, L.: *Manuel de la géographie historique de la France*, Paris, 1929.

in this coastal plain, where the streams run at right angles to the frontier. Its vulnerability made the defence of Belgium a vital interest to France, with the result that the two countries were united in 1919 in demanding the abrogation of Belgian neutrality and the revision of the eastern frontier of Belgium in order to ensure that in the future Belgium should be more effectively defended.

To the south, the restoration of Alsace-Lorraine in 1918 constituted a considerable strategic gain, less perhaps on account of the value of the Alsatian Rhine as a military barrier than through the expulsion from Alsace of the German forces, which before 1914 had been a constant menace. French control over Alsace largely removed also the danger that the defence of the Belfort Gap might be turned by a German attack through the Swiss territory of the Porrentruy salient. Strategic considerations had always mingled with sentiment in the demand for the restoration of the lost provinces.

The really critical section of the frontier was the central section, which after leaving the Lauter crosses the Low Vosges, cuts the Saar to the north of Sarregemuines, runs parallel with but south of the river as far as the banks of the Moselle, crosses the Moselle just north of Sierck, and then forms the southern boundary of Luxemburg till it touches Belgium. Across this part of the frontier ran the historic avenues of invasion from Germany—the route along the Moselle valley between the Hunsrück and the Eifel, and the routes from the Pfalz converging on the Saar valley. This, in the French mind, was the 'mutilated' frontier of 1815. The first Treaty of Paris, signed in May 1814, had left to France both Saarlouis, held since 1684, and Saarbrück, held only since 1793. The second Treaty of Paris, signed after Waterloo, in November 1815, pushed the French frontier back south of the Saar. Both Saarlouis and Saarbrück were then lost. Farther east the frontier was pushed back in 1815 from the line of the Queich, where it had been fixed in 1814, to the line of the Lauter. Thus from a military viewpoint the frontier of 1815–1871 was considerably weaker than that of 1814.

For economic reasons, however, the French were not prepared in 1919 to be satisfied even with the restoration of the 1814 frontier, for it would leave a large part of the Saar coalfield outside France. France wanted the coal above all. The war had revealed the importance of coal for national defence. Not only had the shortage of fuel been—and till the end of 1920 remained—a cause of great anxiety on the home front; in addition, it was a vital element in war potential. From this angle France had cause for anxiety. Before the war she had produced only two-thirds of her coal consumption; the balance had been drawn from Great Britain, Germany, and Belgium. The mines in the north-east, whence came nearly half the pre-war French coal production, had been deliberately wrecked by the Germans during their withdrawal. The restoration of the Lorraine iron-fields would accentuate still further the French shortage of coal, which, it seemed, could only be alleviated by the acquisition of the Saar mines. But the annexation of the entire coalfield would involve a frontier well beyond the 1814 line. It would mean French rule throughout the Saar valley east of Merzig.

To meet strategic requirements it would probably have been necessary to advance the frontier still farther. Foch, in November 1918, proposed a line starting from the junction of the Saar and the Moselle south of Trier and running eastwards to the line of the Queich, reaching the Rhine at Germersheim. At the time, the French Government may have thought of pressing for this strategic frontier,[1] but the proposal was not put forward during the Paris Conference. It was not, however, altogether forgotten, for in March 1919 Tardieu told Philip Kerr that, if the Rhenish provinces were not separated from Germany, France would demand as alternative provision for her security a strategic frontier from just south of Trier to a point on the Rhine some miles north of Landau.[2] But the French, the British, and the Americans alike sought to establish a geographic basis of French security by means other than the annexation of territory to suit military needs; the French sought an advanced military barrier on the Rhine, while the British and Americans deemed that the creation of a demilitarized zone would, with other non-territorial safeguards, give ample protection.

In consequence, the discussion on the Saar at the Peace Conference turned mainly round the economic aspects of the question, and the solution ultimately reached was a compromise between economic and demographic considerations. The French Government claimed at the outset the restoration of the 1814 frontier, including the Landau salient; the ownership of the Saar mines both inside and beyond this frontier; and the subjection of the Saar industrial area beyond the 1814 frontier to a special régime in order to facilitate the exploitation of the mines by the French. Lloyd George was prepared to concede the 1814 frontier; Clemenceau had counted on his acquiescence ever since the London Conference in December 1918.[3] But, perhaps as a lever against the French,

[1] See Cambon's Note of November 26, 1918, in *Miller*, ii, pp. 206–214, and Map constituting Doc. 49, p. 215. See also Malleterre, Gen.: *La bonne Frontière militaire de la France*, pp. 64–65.   [2] *Anglo-French Negotiations*, p. 61.
[3] Ribot, A.: *Journal*, p. 256; Poincaré, R.: *Au Service de la France*, x, p. 378; *Anglo-French Negotiations*, pp. 69, 83. See also Friedensburg, F.: 'Die geheimen Abmach-

Lloyd George insisted that territorial annexation and control of the mines should be regarded not as complementary but as alternative proposals. Lloyd George's acquiescence sharpened the conflict between Clemenceau and Wilson: the latter, against the advice of Colonel House and the American experts, rigidly opposed the 1814 frontier. Clemenceau had perforce to abandon this demand. The President, for his part, conceded from the start that France had a just claim to draw on the Saar mines for coal by way of reparation, and after some hesitation he conceded too, at the instigation of his advisers, that the mines should pass in full ownership to France. At the time he hoped to leave the territory under German administration, but he came to realize that the working of the mines would be impossible under French ownership combined with German rule. Once the French right to reparation in the form of a transfer of ownership was admitted, the establishment of an autonomous government under the League was the soundest form of administration for the territory that could be devised. Wilson arrived at this ineluctable conclusion, but he balanced this concession by exacting French assent not only to a plebiscite at the end of fifteen years, but also to the return of the mines to German ownership if the Saar reverted to Germany. Clearly, apart from the prospect of some impetus to the industrial recovery of France through the assured supply of coal, the solution reached made no contribution to the security of France. The construction of fortifications in the Saar basin was explicitly forbidden, though long after the signature of the Treaty French troops remained in the territory, contrary to the spirit if not to the letter of the Saar clauses.

There was another frontier problem which received much less attention than the Saar question at the Peace Conference—the problem of Luxemburg. Luxemburg, an independent state of 250,000 inhabitants, had been neutralized and demilitarized in 1867. Its status made it the unresisting prey of the German army in 1914. To leave it unprotected was to open the way for renewed invasion, since, by its position of dominance over the Moselle valley, it occupied a position of vital importance for the defence of France. It is at times suggested that the French Government entertained annexationist designs on Luxemburg, but, though a group in France urged annexation and though the activities of the army of occupation gave rise to suspicion, the weight of evidence is against the allegation.[1] Consideration of the question of

ungen zwischen Clemenceau und Lloyd George vom Dezember 1918,' *Berliner Monatshefte*, July–August 1938, pp. 702–715.

[1] On the French attitude, see *Anglo-French Negotiations*, p. 3; Tardieu: *La Paix*, pp. 253–254; Poincaré: *Au Service de la France*, x, p. 336; Ribot, A.: *Journal*, p. 257; and *Miller*, ii, pp. 206–214.

Luxemburg was postponed both by the Council of Ten and by the Council of Four because, as Clemenceau informed M. Reuter during his audience with the Council of Four on 28th May, other problems were deemed more urgent and fundamental. Even Article 40 of the Treaty of Versailles was inserted only at the last moment, after a British member of the Drafting Committee had drawn attention to the omission of any provision relating to Luxemburg. By Article 40 Germany recognized the termination of the customs union between Luxemburg and Germany, adhered to the termination of the régime of neutrality, and accepted in advance all international arrangements which might be concluded by the Allied and Associated Powers relating to the Grand Duchy. Since Luxemburg had been a signatory of the Treaty of 1867, its Government could assert the invalidity of any modification of that Treaty to which it had not assented. Luxemburg did not sign the Treaty of Versailles: its Government held that Article 40 of the Treaty could not bind Luxemburg. Despite Article 40, therefore, the Treaty of 1867 remained in force. The admission of Luxemburg to membership of the League confirmed the political status of Luxemburg as a sovereign and independent state. The application of Luxemburg for League membership on 23rd February 1920 was accompanied by a request for the maintenance of Luxemburg's status of neutrality; by a memorandum of 15th May 1920 the Council of the League recognized that the continued neutrality of Luxemburg was not incompatible with the Covenant. Thus the somewhat anomalous international status of Luxemburg as a neutralized and demilitarized state remained unchanged.[1]

The foreboding that France, if again involved in war with Germany, would prove unable to hold this north-eastern frontier against the invader dominated the minds of Frenchmen from the time of the armistice. Foch prophesied a new and yet more desperate trial if France failed to secure some special protection. 'The battle which we shall have to face in the plains of Belgium will be one in which we will suffer from a considerable numerical inferiority, and where we shall have no natural obstacle to help us. Once more, Belgium and northern France will be made a field of battle, a field of defeat; the enemy will soon be on the coast of Ostend and Calais, and once again those same countries will

[1] On the Luxemburg question at the Peace Conference, see *Miller*, iv, pp. 438–439; xiv, pp. 317–332; xv, p. 149; xvii, pp. 30–33; xix, p. 55. Minutes of the Council of Four on May 28 in Welter, N.: 'Le Grand Duché de Luxembourg après l'Armistice,' *Revue de Paris*, July 15, 1926. See also Aldrovandi, L.: *Guerra Diplomatica*, p. 437. On the customs union with Belgium, *Toynbee, 1920–23*, pp. 68–71, and Malmain, M.: *Les relations commerciales franco-belges de 1919 à 1923*, pp. 289–315. On the status of Luxemburg, Wehrer: 'La Politique de sécurité et d'arbitrage du Grand Duché de Luxembourg,' *Revue de droit international et de législation comparée*, vol. 59, 1932, pp. 326–366, 641–663.

fall a prey to havoc and devastation.' [1] Where, asked Foch, would France find protection against this destiny save on the Rhine? The Rhine forms a continuous potential barrier stretching for 600 miles from Switzerland to Holland. It was, he insisted, the sole barrier provided by nature along the line of invasion, a barrier whose value had been increased by the advance of military technique in so far as the use of the machine-gun compelled the attack to rely on the tank. Only on the Rhine would the Western Democracies find a reliable line of defence, which would both prevent any sudden attack by means of gases or tanks, and would, by the straightness of its course, stop any flanking movement. 'The prime necessity,' he concluded, 'is a natural frontier, a first barrier against a German invasion. There exists but one, the Rhine. It must be held by the Allied forces until a new order of things is established.' [2]

To this general thesis Foch held tenaciously, and Clemenceau, too, until the offer of the Anglo-American Treaty. Yet the actual arrangements proposed for the occupation varied curiously from time to time. Lloyd George complained to Clemenceau early in March 1919 that Foch 'had not explained what his plan really meant.' [3] In his first memorandum, of 27th November 1918, Foch demanded the grouping of all peoples west of the Rhine, including the Rhinelanders, in a common military system. That he soon dropped this proposal is understandable. In this first memorandum he insisted also on the military occupation of the left bank as the essential guarantee of security, and demanded bridgeheads on the Rhine as a guarantee for the payment of reparation. Similarly, in his memorandum of 10th January, while stressing the military value of holding bridgeheads, Foch dwelt on the need to 'ensure the military occupation by Allied forces of the Rhenish provinces on the left bank.' But when protesting against the Treaty, in the plenary session of the Peace Conference on 6th May, he disclaimed all desire to occupy the Rhineland itself. 'To hold the barrier of the Rhine,' he declared, 'would enable us to be the entire masters of the left bank, and to be masters with an inconsiderable expenditure of energy. . . . The occupation of the Rhine must therefore be maintained; I do not say "of the Rhine country." I do not occupy a country; I occupy the passages of the Rhine, which requires very little strength.' [4] Control of the Rhine bridges was indeed the essential French demand; it was this claim which was pressed in the official French Note of 25th February and by Tardieu

[1] *Anglo-French Negotiations*, p. 87.
[2] *Anglo-French Negotiations*, p. 24.
[3] Lloyd George: *Peace Treaties*, i, pp. 286–287.
[4] *Miller*, xx, pp. 176–181. See also Lhopital: *Foch, l'Armistice et la Paix*, pp. 224–225.

in the secret committee appointed on 10th March.   The occupation of bridgeheads on the Rhine would, it was maintained, cripple the offensive power of Germany, which was based on the transport capacity of the Rhine bridges.   'France would never feel safe or protected,' said Tardieu on 12th March, 'so long as it was possible for a German army to cross the Rhine, and this could only be prevented if the Allies had possession of the bridges.' [1]

Eventually, to the intense indignation of Marshal Foch, a settlement was reached on the basis of military occupation for fifteen years, subject to partial withdrawal at the end of each period of five years.   General Mordacq has explained why he advised the method of evacuation inserted in Article 429 of the Treaty.   He had to choose between the withdrawal of troops at the end of each five-year period westwards to a line running parallel with the Rhine, or their withdrawal southwards to a line running perpendicular to the Rhine.   He concluded that the second method was the more advantageous, since French troops would thereby remain in contact with the Rhine till the very end of the fifteen years— a consideration of importance from the point of view of defence, in Mordacq's judgement.   Considerations of offence also dictated, in his opinion, a southerly withdrawal.   The Allies ought to hold Mainz as long as possible; its position at the entrance to the valley of the Main opened the way for the invasion of Germany so as to drive a wedge between the north and the south. [2]

Yet Mordacq's plan of occupation was greeted with derision by military opinion when the conditions of peace became known. Foch was bitterly opposed to the settlement which Clemenceau had accepted.   Throughout April, when the Rhineland negotiations were being concluded, Clemenceau ignored Foch almost completely. The Marshal took advantage of the plenary session of the Conference on 6th May to register his protest.   'I beg leave to say,' he declared, 'that this Section XIV represents a guarantee which I should call equal to zero.'   Foch was not alone in his complaints about the neglect of military advice nor in his criticism of the occupation clauses.   First Wilson, and then, reluctantly, Lloyd George accepted these proposals without—so far as is known—consulting any military advisers.   General Bliss complained bitterly that he had been neglected by President Wilson.   Sir Henry Wilson thought

---

[1] *Anglo-French Negotiations*, p. 64. See, however, General Sarrail's criticism of bridgeheads in an article: 'Les Têtes de pont du Rhin,' *Revue politique et parlementaire*, July 10, 1920, pp. 40–59.   It may be noted that in 1925 Brigadier-General Spears put forward the proposal that a League Commission should be permanently stationed in the demilitarized zone, with authority to supervise the railways to ensure that they should not be adapted to the use of an army bent on military invasion.   He further suggested that machinery might be devised to ensure the destruction of the Rhine bridges if invasion threatened.   See *International Affairs*, May 1925.

[2] Mordacq, J. J. H.: *Le Ministère Clemenceau*, iii, p. 214.

that the evacuation proposals had been drawn up by the 'Frocks' without any soldier being consulted. 'Amazing proposals,' he termed them.[1]   Invited by Lloyd George to express his views on Mordacq's proposals after they had been accepted by the Council of Four, Sir Henry Wilson protested their absurdity in forthright terms.   While the Allies were strong and Germany weak, the Allied troops would hold the shortest and strongest line—the line of the Rhine.   When the Germans had recovered their strength and the Allies had grown weaker, the Allied troops would be required to hold a new line fixed without regard for military considerations.   From a military point of view, he added, 'there is no doubt that if a line is to be held other than the permanent frontier of Lorraine and in the Saar valley, that line must be the Rhine.   If it is thought wise, from a political point of view, to retire from the Rhine in stages, as Germany fulfils her obligations, these withdrawals ought, from a military point of view, to start from the south and not from the north.'[2]   It would appear that because, after the offer of the Anglo-American Treaty, Clemenceau pressed for occupation primarily as a guarantee for the execution of the Treaty, far too little consideration was given to the military aspect of the question.   The problem of security was side-tracked. The criticism levelled against the occupation clauses by soldiers gave rise at first to the belief that only non-military considerations could explain why this particular scheme of evacuation had been inserted in the Treaty.   Thus President Wilson in the American delegation meeting on 3rd June commented that he understood that the conviction prevailed in French military circles that the territory to be evacuated first was the most important from the military point of view; so he concluded that occupation was not really a military question at all.   The real object, he suggested, was 'the control of the navigation of the Rhine.'   General Bliss confirmed Wilson's opinion by adding: 'I think, as you just stated, it is almost entirely a political question rather than a military one, because no essential military objects will be accomplished by the military occupation of the territories proposed to be occupied under the proposed conditions.'[3]   Lloyd George shared the opinion of General Bliss.   'This occupation,' he protested, 'will be of no use to you against Germany; it's only a protection against your military and parliamentary opposition.'[4]

It is hardly unjust to describe the occupation clauses as the expression of an intentional misunderstanding.   Written into the

[1] Callwell, Sir C. E.: *Sir Henry Wilson*, ii, pp. 183–186.
[2] Lhopital: *Foch, l'Armistice et la Paix*, pp. 229–231.
[3] *Baker*, iii, p. 489.
[4] Tardieu, A.: *Le Sleswig et la Paix*, p. 249.

Treaty as a guarantee of execution which might, after the lapse of fifteen years, be of a sudden transformed into a guarantee of security, the Rhineland occupation was naturally regarded by the French from the outset as their essential rampart against Germany.   They were confirmed in this attitude by the miscarriage of the American and British Treaties of Guarantee.   What the military experts thought dangerous in the scheme of occupation was the proposal to evacuate the northern zone at the end of five years.   For this reason, until the Locarno Conference, successive French governments sought to justify the postponement of the evacuation of Cologne, which would normally fall due in 1925.   Inevitably, they looked to German non-fulfilment of Treaty obligations to provide justification for the continued occupation of the whole area.   This intention, it may be, lurked in Clemenceau's mind.   In the French Council of Ministers, on 25th April 1919, he is reported to have turned to Poincaré with the comment: 'M. le President, you are much younger than I.   In fifteen years I shall not be here.   In fifteen years the Germans will not have executed all the clauses of the Treaty, and in fifteen years, if you do me the honour to come to my tomb, you'll be able to say, I am sure, "We are on the Rhine, and we stay there."' [1]   So the feeling that France was seeking, as a measure of security, to prolong the Rhineland occupation—perhaps to make it permanent—continued to embitter Franco-British relations until, in 1925, through Sir Austen Chamberlain's consummate handling of the Cologne incident and of the Locarno negotiations, Great Britain and France came to see eye to eye as to the character of the Rhineland occupation. [2]

Of the French plan for the creation of an independent Rhineland, which was at the outset of the Peace Conference coupled with the project of the Rhineland occupation, little is known save that the left bank of the Rhine was to be detached from Germany and formed into an autonomous state linked with France by a customs union.   Though Tardieu was ready to agree to a plebiscite in the area after a few years, Clemenceau refused to agree to any such compromise.   He admitted that 'everything should be done to make the Rhinelanders prosperous and contented'; they should be relieved of the obligation to pay reparation and should be given economic privileges; but he bluntly told Lloyd George and Colonel House, early in March 1919, that 'he did not believe in the principle of self-determination, which allowed a man to clutch at your throat the first time it was convenient to him, and he would not consent to any limitation of time being placed upon the enforced separation

[1] Mermeix: Le Combat des Trois, pp. 229–230.   Cf. 'Tout cela confirme ce que me disait Clemenceau: "L'Allemagne ne paiera pas et nous resterons"'—M. Barrès, commenting on conversation with Clemenceau (Les grands Problèmes du Rhin, p. 386).
[2] See pp. 162, 367.

of the Rhenish Republic from the rest of Germany.' With the Rhineland Republic, it may be conjectured, Clemenceau looked forward to concluding a special agreement for the occupation of the Rhineland itself. A month before the offer of the Anglo-American Treaty, in consequence of which Clemenceau agreed to set a time-limit to the occupation, he had told the Senate Committee on Foreign Affairs that the military occupation would continue until the Rhineland was disposed to unite with France.[1] It is indeed difficult to see how the control of the Rhine bridges could have been other than extremely precarious without the separation of the Rhineland from Germany, or at least without maintaining permanent control of the principal lines of communication on the left bank. It was almost inevitable, therefore, that French support of the separatist movement should revive as the idea of prolonging the occupation gained ground in the early twenties.

Though the stimulation of separatism was in keeping with the Foch thesis, the occupation of the Ruhr was not. After 1920, as before, Foch kept to the theme: 'With solid bridgeheads on the Rhine, we have nothing to fear.'[2] From 1919 to 1923 he remained at all times reluctant to advance beyond the Rhine into the Ruhr. The Ruhr occupation gave promise, however, of one additional screen against German attack which was abandoned only with the greatest reluctance. Partly as a 'productive pledge,' partly as a measure calculated to obstruct German mobilization, Poincaré sought to secure the transfer of the management of the Rhineland railways to an Inter-Allied Company. In its direction he was prepared to allow representatives of the Rhineland to participate. 'It is unnecessary,' wrote Poincaré to the French Ambassador in London, when first putting forward this suggestion in June 1923, 'to dwell on the value of this pledge from the viewpoint of security.'[3] The importance which he attached to bringing the entire Rhineland railway system under unified Allied control is attested by his efforts, in December 1923, to extend to the British zone of occupation the authority of the Franco-Belgian Railway Régie which had been set up in March to administer the railways in the French and Belgian zones and in the Ruhr. Though for a few weeks the British zone was subjected to a virtual blockade in consequence of the British refusal to assent, Poincaré failed to achieve his purpose. A later attempt to serve the same end in a different way was no more successful. When the London Conference met, in June 1924, to

[1] Lloyd George: *Peace Treaties*, i, p. 286; Ribot, A.: *Journal*, pp. 259–260; *House*, iv, pp. 356–357; *Anglo-French Negotiations*, pp. 63, 67–68.
[2] Le Goffic, C.: 'Deux Entretiens avec le Maréchal Foch,' *Revue universelle*, vol. 37, April 15, 1929, pp. 129–147.
[3] D.D.: *Documents relatifs aux Notes allemandes des 2 mai et 5 juin sur les Réparations* (Paris, 1923), pp. 35–36.

effect the liquidation of the Ruhr adventure, the French military authorities demanded the organization of a separate Rhineland railway administration under Allied control. Eventually they narrowed down their demand to the employment of 5000 French and Belgian railwaymen on certain parts of the railway system. Since this demand was refused, Herriot agreed to be content with the incorporation of the necessary railway personnel in the army of occupation.[1] Thus the attempt to detach the Rhineland railways from the administration of the rest of the German railway system ended in complete failure.

That the French eastern frontier was, as Lord Curzon said, 'in a sense the outer frontier of Great Britain herself' became after the Great War almost an axiom of British policy. It was generally admitted that, if Germany should ever again attempt to invade France, Great Britain would be compelled, in the interests of her own security, to fight alongside the French. For this very reason Poincaré rejected the British proposal in 1922 for an Anglo-French pact limited to the defence of the territory of France. It was, he commented, 'a mystification without any real value'[2]; it would bind Great Britain to do only what she would; even in the absence of a definite commitment, need to do for her own sake.

For France it was not enough that Great Britain should—to quote Lord Curzon's description of the British offer in 1922—promise to come to her aid in the event of 'a repetition of the experience which she had before endured.'[3] France sought to ensure that her experience of the Great War should not be repeated —that, in short, the next war should be fought on German, not French, soil. The creation of an advanced military frontier seemed the only adequate safeguard. It was, the French added, as much a safeguard for Great Britain and the U.S.A. as for France herself. The French Memorandum of 25th February 1919 warned the Allies that, if northern France were overrun, 'the overseas democracies would be debarred from waging a Continental war against any Power seeking to dominate the Continent. They would be deprived of their nearest and most natural battleground. Nothing would remain for them but economic and naval warfare.'[4]

The avowed reasons for British opposition to the French plan are best studied in Philip Kerr's report of his discussions with André Tardieu on 11th and 12th March 1919. The strongest objections would be raised in England, said Kerr, against any proposal for the permanent maintenance of British forces in German

[1] *Cmd.* 2270, p. 120. Bardoux: *Le Socialisme au pouvoir*, pp. 245–254. *The Times*, July 18, August 14, 1924.
[2] *Anglo-French Negotiations*, pp. 133, 166.
[3] *Anglo-French Negotiations*, p. 133.
[4] *Anglo-French Negotiations*, p. 43.

territory. Nor could the British Government ignore the views of the Dominions, whose representatives had told him that they would not leave a man in Europe, nor bind themselves in any way to interfere in purely European questions such as they considered the Rhineland question to be. It would be highly distasteful and difficult for the British Government to maintain the separation of the Rhineland by military force. A vigorous Rhenish demand for reunion would certainly develop; its propaganda would meet with sympathy from some quarters in England. Would the troops of occupation be used to repress such agitation in the Rhineland? 'If local conflicts occur, whither will they lead? If war results from these conflicts, neither England nor her Dominions will have that sympathy with France which animated them in the last war.' Any settlement which imposed an undue burden on Great Britain, or committed the country to obligations such as the permanent separation of the Rhenish provinces from the rest of Germany against their will, would offend the British sense of justice and fair play and so lead to the estrangement of Great Britain and France.[1]

It is no disparagement of this reasoning to add that the French plan ran counter to the traditional interests of Great Britain in western Europe. 'All our greatest wars have been fought,' declared Sir Austen Chamberlain, 'to prevent one great military Power dominating Europe, and at the same time dominating the coasts of the Channel and the ports of the Low Countries.'[2] The implied principle applied as much to France as to Germany. 'The experience of the past,' wrote the Historical Adviser to the Foreign Office, 'has always shown that the independence of Holland and of Belgium is closely connected with the political condition of the Rhineland. In the old days it was for this reason always necessary for England to oppose by every means French domination over the Rhine provinces, for with France stationed at Coblenz and Cologne the real independence of Belgium, military, economic, and political, must inevitably disappear. This is as true now as it ever was in the past.' Small Rhineland states under the influence of France, he continued, 'might be nearly as dangerous to Belgian independence as if this district were actually annexed to France.'[3] British statesmen may be assumed to have viewed French domination of the Rhineland with as little equanimity in the twentieth as in the nineteenth century.

The need of some special protection for France was, however, disputed neither by the British nor by the American delegation at the Peace Conference. One form of protection met with general

[1] *Anglo-French Negotiations*, pp. 59–69.
[2] 182 *H.C. Deb.*, March 24, 1925, col. 315.
[3] Headlam-Morley, Sir J.: *Studies in Diplomatic History*, p. 167.

agreement—the demilitarization of the left bank of the Rhine, which was stipulated by Articles 42–44 of the Treaty of Versailles. In later years the belief developed that the demilitarization of the Rhineland was part of the price paid to induce France to drop her demand for its separation from Germany; but in fact the establishment of the demilitarized zone was taken for granted from the very outset of the Conference, and was included among the military terms of peace before the Rhineland discussions had really commenced. It was, Lloyd George said, 'the original British proposition' [1] for the solution of the Rhineland problem. It was a natural expression in the twentieth century of that concern for the independence of the Low Countries which had for centuries constituted the foundation of British policy towards Europe. This, indeed, was the burden of Sir James Headlam-Morley's advice in 1925: 'If Germany were to recover her full military power, then, as in the past, the German army, occupying the country between Cologne, Aachen, and Trèves, would be a spearhead directed at France and Belgium. It is the obvious dictate of wisdom and foresight to avoid this danger in the future. This is done by Articles 42–44 of the Treaty of Versailles.' [2]   But, in Great Britain, France was commonly regarded as the sole beneficiary of Articles 42–44. Sir Austen Chamberlain's declaration—'The peace of the world and the peace of the British Empire depends upon the observance and maintenance of that Treaty provision' [3]—remained unique in the annals of British foreign policy.

In 1919 the French, the Socialists apart, denied that the mere demilitarization of the Rhineland could suffice for the security of France. The first of their reasons may be stated briefly. Attention was drawn to the danger that if the bridges of the Rhine were not guarded they might be suddenly seized by German forces, which could then deploy on the left bank. The conclusion was drawn that demilitarization could provide no satisfactory alternative to Allied control of the Rhine bridges.

On the second reason for the French attitude it is necessary to dwell. The French realized that the permanence of the régime would depend on the determination of the Allies to maintain it. They asked, accordingly, what guarantees were proposed to ensure German observance of the obligation of demilitarization. Clemenceau, in March 1919, demanded the institution of a Joint Commission of Inspection to watch over the zone; he demanded, too, that in the event of the entry of German troops into the zone, France should be entitled to occupy the Rhine bridgeheads, and

---

[1] *Anglo-French Negotiations*, p. 92.
[2] Headlam-Morley, Sir J.: *Studies in Diplomatic History*, p. 168.
[3] 182 *H.C. Deb.*, March 24, 1925, col. 317.

to call on Great Britain and the U.S.A. for military assistance under the proposed Anglo-American Treaty of Guarantee. In return for a guarantee of the demilitarized zone along these lines, Clemenceau was probably prepared to drop quite definitely the occupation of the Rhine as the basis of French security.[1] Lloyd George at that time, though opposed to granting France the contingent right to occupy the Rhine bridgeheads, was willing to give a British guarantee of the maintenance of the zone.[2] President Wilson was not prepared to go quite so far; in his Note of 28th March 1919 he proposed only to stigmatize any violation of the zone as a hostile act against the signatories of the Treaty, and to pledge the United States to come immediately to the assistance of France in the event of any unprovoked movement of aggression against her by Germany.   This proposal fell short of the conditions that would, in Clemenceau's judgement, justify the abandonment of military occupation, for which, accordingly, Clemenceau continued to press.   The outcome has been recorded; the President agreed to the equivocal occupation clauses of the Treaty, and Clemenceau to the formula of Wilson's Note of 28th March, which was incorporated in the Treaty as Article 44.   A correct interpretation of this Article and of the draft Treaties of Guarantee would seem to be that they would have given rise to a right, but not an obligation, on the part of Great Britain and the U.S.A. to treat violation of the demilitarized zone as a *casus belli*.

The question of a British guarantee of the demilitarized zone came to the fore again as a major issue during the negotiations for an Anglo-French Pact in the first months of 1922.   The British draft treaty submitted by Lloyd George to Briand would have pledged immediate military aid by Great Britain 'in the event of a direct and unprovoked aggression against the soil of France by Germany.'   It was thus more restricted in scope than the abortive Treaties of Guarantee, which had not made assistance conditional on an actual invasion of the territory of France.   Both Briand and Poincaré demanded that German violation of the demilitarized zone should be held to constitute an act of aggression against France—and against Britain, added Poincaré—just as much as an actual invasion of French soil.   On this proposal Lord Curzon commented that, in his view, British public opinion would not consent to go to war automatically for the defence of the demilitarized zone if it were assailed.   'I do not say,' he added, 'that on an appreciation of the circumstances of the case, if and when it arose, they might not both be willing and be bound to

[1] This would appear to be the significance of Tardieu's proposal of March 20, 1919: *Miller*, vii, Doc. 559, p. 29.   See also *Miller*, vii, pp. 57–59.
[2] See his Memorandum of March 26, 1919: *Anglo-French Negotiations*, p. 82.

do so. But they would not accept in advance an obligation so formidable and so ill-defined.' The British Government was prepared to give a pledge only to 'concert' with France in the event of any threatened violation of the zone.[1]

In 1925, by the Treaty of Locarno, France appeared to have secured the long-sought guarantee. The events of March 1936 revealed its delusive nature. The interpretation of the relevant articles of the Treaty of Locarno provides a feast for legal wits: they may be construed to support the conclusion that they afforded 'no guarantee of demilitarization as such.'[2] Yet that the intention in 1925 was to embody in the Treaty a firm guarantee of the demilitarized zone admits of no doubt. The following explanation of the paradox seems reasonable. The foundation of the Locarno Treaty was the undertaking by Germany and France not to attack each other. Briand doubtless insisted on reserving the right of France to take immediate action in the event of German violation of the zone, and desired that Great Britain also should bind herself to take immediate action in such circumstances. Chamberlain, with the Frankfort incident in mind,[3] may well have objected that immediate action could be permitted only in the event of a violation indicative of an intention to repudiate Articles 42–43—i.e. in the event of what might be called, in the terminology of the London Agreements concluded in August 1924,[4] a 'flagrant' breach. Stresemann probably suggested thereafter that not all flagrant breaches of Articles 42–43 could reasonably entitle France to take immediate action; the construction of fortifications could not take place so quickly as to preclude appeal to the Council of the League. Hence the wording of Article 2 of the Treaty of Locarno:

'. . . Germany and France mutually undertake that they will in no case attack or invade each other. . . .

'This stipulation shall not, however, apply in the case of:

'(1) The exercise of the right of legitimate defence, that is to say, resistance . . . to a flagrant breach of Articles 42 or 43 of the said Treaty of Versailles, if such breach constitutes an unprovoked act of aggression and by reason of the assembly of armed forces in the demilitarized zone immediate action is necessary. . . .'

Thereafter, in the process of interpretation, the word 'flagrant,' bequeathed by the Dawes Report, lost its original status. It was felt to have no meaning save that derived from the words which followed. The crucial question became: by what criterion could it be determined whether the assembly of armed forces in the demilitarized zone made immediate action necessary? The answer

---

[1] *Anglo-French Negotiations*, pp. 125, 131, 158.
[2] Wolfers, A.: *Britain and France between Two Wars*, p. 48.
[3] See p. 70.   [4] See p. 78.

seemed clear: immediate action was necessary only to meet an imminent threat of invasion; the delay involved in an appeal to the League would not be dangerous if armed forces entered the zone without seeking to cross the frontier. Thus the pith of the Locarno Treaty suffered decay.

On 7th March 1936, when German troops entered the demilitarized zone, the Flandin Ministry decided against independent action. Financial considerations are said to have been decisive; but misgivings concerning the bearing of the Treaty, together with memories of Frankfort and the Ruhr, may well have influenced the decision to appeal to the League and to consult the other Locarno signatories. For France this hesitation was fatal. Her failure to act might be held to signify that the German violation was not a breach of such flagrant character as to bring into play the obligation of the Guarantor Powers to come immediately to her aid. To delay was to play into the hands of Great Britain. On the British attitude Sir Austen Chamberlain's comment may perhaps be recalled: 'That has happened against which we guaranteed France, and Press and public opinion seek excuses for evading our pledge.' [1] The demilitarized zone abolished—just another of the injustices of Versailles gone—anyhow it could not last; better to rebuild without further fuss on the basis of the proposals refurbished for the occasion by the German Chancellor.

CHAPTER XVI

SECURITY: THE EXPLORATION OF POLITICAL GUARANTEES

THE denial in 1919 of the so-called physical or material guarantee of security which alone, in the judgement of Marshal Foch, could afford France protection, made imperative the effort to allay French apprehension by the proffer of some alternative safeguard against future German invasion. The abortive British and American Treaties of Guarantee, whereby Lloyd George and President Wilson induced Clemenceau to drop the demand for the permanent occupation of the Rhineland, formed the prelude to a prolonged endeavour to solve the problem of French security—or, more broadly, the problem of European security— by the method of 'political guarantees,' i.e. by the interchange between states of pledges of assistance against attack. No useful purpose would be served by relating once again the tortuous

[1] Petrie, Sir C.: *Life and Letters of Austen Chamberlain*, ii, p. 408.

history of the protracted negotiations directed towards the creation of a system of European security; that history has been related in numerous works, and until access is permissible to official sources of information it is improbable that new facts will emerge to lend new interest to the familiar record.   In this chapter nothing more is attempted than to review from the special angle of Anglo-French relations the major problems encountered in the endeavour to make provision for the security of France through the medium of political guarantees.

If the purpose be to steer clear of the tangles of diplomatic negotiation, perhaps the most hopeful point of departure is to consider the divergent British and French conceptions of security. A suitable text may be found in the phrase used by Sir James Headlam-Morley with regard to the Locarno Treaties.   They had as their object, he wrote, 'not security in war, but security against war.' [1]   The phrase indicates neatly the difference of approach to the problem of security which hindered the conclusion of any agreement equally satisfactory to the two countries.   What appeared from the British viewpoint a fitting solution was from the French viewpoint no solution at all.   A divergence of judgement concerning the conditions of security is apparent at every stage of the negotiations from 1919 to 1936.

From the first months of peace the French viewed the renewal of war as a very real danger of the immediate future.   They were in no doubt as to the quarter from which danger threatened.   They sought first and foremost, therefore, security in the war which seemed to them imminent—security above all, it must be repeated, against invasion.   It may be noted that this military preoccupation with defence against invasion was itself in large measure a legacy of the war.   Before 1914 French strategists, like those of other countries, had concentrated on one objective—to meet and defeat the enemy in battle; where the fighting took place concerned them little.   But after the war a population which had known the horrors of invasion was intent on obtaining safeguards against a repetition of that experience; while for strategists, aware in 1918 as they had not been in 1914 of the dependence of military power on industrial production, it was essential to prevent the industrial areas adjacent to the north-eastern frontier from passing in time of war into the hands of the enemy.

This change of attitude was one factor which made 'security' far more difficult of attainment after the war than before.   Since the protection of an advanced military frontier had been denied, there appeared only one way of assuring the integrity of the national territory.   That was to confront the would-be invader with a

[1] Headlam-Morley, Sir J.: *Studies in Diplomatic History*, p. 8.

superior military force at the very start of hostilities. For that force to be available as soon as war began, it needed to be maintained and trained in time of peace. Superiority attained slowly as war proceeded would be of no avail; it would hold out no more than the hope of victory after a long struggle conducted again on the devastated soil of France. It was this line of reasoning which led the French to impugn the efficacy of any pledge of military assistance the execution of which was not worked out in detail in a supplementary military convention. Foreign reinforcements could serve to prevent invasion only if ready to co-operate with French forces at the very outset of war in accordance with a prearranged plan. Assistance given gradually, at a pace set by the slow process of mobilization in time of war, would leave France to bear alone the brunt of the attack during the most critical phase—the initial hostilities. This thesis was first advanced by Clemenceau and Foch in 1919: it was reiterated by Briand and Poincaré in 1922; its fullest exposition is to be found in the observations of the French delegation in the Permanent Advisory Commission during the discussions which preceded the Draft Treaty of Mutual Assistance in 1923.[1] In the light of this thesis the Locarno Treaty of Guarantee was an illusory safeguard, because the very nature of the Treaty— the assumption of an obligation by Great Britain and Italy towards both France and Germany—excluded the possibility of any supplementary military convention. It was not until March 1936— seventeen years to a day after the offer of the original British Treaty of Guarantee—that the British Government gave its consent to the Anglo-French staff conversations which the French had at all times deemed indispensable. The French attitude was never more bluntly expressed than by Balfour in the well-known British statement on the Geneva Protocol: 'Brute force is what they fear, and only brute force enlisted in their defence can (as they believe) give them the security of which they feel the need.' Enlisted, it must be added, on the first day in accordance with a prearranged plan.

Linked with this military preoccupation there was in the French conception of security a secondary element—the sense of the vital import to France of the preservation of the territorial settlement in eastern and central Europe. 'She sees, and sees rightly'—to quote again the Historical Adviser of the Foreign Office—'that the future of Europe is bound up with the defence of the new states, and she has therefore taken the obvious course of making alliances and military arrangements by which they are, in case of danger, assured of the full support of the French army.'[2] Exposed

---

[1] *Report of the Temporary Mixed Commission*, August 20, 1923, pp. 14 et seq. Cf. *Cmd.* 2169, pp. 52, 73–75, 148–150.
[2] Headlam-Morley, Sir J.: *Studies in Diplomatic History*, pp. 183–184.

like France to German invasion, Poland and Czechoslovakia saw eye to eye with France on the question of security. Their armies were held in readiness to meet attack; they welcomed mutual arrangements for prompt military assistance in the event of war. Their subjugation would assure Germany the domination of eastern and central Europe; that the subjection of France would speedily follow was, until the apostasy of Munich, a well-founded article of French faith. First Sadowa, then Sedan—this theme recurred time and again. Hence the treaties which linked France with the new states—those of 19th February 1921 with Poland and of 25th January 1924 with Czechoslovakia—which, though providing for consultation and for the pursuance of a common policy in any critical situation, imposed no military obligations; and the Locarno Treaties of 16th October 1925 with the same countries, which comprised reciprocal pledges of military assistance in the event of unprovoked attack by Germany. Till 1938 France steadily refused to divorce the organization of security in western Europe from the stabilization of the territorial settlement in eastern Europe. Germany, however, had accepted her new frontiers under duress, and it was apparent that she would press for their revision as soon as she regained her military strength. Security from the French viewpoint involved, therefore, the maintenance of the European territorial settlement in the face of opposition from potentially the most powerful of European states. Therein may be found a second reason for the intractable character of the problem of French security.

In the conjunction of these two elements in the French conception of security—preoccupation with defence against invasion, and concern for the stability of the territorial settlement—lay the genesis of the French thesis regarding the interconnexion between disarmament and security. From 1920 to 1935 the armed forces of Germany were limited by the military clauses of the Treaty of Versailles; those of France and her allies were subject to no regulation. During those years the peace of Europe rested on the armed preponderance of France. The extension of disarmament to countries other than Germany would modify to Germany's advantage the existing distribution of military power. It would sound the knell of French ascendancy on the Continent. The institution of some new safeguard seemed imperative to replace that which France would be called upon to abandon. As the prerequisite of disarmament, France sought, therefore, to vest her own armed preponderance, which in existing conditions constituted the guarantee of peace, in a collectivity of states organized in a system of compulsory arbitration and mutual defence. That was the primary signification of the French proposals for the organization of a system of collective security. They were designed to ensure that the superiority of the collective force mobilized against the aggressor should be immediately realizable, not achieved slowly in a war of attrition. Thereby they reflected the two essential elements in the French conception of security.

Enough has been written to indicate the character of the complex problem in the solution of which Great Britain was invited to participate. That invitation brooked no refusal. British participation was not, indeed, motivated—not, at least, until the rearmament of Nazi Germany—by any conviction of immediate and direct danger threatening Great Britain herself from the Continent. Nevertheless, Great Britain had both a particular and a general interest to serve in seeking to meet the French demand for security. Her particular interest coincided with that of France—to prevent Germany from ever combining control of the Channel ports with control of the North Sea ports. Her general interest was to foster the spirit of conciliation by the exercise of a restraining influence on France; the assurance of British support in the event of war was at all times the condition of keeping France from extreme courses. Almost each advance to France was occasioned by the desire to bring French policy into line with British policy: in 1919 to induce France to abandon the military frontier on the Rhine; in 1922 to secure the alignment of France with Great Britain on the problems of reparation and reconstruction; in 1925 to secure the evacuation of Cologne and, more generally, to effect the final liquidation of the Rhineland programme; in 1936 to open the way for the resumption of negotiations with Germany after the reoccupation of the demilitarized zone. Isolation was never for Great Britain a practicable policy; to have left France in the lurch might at any time have precipitated France along one of two courses—either an understanding with Germany without British participation, or an attempt to utilize the artificial military superiority of France in order to keep Germany suppressed. Neither course could fail to be detrimental, and possibly disastrous, to Great Britain, the first in the long run, the second more immediately. The desire to attend to imperial and oceanic problems neither unduly encumbered by European commitments nor embarrassed by European complications dictated as the objective of British policy the reconciliation of France and Germany through the mediatory influence of Great Britain. No advance could be made towards this objective save through willingness on the part of Great Britain to participate in the organization of European security.

For these reasons Great Britain was prepared to give a pledge that she would come to the assistance of France in the event of German aggression. But, judged by the French criteria, an unadorned pledge constituted no guarantee of security such as would justify the reduction of national armaments. Great Britain declined, nevertheless, to be lured further along the road of Continental commitments. To most Englishmen a military convention with France—which was, after all, an indispensable condition of effective British participation in the defence of French territory—was simply unthinkable. Nor was there any division of opinion among Englishmen as to the wisdom of refraining from any specific commitment concerning the British attitude in the event of a disturbance of peace in eastern Europe. In 1922 the negotiations for an Anglo-French Pact broke down from failure to reach agreement on these two questions. Only by evading them were the Locarno negotiations brought to a successful conclusion. British policy with regard to the problem of security moved only within certain limits, which remained constant throughout the years of French ascendancy.

The objection to any agreement to hold staff conversations—and *a fortiori* to a military convention—was stated by Lord Curzon in his memorandum of 1st February 1922 on the French draft treaty: 'It will lead to the impression, and almost certainly to the demand, that each country shall maintain a certain proportion of forces, to be provided or utilized in a particular way. It will convey the idea, in a more concrete form than it would be prudent or safe to admit, of a military obligation the definition of which will rest not with Cabinets or Parliaments, but with the General Staffs.' [1] A conscientious War Minister might well regard this as less an objection to staff conversations than to the signature of the treaty itself. [2] Perhaps a more pertinent objection from the British viewpoint was that staff conversations or a military convention might in time of crisis be found to constitute a commitment far more automatic in operation than the simple engagement of a treaty. The latter would, in the event of war, leave within the discretion of the British Government the decision whether the circumstances which had arisen were such as to call into play the obligations of the treaty. [3] The consequences of staff conversations might be, as *The Nation* commented during the Locarno negotiations, 'to transfer the control of events, in times of political crisis, from the statesmen to the general staffs. When once a definite plan of joint operations has

---

[1] *Cmd.* 2169, p. 160.

[2] Lord Haldane: 'If you enter into covenants, if you say we guarantee the frontiers of certain Powers, however unlikely it may seem to the lay mind that those guarantees will have to be put into force, . . . the War Staffs of the three Services will set to work and get out plans for them, and, what is more, I should deplore the day in which they ceased to do that' (69 *Lords Deb.*, November 16, 1927, col. 102).

[3] Cf. Sir John Simon's statement on the Locarno Treaty: 281 *H.C. Deb.*, November 7, 1933, col. 61.

been concerted and the military preparations of each party adjusted thereto, it becomes exceedingly difficult, without an appearance of treachery, to refuse the promised assistance, whatever doubts may be entertained as to the legal or moral existence of the *causa* (sic) *foederis*.' [1]

The Gladstonian dictum that 'England should keep entire in her own hands the means of estimating her own obligations upon the various states of facts as they arise' was not then wholly ignored—so, at least, a Frenchman might judge—even in the conduct of British policy with regard to western Europe. As regards eastern Europe the dictum was observed in its pristine purity. The maintenance of the territorial settlement in north-western Europe was a vital British interest; that settlement, in any event, bade fair to be definitive. But no direct threat to the security of Great Britain would be involved in the modification of frontiers in eastern Europe, while there the frontiers were still the subject of acute contention. In the west the British stake was great, the risk of a guarantee seemingly small; in the east the stake seemed small, the risk undoubtedly great. 'The British people,' Lloyd George explained to Briand, in December 1921, 'were not very much interested in what happened on the eastern frontier of Germany: they would not be ready to be involved in quarrels which might arise regarding Poland or Danzig or Upper Silesia. On the contrary, there was a general reluctance to get mixed up in these questions in any way. . . . He did not think, therefore, that this country would be disposed to give any guarantees which might involve them in military operations in any eventuality in that part of the world.' [2] Successive Foreign Secretaries might vary the language; but until the reversal of British policy in March 1939 the theme remained unchanged. No principle of British policy was reiterated with greater frequency than the inability of the British Government to enter into new European commitments beyond those comprised in the Covenant and the Treaty of Locarno.

The failure of Great Britain and France to adopt a common standpoint on these questions may well be regarded as the outward expression of divergent conceptions of security. 'There is not, and there cannot be, any uniform notion of security. Everyone defines it in his own way,' remarked Jean Fabry during the debates on the Locarno Treaties.[3] For France, as a Continental state, adequacy of military preparation constituted the essential criterion of security. The Channel relieved Great Britain of the necessity of thinking of security in this manner, at least as far as land armaments were concerned. What Englishmen had to fear was not

[1] *The Nation*, July 8, 1925.   [2] *Anglo-French Negotiations*, pp. 112–113.
[3] *Chambre: Débats*, February 25, 1926, col. 970.

invasion, but entanglement in a war of European origin. While French policy, therefore, was directed primarily towards the elaboration of military safeguards against Germany with a view to the attainment of security in war, the aim of British policy was to promote relationships of confidence and mutual trust as a specific against war. 'British opinion,' commented *The Times*, in 1924, on the occasion of the publication of the French Yellow Book on the Anglo-French negotiations, 'is not pacifist in the sense of making light of the necessity of military precautions for defence. But military machines alone are not sufficient. They must be supplemented by continuous effort to establish such relations between the peoples as shall steadily diminish the necessity and the occasions for resorting to arms. That is the idea which lies behind the rather wavering and uncertain policy of the last few years.' [1] No less, it may be added, was this the inspiration of the Treaty of Locarno, despite its fallacious guise as a treaty of guarantee.

This brief review may suffice to indicate the difficulties inherent in the elaboration of any solution of the problem of security acceptable alike to the exponents of security in war and the exponents of security against war. The antagonistic character of these two conceptions of security provided the theme of MacDonald's peroration to his famous speech at Geneva on 4th September 1924. 'Our interests for peace,' he declared, 'are far greater than our interests in creating a machinery of defence. A machinery of defence is easy to create, but beware lest in creating it you destroy the chances of peace.' It was this clash between opposed conceptions of security which gave rise to the Anglo-French controversy regarding the propriety of concluding defensive alliances. From the French viewpoint the conclusion of defensive alliances designed to guard against attack by a designated country constituted the essential condition of security. Such alliances envisaged assistance to be given in specified circumstances, and so plans could be drawn up in connexion therewith to ensure that effective assistance should be forthcoming immediately in the event of war. But to the vast majority of Englishmen the defensive alliance was taboo because based on the hypothesis of war: it was the evil device which, reintroduced into the politics of Europe, would promote the formation of competing groups, and so impede the development of that spirit of mutual understanding and willing co-operation which would constitute the best surety of peace.

The negotiations for an Anglo-French Pact broke down in July 1922. By then it had become evident that British and French views concerning the conditions of security differed so widely as

[1] *The Times*, March 10, 1924.

to preclude any solution of the problem of French security through the medium of a bilateral agreement concerned solely with the danger of German aggression. The breakdown of the negotiations for an Anglo-French Pact coincided, however, with the resumption, on the initiative of Lord Robert Cecil, of the effort to organize an efficient system of security within the framework of the League. The hope was entertained that it would be possible to meet the German danger by a multilateral agreement designed to provide security against aggression from any and every quarter. The rejection in swift succession of the first tentative plan—the Draft Treaty of Mutual Assistance—in 1924 by the British Labour Government, then of the second—the Geneva Protocol—in 1925 by the British Conservative Government demonstrated that this fresh line of approach presented new difficulties while failing wholly to obviate those which beset the old. The British attitude to the French proposals presented at the Disarmament Conference eight years later—the Tardieu Plan of February 1932, and the Herriot Plan of November 1932—revealed that time had not lessened the rift between the views of the French and the British Governments. The exploration of the problem of security from this new angle had, however, the not unimportant consequence of achieving a measure of reconciliation between the French Radical Socialists and that section of the British public which had, in the first days of peace, been most critical of the French standpoint.

This series of plans for developing the potentialities of the Covenant provides the most eloquent testimony of French misgivings concerning the degree of security afforded by the League as established in 1919. Neither Article 10 nor Article 16—the two articles which determined the character of the League as an organization of security—were of French origin. Article 10 owed its place in the Covenant to President Wilson; Article 16 derived from the Report of the Committee on the League appointed by the British Government in 1918, under the chairmanship of Sir Walter Phillimore. During the Great War British and American sponsors of the League had alike recognized the necessity of forceful collective action to restrain future aggression. But in the drafting of the Covenant the provisions for mutual guarantee and assistance shrank to pale shadows of the intentions of their authors. Article 10 purported to provide a guarantee of 'the territorial integrity and existing political independence' of all members. From the very outset British advocates of the League had contested both the expediency and the practicability of this form of guarantee. An interpretation of Article 10 acceptable to Great Britain was, however, facilitated by the absence of any precise indication of the means whereby the guarantee should be made effective. Accordingly the article was widely understood to establish no more than a general principle: each member remained free to decide for itself to what degree it would uphold this principle by the employment of military force. Article 16 provided for the application of sanctions against any state which resorted to war without first observing the procedures of peaceful settlement prescribed by the Covenant. In the intention of the Phillimore Committee the delinquent state was to have become automatically involved in a state of war with the other members of the League, who were to agree to take jointly and severally all measures—military and economic—necessary to check such wrongful resort to war. In the process of insertion in the Covenant the edge of this forceful provision was blunted; the interpretative resolutions of October 1921 served only to lay bare the elements of weakness native to Article 16. The members of the League would not automatically be at war with the delinquent state; such a state would be deemed to have committed an act of war against them, but—a concession this to American constitutional requirements—the onus of a declaration of war would remain with the governments of the member states. It followed that no obligation to restrain aggression by military action could be presumed to devolve on the members of the League. Only the obligation to apply economic sanctions was beyond dispute, and even in that respect common action was contingent on a unison of view in the designation of the aggressor. In the event of war each member remained free to judge for itself which of the contestant states had committed a breach of the Covenant and which state was engaged in a war of legitimate self-defence.[1] Hence the guarantees contained in Article 16 became, as M. Politis later observed, 'vague as regards their principle and fortuitous as regards their application.'[2] From the first moment of the Covenant's publication French criticism concentrated on the delay and uncertainty which would attend the rendering of assistance to any victim of aggression. 'Everything has been omitted which might involve automatic action on the part of the Associated Powers,' commented Jules Cambon, when he first read the Covenant. 'Very well; but there will be plenty of time for Belgium and France to be swallowed up, before the mere decision that the League of Nations should intervene.'[3]

To summarize the provisions of the successive plans for strengthening the Covenant would involve too wide a digression. It must suffice to indicate the general character of the arrangements

[1] On Articles 10 and 16, see Zimmern, Sir A.: *The League of Nations and the Rule of Law*, pp. 244–247, 279–280, and references there cited; Schiffer, W.: *L'Article 16 du Pacte de la Société des Nations* (Geneva Research Centre, 1938).

[2] *C.R.L.A.: Pol. Comm.*, p. 44.

[3] Tabouis, G.: *Jules Cambon*, p. 325.

which, in the French view, were essential to enable the League to operate effectively as a guarantee of the security of its members. The first necessity was to make sure that there should be no hesitation in deciding which state was the aggressor. The aggressive act, the commission of which was to be countered by the application of sanctions, should therefore be precisely defined. Furthermore, a procedure should be devised whereby in time of crisis the designation of the aggressor would become rather a matter of automatic registration than of individual judgement; otherwise opinions might vary whether the act complained of did in fact constitute aggression within the accepted definition. Should this procedure necessitate at any stage a vote within the Council of the League— this should be avoided if possible, since a vote would imply the possibility of diversity of opinion—a majority vote should suffice. Provision having thus been made for the immediate and indubitable designation of the aggressor, no doubt should be allowed to linger about the obligation of signatory states to apply both economic and military sanctions at the behest of the Council. The intention of such arrangements was to restrict to the utmost extent the discretion of the individual governments and to cause them to act together with clock-work precision in the application of sanctions.

Yet even a general treaty framed on such lines would not suffice to ensure assistance of that immediately effective character which was essential from the French viewpoint. The inadequacy of any such scheme from the angle of military security—security in war— was never more bluntly stated than by Ramsay MacDonald in his comments as British Foreign Secretary on the Draft Treaty of Mutual Assistance.[1] Economic pressure would be slow in operation. Plans of military co-operation could not be drawn up to meet the varied hypothetical circumstances in which the League might be called upon to take action. A prolonged delay would therefore intervene before military pressure could be brought to bear on the aggressor state. MacDonald's purpose, it is clear, was to demonstrate the futility of seeking a solution of the problem of security based on the pitting of collective force against an aggressor.[2] The French reply may be seen, not in the Geneva Protocol, which as regards the organization of security marked little advance on the Draft Treaty, but in the Plans submitted by Tardieu and Herriot to the Disarmament Conference in 1932. They provided that the signatory states should hold at the disposal of the League, constantly ready for action, specialized air units, together with contingents of long-service troops equipped with

---

[1] *Cmd.* 2200, pp. 11-13.
[2] The Draft Treaty was, Macdonald declared on another occasion, 'a war-preparation document' (Labour Party: *Report of Annual Conference, 1924,* p. 108).

powerful weapons of war denied to national armies. The naval Powers were to engage to furnish stipulated naval assistance to any victim of aggression, and the League itself was to maintain permanently an 'organically international air force,' the staff of which was to be recruited directly by the League. Such provisions constituted a bold elaboration of the ideas which had been advanced in the original French plan for the League drawn up in 1918.[1]

To endow the League with the rudiments of executive authority, to equip it with instruments of action—these were two of the three principal objectives of French plans for strengthening the Covenant. But merely to embroider Article 16 was insufficient to complete the conversion of the League into an organization designed to afford, in all circumstances, efficient military protection against aggression. For Article 15, para. 7, entitled the League to retire into an attitude of passivity should war break out over a dispute in respect of which the Council had failed to reach a unanimous report. In such an event the victim of aggression might have to rely solely on its own national forces for defence. As long as no certainty existed of the forceful intervention of the League in every instance of war, no state could dare reduce its armaments below the level deemed necessary for effective national defence. The effective organization of security within the framework of the League required, therefore, the closure of this 'gap in the Covenant'—i.e. the complete proscription of the right of private war. Its necessary counterpart was the compulsory settlement by peaceful means of all international disputes. 'Compulsory arbitration,' eschewed by the makers of the Covenant, emerged therefore as the fundamental basis of the Geneva Protocol. Not only was it 'part of a great machinery of pacific settlement'; it provided also the essential control mechanism in the organization of sanctions. Compulsory arbitration formed the third objective of French plans for the development of the League.

The idea of compulsory arbitration possesses a special import in the history of Anglo-French relations; it facilitated the transition of the British Left from pseudo-pacifism to the advocacy of collective security. It may, then, be well to emphasize at this stage the remarkable contrast between popular British and French ideas of the League in the early twenties. From the first the French partisans of the League had taken their stand by that conception of collective security based on armed force which President Wilson had impugned as 'international militarism.'[2] This notion of collective security remained an alien on English soil throughout the decade which followed the War; not until the thirties was it really naturalized into

---

[1] On this aspect, see especially Aubert, L.: 'Security,' *Foreign Affairs*, October 1932. For the text of the French draft for the League, see Miller, D. H.: *Drafting of the Covenant*, ii, pp. 238–246.

[2] Miller, D. H.: *The Drafting of the Covenant*, ii, p. 294.

the main stream of English thought. At the time of the Geneva Protocol a well-known publicist discerned in England a 'genuine bewilderment at the suggestion that if peace is to be obtained, it must be paid for by certain sacrifices, the assumption of certain obligations.' [1] The very idea that there existed any need for an organized system of guarantees of mutual assistance against aggression ran counter to convictions deep-rooted in the traditions of British liberalism. It appeared to imply that fear and distrust were the sentiments which the peoples of different countries would necessarily and normally entertain towards one another. It laid the stress on military preparation to restrain the would-be aggressor by external coercion rather than on the elimination of the motives that would lead to aggression. It was indicative of the wrong attitude of mind in the search for peace. The aim should be not to organize force on a new plane, but to get rid of force as a factor in international relations. Enmities should, therefore, be dissipated through reconciliation and the cultivation of good will. The best guarantee of peace lay in the determination of men of all nations to prevent the recurrence of war. Of that universal feeling the League was the symbol. Trust in the League—'a purified and extended League'—was therefore widely preached and loudly acclaimed, but rather by way of moral exhortation than as the advocacy of a clearly conceived policy, for few were curious to inquire what the League meant in terms of machinery and of obligations. [2]

Fervour rather than clarity would seem, indeed, to have marked popular peace propaganda in Great Britain after the Great War. In 1924 the assumption of governmental responsibilities debarred the Labour Party from continued advocacy of Treaty revision, hitherto its main plank in foreign policy. The Geneva Protocol came as a timely rallying-cry to fill the gap. It represented the almost inevitable point of convergence between the mystical British cult of peace, half-religious in its inspiration but lacking a concrete programme save for the insistent demand for disarmament, and the more precise and rational French doctrine of '*la Paix par le Droit.*'

[1] Angell, Norman: 'The Public and the Geneva Minimum,' *The Nation*, May 30, 1925.
[2] One illustration of this state of mind must suffice. At the Annual Conference of the Labour Party in 1922 a resolution was presented urging that the 'Socialist and Labour parties of all countries should agree to oppose any war entered into by any Government, whatever the ostensible objective of the War.' Tom Kennedy moved the addition of the reservation: 'but should be free to support any nation forced by armed aggression to defend its independence or its democratic institutions.' The League, he urged, should possess means of enforcing its decisions; peace could not be ensured by preaching 'outworn ethical platitudes.' Kennedy's amendment was defeated on a card vote: 3,231,000 against, 194,000 for. The original resolution was carried by show of hands (*Labour Party: Report of Annual Conference, 1922,* p. 203).

Yet though, from 1924, the British Labour Party and the French Socialist Radicals were united in their homage to the Geneva Protocol, the assumption of an identity of view between the two parties is hardly well founded. For on the British side the sponsors of the Geneva Protocol inclined to the belief that the system of compulsory pacific settlement would command such support among the people of all nations as to make the provision for sanctions a work of supererogation. The commitments of the Protocol, declared MacDonald, though 'black and . . . big on paper,' would in practice involve no risk: sanctions indeed were 'a harmless drug to soothe nerves,' and could probably never be applied with success.[1] It need, then, occasion no surprise that until 1934 the Party saw no necessity to resolve the contradiction between allegiance to the Protocol and the continued advocacy of resistance to all war. On the French side there is little to warrant the assumption that the Geneva Protocol would have been accepted as in itself an effective guarantee of security. Léon Blum's comment on the devotion to the Geneva Protocol proclaimed by successive French Governments was not lacking in justification: 'If the Protocol were more than a mere matter of hope and regret, it would not satisfy us any more than all the rest.'[2] The Protocol would have bound the signatory states 'to co-operate loyally and effectively in support of the Covenant of the League of Nations, and in resistance to any act of aggression, in the degree to which its geographic position and its particular situation as regards armaments allow.' 'To co-operative loyally and effectively': this phrase originated in the refusal of the British delegation to give any undertaking in advance regarding the nature or the extent of the assistance which Great Britain would render to the victim of aggression.[3] Such a general pledge hardly constituted that concrete commitment, precisely assessable in terms of material assistance, which the French had declared the essential condition of disarmament on their part. Dr. Benes had not failed in his report to draw attention to the need of more definite assurances: 'Many states would require to know what military support they could count on.' The knowledge that the Protocol would not, unless reinforced by a supplementary Pact, be accepted by the French as an adequate solution of the problem of security was one of the considerations which resulted in its rejection by Austen Chamberlain.[4]

While the Labour Party progressed, though by a circuitous route,

[1] 210 *H.C. Deb.*, November 24, 1927, col. 2099–2100.   MacDonald, J. R.: *Protocol or Pact.*

[2] Blum, L.: *Peace and Disarmament*, p. 131.

[3] Baker, P. J. N.: *The Geneva Protocol*, p. 135.   Parmoor, Lord: *A Retrospect*, pp. 234–236.

[4] 182 *H.C. Deb.*, March 24, 1925.

to the wholehearted advocacy of collective security, successive British Governments of Conservative composition remained, save for the Abyssinian episode, consistent in their deprecation of any emphasis on the coercive functions of the League. Their attitude signified not merely a refusal to advance to the position of the Geneva Protocol, but even a retreat from the position of the Covenant. For the Covenant and Protocol alike involved the exercise of coercive power by the League; the Protocol differed from the Covenant in the extension of coercion to a wider range of disputes. But the difference constituted a vital distinction which deserves elaboration.

Article 16 owed its place in the Covenant to the British conviction that the War might well have been avoided had the Austro-Serb dispute been submitted to a conference of the European Powers. The intention of the Phillimore Plan was not the mobilization of overwhelming force to ensure that aggression should never pay; its more modest purpose was to ensure the submission of all international disputes to some procedure of peaceful settlement and to procure at least a period of delay before resort to war. 'The moratorium,' said Lord Phillimore, 'is the essence of the whole matter.'[1] It would afford an interval for mediatory activity in the presence of a beneficent and watchful world opinion. Should war ensue, despite the due observance of the precautions of the Covenant, the members of the League might, regretfully, but with a clear conscience, stand aside. It was, as has been noted, this contingent right to stand aside which the Protocol abolished. There remains for consideration the question why the British Government not only rejected the Protocol, that 'perfectly proportioned offspring of the Continental mind,'[2] which yearned after the more perfect organization of security, but also contemned the Covenant, that product of Anglo-Saxon statesmanship which aimed at the more assured maintenance of peace.[3]

A partial explanation may be found in the influence of external circumstances. For the League as it came into being in January 1920 differed in two vital respects from the League as it had been envisaged during the War.

There was, in the first place, a difference of setting. Throughout the War discussion had tended to proceed on the somewhat optimistic assumption that the future territorial settlement would afford substantial satisfaction alike to victor and vanquished. It seemed at the time not unreasonable to conclude that in the improbable

---

[1] Phillimore, Sir W.: 'A League of Nations,' *Quarterly Review*, January 1919.
[2] Zimmern, Sir A.: *The League of Nations and the Rule of Law*, p. 355.
[3] For a survey of British policy with regard to the League, see Charvet, J.: *L'Influence britannique dans la Société des Nations*, Paris, 1938; and the more scholarly and judicious work of Schwoebel, J.: *L'Angleterre et la sécurité collective*, Paris, 1938.

event of an attempt to disturb the settlement by force the great mass of public opinion throughout the civilized world would be clamant against the aggressor. The territorial settlement proved, however, not only the subject of fierce resentment within the defeated countries, but of widespread disapproval beyond their confines, notably in Great Britain. In these circumstances the fear might well be entertained that to emphasize the coercive functions of the League would involve its conversion from the repository of world public opinion into an instrument in the hands of the defenders of an unjust *status quo.* 'The need for force in the relationship of peoples,' commented an English writer, 'is in inverse ratio to their contentment. A League of Nations worthy of the name could have been created only as the framework and expression of a settlement which had won the general assent of civilization.' [1] *The New Statesman* was expressing a point of view not restricted to the circle of its readers when it objected to the Geneva Protocol that it evoked 'the disagreeable possibility of our being called upon to coerce those with whose grievances we sympathize.' [2]

There was, secondly, a difference of composition. The United States had refused to become a member. British apprehension concerning the effect on Anglo-American relations of British participation in the application of sanctions without American co-operation requires no emphasis. The position of the British Government is well illustrated by the approach which was made to the American Government with regard to the Geneva Protocol. Acting on instructions from the Foreign Secretary, the British Ambassador broached the question of the Protocol in an interview, on 5th January 1925, with the American Secretary of State. [3] He pointed out that

'the putting into effect of the Protocol without modifications might leave the way open for the development of situations which would be embarrassing with respect to the relations between Great Britain and the United States. [Great Britain] might be called upon to blockade some country and come into antagonism with the interests of the United States in consequence. It was a cardinal point in British policy to maintain friendly relations with the United States and to co-operate with this Government wherever possible, and there might be interference with this policy if contingencies should arise in which through the operation of the Protocol the British Government was brought into opposition to the interests of the United States. On the other hand, it seemed to the British Government that it would not be well to throw out the Protocol entirely, for if this were done there would most probably be a continuance of competitive armament in Europe which the countries concerned could not afford. The

---

[1] Brailsford, H. N.: *After the Peace*, p. 64.
[2] *The New Statesman*, November 15, 1924.
[3] *U.S.A. Foreign Relations*, 1925, i, pp. 17–18.

only alternative to such a competition in armament, with all its possible consequences, would seem to be the adoption in some form of such an arrangement as the Geneva Protocol proposed. The British Government were seeking for modifications which might suit the purpose and would be very glad to know the position of the United States.'

The American Secretary replied that 'there was one thing he believed could be depended on, and that was that this Government from its very beginning had been insistent upon the rights of neutrals and would continue to maintain them.' He 'did not believe any Administration, short of a treaty concluded and ratified, could commit the country against assertion of its neutral rights in case there should be occasion to demand their recognition.' The Ambassador suggested three days later that 'it would be well for the British Government to say frankly to its associates in the League that there could be no hope of applying the sanctions successfully in opposition to the views of the United States as they might be entertained by its people when a contingency arose.' The Secretary insisted that the United States must be kept out of the discussion. It is legitimate to conclude that the attitude of the American Government was one factor which influenced the British Government in its decision to abandon the intention which it had at first entertained of submitting amendments to the Protocol.[1] Thenceforward through the hesitancy of Great Britain the organization of a system of European security appeared inextricably linked with the direction of American policy.

The abstention of the United States influenced Great Britain also indirectly, through the attitude of the Dominions. For the War had wrought a transformation within the Empire, and the British Cabinet could no longer mould by its own volition the foreign policy of the Empire as a whole. 'It must be remembered,' Lord Curzon observed to the French Ambassador in 1921, 'that British foreign policy was now not the policy of the Cabinet in Downing Street alone, but was the policy of the Empire, and the points of view of the Prime Ministers of our distant Dominions had also to be seriously considered.'[2] The Dominions, unconscious consumers, like the U.S.A., of the security generated by the French army, and fearful of entanglement in European quarrels, exerted their influence in the direction of a 'non-coercive League.' The fate of the League would be sealed, declared General Smuts on the eve of the Abyssinian crisis, 'if ever an attempt were made to transform it into a system to carry on war for the purpose of preventing war. I cannot conceive the Dominions, for instance, remaining in such a League and pledging themselves to fight the

[1] 210 *H.C. Deb.*, November 24, 1927, col. 2102–2103.
[2] *Anglo-French Negotiations*, p. 109.

wars of the Old World; and if the Dominions leave it, Great Britain is bound to follow.'[1]

British deprecation of any emphasis on the coercive functions of the League cannot, however, be explained solely by reference to external circumstances. For the British Government did not seek refuge in an attitude of mere negation to proposals involving an unwelcome extension of its responsibilities; it rebutted them with the affirmation that the exercise of coercive power by the League would detract from its efficacy as an agency for the maintenance of peace. 'Anything which fosters the idea that the main business of the League is with war rather than with peace is likely to weaken it in its fundamental task of diminishing the causes of war'—so read the famous declaration on the Geneva Protocol. This passage may perhaps be ascribed in some measure to a belief in the wholesome psychological effect of averting the mind from the contemplation of the more grim contingencies of international affairs. But it would suggest also that, within the framework of the League, no less than in the direct discussion of the problems of Anglo-French relations, there emerged a conflict between the conceptions of security in war and security against war. For to convert the League into a machine efficient for purposes of military defence entailed the standardization of its procedure to ensure speed in the rendering of military assistance. Such standardization, in the judgement of the British Government, was calculated to endanger the development of the League. A definition of aggression? The determined aggressor would find no difficulty in circumventing the definition; it would prove 'a trap for the innocent and a signpost for the guilty.'[2] A procedure for the designation of the aggressor? The imperative necessity was rather to preserve a flexibility corresponding to the infinite variety of possible eventualities. 'The elaboration and multiplication of rules,' observed the British Government in its *Observations on the Programme of Work of the Committee on Arbitration and Security*,[3] 'must tend, not only to turn the Council into an automaton but to weaken its power of initiative in any contingency not wholly provided for in such rules.' The speedy application of sanctions? There existed, as M. Rutgers noted in his Memorandum on the Covenant submitted to the same Committee, a certain danger in fixing in an immutable form the measures which might be taken in application of Article 16. An inexorable procedure might entail the application of sanctions at a moment 'when there was

---

[1] *International Affairs*, 1935, p. 8. For the attitude of the Dominions, see *Toynbee*, 1924, pp. 27-36, and *1925*, pp. 4-8; Dewey, A. G.: *The Dominions and Diplomacy*; Toynbee, A. J.: *The Conduct of British Empire Foreign Relations*.
[2] Sir Austen Chamberlain: 210 *H.C. Deb.*, November 24, 1927, col. 2105.
[3] Printed in League of Nations Publications, 1928, ix, 3.

still room for doubt as to whether there had really been resort to war, and for hope that the mediation of the Council might stop the hostilities which had begun.'

Indeed, the French plans might be taken to afford a demonstration that the League could operate as an effective guarantee of military security only if transformed into an organic institution capable of decision and action independently of the vagaries of its constituent members—only, in short, if endowed with the lineaments of a super-state. Against any such development within the League the British Government maintained a firm resistance. They remained adamant in their determination that the League should remain, in the words of *The Times'* leader on the Tardieu Plan, 'a society of free nations, each retaining its own independent sovereignty, seeking by voluntary co-operation to further their common interests —the greatest of which is peace—and to settle their differences by the peaceable methods of arbitration and discussion.' [1] This attitude to the League was born of the conviction that the people of different nations could not be brought to act together at the behest of an international council. Not the existence of formal obligations, but the disposition prevalent among its citizens in the hour of need would determine whether, and to what extent, a state would render assistance to the victim of aggression. From this viewpoint the Abyssinian episode constituted not an aberration, but an illustration of British policy, for in 1935 it had become apparent that the principle of Article 16 had become, as regards economic though not as regards military sanctions, a 'living reality' in the minds of the British people. On the same line of reasoning was based the British rejection of compulsory arbitration. The limiting factor in the extension of arbitration, commented the British Government in the course of the *Observations* already quoted 'is the extent to which public opinion in any particular country can be counted on to accept and to carry out loyally a decision which is unfavourable to its own contentions. . . . An arbitration treaty which goes beyond what the public opinion of a country can be counted upon to support when the interests of that country are in question, and when a decision unfavourable to those interests is pronounced, is a treaty which is useless.' Was it not a conviction that the efficacy of the League would depend on the lively support of public opinion that prompted Sir Austen Chamberlain's warning that to pile obligation on obligation would accomplish only the transformation of its members from 'living nations' into 'dead states'? [2]

The Statement on the Geneva Protocol, read by the British Foreign Secretary before the Council of the League on 12th March

[1] *The Times*, February 8, 1932.   [2] Chamberlain, Sir A.: *Peace in our Time*, p. 184.

1925, marked the close of the second stage of the negotiations relating to the problem of security which had opened with Briand's visit to Lloyd George in December 1921. Discussions extending over three years had served to show that neither the old-fashioned device of a defensive alliance nor the new-fangled system of general guarantees within the framework of the League would avail, given the limitations of the British outlook, to provide a solution of the problem of security as that problem was understood by France. It may be well to recall what were, from the French viewpoint, the postulates of an efficient solution: an organization of security European in its scope, and the assurance of immediate military assistance in the event of attack. Great Britain was prepared to underwrite the territorial settlement in eastern Europe neither directly by the acceptance of specific commitments, nor indirectly by a pledge of resistance against aggression in general; nor was there any prospect of British assent to those conditions which alone would suffice to assure immediate military assistance—the conclusion of a military agreement by way of supplement to a defensive alliance, or the standardization of League procedure to ensure the automatic operation of a general system of guarantees.

His hearers perhaps experienced a sense of relief when the British Foreign Secretary concluded his critical examination of the Geneva Protocol with the adumbration of a solution which would be viewed with approval by His Majesty's Government. Though the passage is famous, it must be quoted at length:

'Since the general provisions of the Covenant cannot be stiffened with advantage, and since the "extreme cases" with which the League may have to deal will probably affect certain nations or groups of nations more nearly than others, His Majesty's Government conclude that the best way of dealing with the situation is, with the co-operation of the League, to supplement the Covenant by making special arrangements in order to meet special needs. That these arrangements should be purely defensive in character, that they should be framed in the spirit of the Covenant, working in close harmony with the League and under its guidance, is manifest. And in the opinion of His Majesty's Government these objects can best be attained by knitting together the nations most immediately concerned, and whose differences might lead to a renewal of strife by means of treaties framed with the sole object of maintaining, as between themselves, an unbroken peace. Within its limits no quicker remedy for our present ills can easily be found, nor any surer safeguard against future calamities.' [1]

Here in embryo was the Treaty of Mutual Guarantee signed at Locarno on 16th October 1925.

The suggestion that, within the framework of the Covenant,

[1] *Cmd.* 2764.

the nations immediately affected should conclude agreements for meeting 'a specific danger in a particular area' was certainly not new. The Draft Treaty of Mutual Assistance had provided for the conclusion between any two or more signatories of complementary defensive agreements defining in advance the assistance they would render each other in specific instances of aggression. Such treaties were to be subject at the time of their negotiation to the approval of the Council; thereafter the signatories were to be free to put immediately into operation the plan of assistance agreed upon should the contingencies envisaged therein arise. The Geneva Protocol reproduced this authorization of special agreements, though it withheld from the signatories the right to take military action until the Council itself had resolved on the application of sanctions.

What then was there in the Locarno Treaty which was new, and which caused it to be greeted with such jubilation? The Treaty of Locarno differed from the regional pacts hitherto envisaged in that it was from the first, to use the jargon of the time, 'an open treaty.' It was directed, not against a particular state, but against the unknown aggressor within a defined area. It was, to quote the *Observations* presented by the British Government to the Committee of Arbitration and Security, 'no mere alliance between a group of friendly states with a community of interests': it created 'a bond between nations which were recently at war with one another. It is directed solely to prevent a recurrence of that calamity and to preserve the peace within a group of states whose interests have often conflicted and whose territories have frequently been the theatre of war.' There was indeed some justification for regarding the Locarno Treaty as the application of the Geneva Protocol on a small scale. It was, however, less juridic in its inspiration. Like the Protocol, it ruled out war and provided for the punishment of the transgressor. But, unlike the Protocol, it made no provision for the 'compulsory arbitration' of disputes; unlike the Protocol, therefore, it did not open up the forbidding vista of sanctions for the enforcement of an arbitration award. The arrangements for the designation of the aggressor were more flexible than in the Geneva Protocol; the decision as to which state was the aggressor was entrusted to the Council of the League; but in the event of urgency immediate assistance was to be rendered in advance of the findings of the Council.

Arguments could be adduced to demonstrate that the organization of security on a regional basis possessed considerable advantages over any more general scheme. It could be urged that states, while hesitating to accept a general pledge to intervene in every disturbance of the peace, would be prepared to shoulder onerous and rigid commitments if they applied only to the area within which their vital interests were concerned. The rendering of mutual assistance, which was merely optional under the Covenant, might be made obligatory as between a defined group of states within a specific area. It could be maintained that the more limited scheme would be both more effective as a deterrent against aggression and more reliable in the event of aggression than a general system of guarantees: more reliable because under a general system the obligation of assistance would be spread over a large number of states, each of which would be inclined to regard its obligation as *pro tanto* reduced; more effective as a deterrent because the uncertainty of the operation of the more general scheme might tempt the aggressor to hazard the risk that it would not be operated.

Throughout the decade during which the west European settlement remained under the ægis of Locarno, the British Government proffered the Treaty of Locarno as an example which if applied elsewhere would allay tension in other danger zones. To the query 'How may security be promoted?' the British Government replied in 1928: 'His Majesty's Government look forward to the gradual growth of this system, convinced as they are that the easiest way of attaining a universal sense of security is for each state to provide itself with the necessary guarantees in that quarter where its main interests, and consequently its principal danger, lie. If the system is gradually extended until it includes every state which feels that its security is not already amply safeguarded, there will eventually be woven a network of guarantees against the rupture of the peace in any part of the world.' Nevertheless the Locarno Treaty of Mutual Guarantee remained unique, despite all efforts from 1928 to 1935 to further the conclusion of similar treaties in other areas of Europe. The Treaty was the outcome of the special conditions which prevailed in western Europe in 1925. Momentarily, Great Britain, France, and Germany possessed in common, though each for different reasons, an interest in the maintenance of peace based on a guarantee of the territorial settlement against disturbance by force. It was not possible by the conclusion of further treaties on the Locarno model to secure acquiescence in the territorial settlement elsewhere in Europe: such acquiescence provided the necessary condition, and could not be realized as a consequence, of such treaties.

Consideration of the degree to which the group of treaties concluded at Locarno themselves provided an adequate solution for the wider problem of European security must be postponed to the next chapter. But even in the west the Locarno Treaty of Mutual Guarantee provided no final solution of the problem of security as the French understood security. The immediate arrival of effective military assistance was not ensured by the Treaty, since it could not, for reasons noted earlier in this chapter, be supplemented by a military agreement. In view of the diminutive size of the British army, barely sufficient for Imperial needs, France would still, during the initial period of hostilities, have to rely for military defence on her own unaided efforts. In the course of the debates preceding the Draft Treaty of Mutual Assistance, veiled reference had been made, on more than one occasion, to the inadequacy of British military strength as backing for a British guarantee. The opinion expressed by the Belgian and French members of the Permanent Advisory Commission may be quoted in this connexion: 'The relative value of foreign intervention will depend upon the peace-time military organization of the co-operating state. If a long war is to be avoided, the initial operations must be regarded as decisive. . . . Those countries which only maintain small professional armies, and for which mobilization involves the training of their national man-power, will not be able to put any considerable effectives into the field until after several months, if not longer.' [1] This advisory opinion, expressed with regard to the Draft Treaty of Mutual Assistance, bore no less forcibly on the Locarno Treaty. After its conclusion France proceeded to reduce her armed forces to the minimum level compatible with the effective defence of the frontier. For disarmament below that level the Locarno Treaty provided no justification. Its aim was not security in war, but security against war; for security in war, in the opening stages, France still of necessity looked to her own armed forces.

In November 1932 the conviction that the organization of security required further elaboration, in order to ensure immediate and effective military assistance in the event of aggression anywhere in Europe, resulted in the production of the Herriot Plan. Various aspects of the Plan have been examined elsewhere in this book. It may justly be held to have constituted the most courageous and thorough attempt to work out an organization of collective security at once universal in scope and yet capable of immediate and effective operation within the continent of Europe. Its presentation was prompted by the development of American policy in the first days of the Disarmament Conference. In 1932 there was across the Atlantic a growing recognition that the United States could not remain indifferent to the creation of a system of security in Europe. The most promising approach—indeed, the only possible approach—was to bring within the embrace of a single plan the Kellogg Pact, the Covenant of the League, and some special

[1] *Report of the Temporary Mixed Commission*, August 1923, p. 14.

arrangement adapted to the conditions of the European continent. The purpose of the Herriot Plan was to effect this integration. It contemplated the division of the states of the world into three concentric circles. The outermost circle was to include all the Powers represented at the Disarmament Conference—by implication, therefore, the U.S.A. In the event of a breach, or threat of breach, of the Kellogg Pact these Powers were to concert together 'with a view to appealing to public opinion and agreeing upon the steps to be taken.' In application of the Kellogg Pact they were to break off all financial and economic relations with an aggressor state and to refuse recognition 'of any *de facto* situation brought about in consequence of the violation of an international undertaking.' The second circle was to consist of members of the League who were to be required to give full effect to their obligations under the Covenant and under supplementary treaties. For the innermost circle of European states a special organization was proposed. They were to enter into political agreements providing for mutual assistance against aggression and for the peaceful settlement of disputes; and they were to accept special military arrangements, involving on the one hand the reorganization of their national armies and on the other the provision of military forces at the disposal of the League. Great Britain was included, not within the innermost circle of Continental states, but within the second circle of states bound by the obligations of the Covenant and of supplementary treaties. The fate of the Herriot Plan belongs to the general history of the Disarmament Conference; the discussion to which it gave rise cannot be summarized here. It may, however, be noted that more than one of the European states intimated its refusal to enter into special Continental arrangements unless Great Britain fully participated.

CHAPTER XVII

THE EUROPEAN FRAMEWORK

THE Great War resulted in the breakdown of the three great empires which had in 1914 dominated eastern and central Europe. From their ruins emerged the small national states whose existence was consecrated by the Treaties of Versailles, Saint-Germain, and Trianon. It is beyond the competence of the writer to explore the many political and economic problems to which this reorganization of the European states system gave rise. An adequate study would involve prolonged research. It is, therefore, in a somewhat tentative spirit that questions relating to eastern and central Europe are taken up in this chapter. No comprehensive survey is here proposed: nothing more is attempted than a sketch of the general trends of British and French policy towards the eastern neighbours of Germany.

For twenty years it has been widely regarded as the principal merit of the European settlement after the Great War that it endeavoured to give satisfaction to the national aspirations of the suppressed peoples of eastern and central Europe. The view is now commonly advanced that what has in the past been regarded as the principal merit of the settlement was in fact its fundamental defect, because the principle of national liberation 'was utterly at variance with twentieth-century trends of political and economic organization.' [1]

It is not without profit to consider why the liberation of the suppressed nationalities of Europe came to be adopted as a principal war aim of the Allies. That peace would be best assured by re-drawing the map of Europe along the lines of national division appeared a common-sense conclusion from the history of the last hundred years. Had not the primary cause of war throughout that period been the demand for national freedom in 'the deadlands of Europe'? This line of reasoning, developed in almost every writing on war aims, was most succinctly expressed by Sir Herbert Samuel: 'Unrest among a subject population, repression by the ruling power, sympathy and angry resentment in the neighbouring kindred state, alarm and answering resentment among the dominant people nervous for their ascendancy, sterner repression as the result, and greater unrest again—this is the unhappy circle of events which, constantly recurring wherever national liberty is denied, maintains animosity and predisposes to war.' [2] Only in the speeches of President Wilson was the demand for national liberation given doctrinal form. To President Wilson the nation was a moral entity living within a community of nations the peace of which depended on equal respect for the rights of each member great and small; among these rights was numbered first and foremost the right to freedom from foreign rule. President Wilson spoke the language of moral obligation, whereas to the statesmen of the Entente the vague principle of national self-determination was rather a political maxim to be applied with due regard to time and circumstance. It may be added that the idea of national liberation could alone give meaning to the struggle which the Allies were waging from 1914 to 1918. Both in England and France it was admitted that a German triumph might bring peace and prosperity to the Continent—peace and prosperity to the

[1] Carr, E. H.: *Conditions of Peace*, p. 49.
[2] Samuel, Rt. Hon. H.: *War and Liberty*, p. 16.

Continent from the English Channel to the Dniester under a *Pax Germanica*. 'There might be a Europe, there might be a rich and fairly peaceful Europe under Germany's domination: but the peace would be . . . an iron peace, and the riches would be produced for German masters by masses of men without freedom and almost without nationality.'[1] That small states would henceforward 'only be able to maintain their independence with the utmost difficulty' was a peculiarly German doctrine; neither the interests nor the inclinations of Great Britain and France permitted its currency in the countries of the Entente. Great Britain is fighting, Asquith declared at the outset of the struggle, 'to withstand, as we believe in the best interests not only of our own Empire but of civilization at large, the arrogant claim of a single Power to dominate the development of the destinies of Europe.'

Comparatively little is known of any plans drawn up in 1914–1918 by the British and French Governments for the reorganization of Europe after the War. Probably there is little to know; the elaboration of detailed plans seemed futile until victory was assured. No memoranda are available to indicate the views of the French Government concerning the political settlement of Europe as a whole. For Great Britain all that is available are the papers drawn up in connexion with the consideration of war aims and peace terms by the British Cabinet in October 1916, and by the Imperial War Cabinet in March 1917. But these are sufficient to show that to British statesmen the idea of re-drawing the map of Europe along the lines of national division commended itself the more because it would tend, so it seemed, to lessen the power of Germany in eastern and central Europe. A durable peace, Balfour advised in October 1916, can best be secured 'by the double method of diminishing the area from which the Central Powers can draw the men and money required for a policy of aggression, while at the same time rendering a policy of aggression less attractive by re-arranging the map of Europe in closer agreement with what we vaguely call the principle of nationality.'[2] The British Cabinet held the view—so General Smuts informed Count Mensdorff in December 1917—that no peace could be satisfactory which left Germany in a position of military predominance on the Continent. 'The political dispositions of Central Europe after the war,' General Smuts added, 'should afford some safeguard against its re-establishment.'[3] The territorial changes which the British Government had in mind were outlined by Balfour in a speech in the Imperial War Cabinet on 21st March 1917. Since the speech has

[1] Murray, G.: *Faith, War and Policy*, p. 238.
[2] Lloyd George: *War Memoirs*, ii, pp. 877–888.
[3] Lloyd George: *War Memoirs*, v, p. 2467.

not been published in any easily accessible work, it may be worth while quoting at length the relevant extract. 'I frankly admit,' Balfour declared, 'that when the Germans say that we are fighting for a cause that means their destruction, it is not true in one sense: we are not destroying a German Germany, but we are trying to destroy the rather artificial creation of the modern Prussia, which includes many Slav elements which never belonged to Germany until about 140 years ago and ought, really, not to belong to Germany at this moment. . . .' Balfour welcomed the prospect of detaching from Germany her Polish provinces. 'Personally,' he added, 'from a selfish Western point of view, I would rather that Poland was autonomous under the Russians, because if you make an absolutely independent Poland, lying between Russia and the Central States, you cut off Russia altogether from the West. Russia ceases to be a factor in Western politics, or almost ceases. She will be largely divided from Austria by Roumania. She will be divided from Germany by the new Polish State; and she will not be coterminous with any of the belligerents. And if Germany has designs in the future upon France or the West, I think she will be protected by this new State from any action on the part of Russia, and I am not at all sure that that is to the interests of Western civilization. It is a problem which has greatly exercised my mind, and for which I do not see a clear solution. These are disjointed observations in regard to Poland; they lead to no clear-cut recommendation on my part. I am not pleading for a cause; I am trying to lay before the Cabinet the various elements in the problem as they strike me.' [1] In Balfour's view, then, the interests of Europe would best be served if Poland, while enjoying a large measure of autonomy, were to remain an integral part of the Russian Empire, for only so would Russia remain a European Power so placed as to exercise direct pressure on Germany. But when the October Revolution had dispelled the possibility of such an arrangement, British and French thought moved towards complete independence for Poland. Perhaps the most striking statement in Lloyd George's speech of 5th January 1918 was the declaration: 'An independent Poland, comprising all those genuinely Polish elements who desire to form part of it, is an urgent necessity for the stability of Western Europe.'

The application of the principle of national self-determination in the Danubian basin was the cause of more prolonged perplexity. In 1916 the Foreign Office looked forward without misgiving to the break-up of the Dual Monarchy and to the inclusion of German Austria in Germany. The Austrians, it was held, would swell the

---

[1] *U.S.A. Foreign Relations, Lansing Papers, 1914–1920*, ii, pp. 27–28. Cf. *House*, iii, p. 48; and Lloyd George: *War Memoirs*, ii, pp. 877–888.

Catholic population within Germany and so create a counterpoise to Prussia. But Balfour was of a different mind, and his views came to prevail within the Cabinet. Fearing the fusion of the German-speaking population within a single powerful state, Balfour desired the maintenance of the Dual Monarchy. The British ideal for central Europe was an Empire liberalized by the grant of autonomy to the subject nationalities and redeemed from the domination of Prussia. This was the theme of Lloyd George's speech of 5th January 1918; this, too, was the sense of the tenth of the Fourteen Points. But Balfour in his speech to the Imperial War Cabinet in May 1917 had frankly confessed himself baffled by the obstacles to any such settlement. Transylvania had been promised to Roumania—that would break up historic Hungary; Bosnia and Herzegovina had been promised to Serbia, and Dalmatia to Italy—that might not break up the historic Austria; but the secession of Bohemia would do so—and the Czechs, Balfour admitted, had such a hatred of German civilization that they, too, would claim their freedom. As long as hope could be entertained of a separate peace with Austria, Allied statesmen refrained from any step likely to contribute to the entire collapse of the Habsburg Empire. But before the cessation of hostilities the foundations of the Czechoslovak state had been laid by the recognition of the Czechoslovaks as an allied and belligerent nation.

The controversy between Lloyd George and Clemenceau at the Peace Conference regarding the eastern frontiers of Germany is well known. 'I would therefore take as a guiding principle of the peace,' declared Lloyd George in his Memorandum of 26th March, 'that as far as is humanly possible the different races should be allocated to their motherlands, and that this human criterion should have precedence over considerations of strategy or economics or communications, which can usually be adjusted by other means.' Clemenceau's reply, five days later, was indicative of his determination to endeavour to strengthen Poland and Czechoslovakia as barriers against the expansion of German power in eastern and central Europe. 'Our firmest guarantee against German aggression,' he remarked in the Council of Four, 'is that behind Germany, in an excellent strategic position, stand Czechoslovakia and Poland.' [1] But this controversy between the British and French premiers at the end of March conveys a somewhat distorted impression of the relations of the British and French delegations on frontier questions. Neither the question of the Czech–German frontier, nor indeed even the problem of Austria, provoked any conflict of opinion between the British and the French. The inclusion within Czecho-

[1] Aldrovandi, L.: *Guerra Diplomatica*, p. 405.

slovakia of the German-inhabited territories of Bohemia was never in doubt. Even before the Peace Conference opened, Dr. Benes is said to have obtained from the three European Great Powers— from France on 28th September 1918, and from Great Britain and Italy on 7th January 1919—pledges of support for the Czech claims to these borderlands.[1] All the members of the Commission on Czechoslovak claims, British, French, Italian, and American alike, agreed in recommending that the historic frontier of Bohemia should in principle be adopted as the frontier of the new state. The considerations which they advanced in support of their recommendation are not without interest:

(a) *Economic reasons*. The whole of the region occupied by the Germans of Bohemia is industrially and commercially dependent upon Bohemia rather than upon Germany. The Germans of Bohemia cannot exist without the economic co-operation of the Czechs, nor the Czechs without the economic co-operation of the Germans. There is between them a complete interdependence in this respect. . . .

(d) *Reasons of national security*. These reasons depend on geographic considerations. The chain of mountains which surrounds Bohemia constitutes a line of defence for the country. To take away this line of mountains would be to place Bohemia at the mercy of the Germans.[2]

On the question of German Austria there appears also to have been remarkably little difference of opinion, and still less discussion, at the Peace Conference. Until March the question of Austria attracted curiously little attention. Though in December 1918 Pichon had declared in the Chamber his determination to prevent the inclusion of the Austrian Germans within Germany, no action was taken until, on 4th March 1919, the Austrian Constituent Assembly proceeded to accept as part of the organic law of Austria the resolution: 'German Austria is a constituent part of the German Reich.' At this stage the French Government intervened.[3] On 11th March Tardieu notified his colleagues Philip Kerr and Dr. Mezes of the French desire to require from Germany an undertaking 'to recognize the independence of German Austria, and to undertake to do nothing, either of a political or of an economic nature, which directly or indirectly could violate this independence.' Kerr replied mildly that he had no instructions; he thought that such a provision might be accepted as a temporary measure pending the settlement of Austria-Hungary and the setting up of the League of Nations.[4] Clemenceau, however, waited till the end of April

[1] Vondracek, F. J.: *The Foreign Policy of Czechoslovakia*, p. 24.
[2] Seymour, C.: 'Czechoslovak Frontiers,' *Yale Review*, Winter, 1939. This article contains the best review of the drawing of the frontiers of Czechoslovakia at the Peace Conference.
[3] Ball, M.: *Post-War Austro-German Relations*, pp. 9–11, 20. See also Allizé, H.: *Ma Mission à Vienne*, pp. 32 et seq.
[4] *Anglo-French Negotiations*, pp. 59, 67.

before submitting to the Council of Four the resolution which was the origin of Article 88 of the Treaty of Versailles: 'Germany acknowledges and will fully respect the independence of Austria. . . .'[1] Of the discussion preceding the adoption of Clemenceau's resolution no record has been published.

In the fixing of the German frontiers in eastern and central Europe only the question of the Polish-German frontier gave rise to acute Franco-British controversy. The divergent attitudes of France and Great Britain first became evident during the preparation of armistice terms. In the Supreme War Council on 2nd November 1918 Pichon proposed that the Germans should be required to evacuate all the territories which had formed part of the Kingdom of Poland before 1772. Balfour replied that the Allies were committed only 'to reconstitute a Poland composed of Poles'; the 1772 frontier, he added, would involve not only the inclusion of territory not inhabited by Poles, but the exclusion of Polish-inhabited territory.[2] French insistence on the frontiers of 1772 thereafter ceased; Cambon's note of 26th November 1918, which outlined the French demands, required no more than a strict application of Balfour's principle.[3] But Point X of the Fourteen Points involved a further complication. 'An independent Polish state should be erected which should include the territories inhabited by indisputably Polish populations, which should be assured a free and secure access to the sea. . . .' Free and secure access to the sea? It was the unanimous view of the experts of the Polish Commission—British, French, Italian, and American—that 'free and secure access to the sea' could be assured to Poland only by incorporating within Poland not only the German-inhabited town of Danzig, but also the German-inhabited Kreis of Marienwerder, which was traversed by the Danzig-Mlawa-Warsaw railway.[4] Challenged on this point by Lloyd George, and invited by the Council of Ten to reconsider its recommendations, the Commission reaffirmed its view. Lloyd George nevertheless prevailed on Wilson and Clemenceau to agree to the establishment of a special régime in Danzig, and to a plebiscite to determine the fate of Marienwerder, which in the outcome remained German. As regards Danzig, the writer of the authoritative study on *The Peace Settlement in the German-Polish Borderlands* has recorded his conclusion that in the vagueness of the hastily drafted Danzig clauses of the Treaty of Versailles may in the ultimate analysis be found the origin of the recurring Polish-Danzig disputes.[5]

[1] Almond, N., and Lutz, R. H.: *The Treaty of Saint-Germain*, pp. 630–631.
[2] Mermeix: *Les Négociations secrètes*, p. 247.
[3] *Miller*, ii, pp. 206–214.
[4] *Miller*, vi, p. 350.
[5] Morrow, I. F. D.: *The Peace Settlement in the German-Polish Borderlands*, pp. 174–175.

With the outcome of Lloyd George's efforts with regard to Danzig it is of interest to compare the settlement eventually reached with regard to Upper Silesia. In response to German protests, Lloyd George insisted on a plebiscite also in this area, which according to the initial conditions of peace was to have been ceded outright to Poland. The voting on 20th March 1921—60 per cent for Germany, 40 per cent for Poland—precipitated a prolonged Anglo-French dispute. In the industrial area the communes which had voted for Poland were inextricably intermixed with those which had voted for Germany. Ought the industrial area to be divided between the two countries? Neither Great Britain nor France inclined to this view: but whereas France desired the transfer of the area to Poland, Great Britain insisted on its retention by Germany. Neither country took its stand by a strict interpretation of the plebiscite. On 12th August the Supreme Council escaped from the deadlock by inviting the Council of the League to recommend the line of the frontier between Poland and Germany. Two months later the League Council made its recommendations. A frontier was proposed which cut through the industrial area in order to conform as precisely as possible with the wishes of the inhabitants expressed in the plebiscite, while a general convention was to be concluded between Poland and Germany to safeguard the continuity of economic activity. The Upper Silesian Convention, both in its negotiation and subsequent operation, is justly regarded as a model international experiment.[1]

In the twenty years from the signature of the Treaty to the outbreak of the present war four periods may be distinguished in the course of Anglo-French relations in their bearing on the maintenance of the territorial settlement.

The first period, the pre-Locarno years from 1920–1925, was marked by the adoption by Great Britain and France of apparently antithetical policies; the objective of the one, as has already been written, was economic reconstruction, of the other political stabilization. The speech delivered by Dr. Benes in the Czech Parliament after the close of the Genoa Conference illustrates the Continental non-German view of the discordant policies of the two Great Powers:

'Two political tendencies are in process of development in Europe at the present time. The first, the outcome of the last War, aims at the maintenance of the treaties of peace and of the alliances to which they have given rise; it is based on the calculation that gradually in the course of time, by an evolutionary process, the psychology of war and reciprocal

[1] For a full study, see Kaeckenbeeck, G.: *The International Experiment in Upper Silesia.*

enmity will disappear. Through the progressive execution of the treaties of peace, mutual confidence will develop again; a final reconciliation and the necessary collaboration between nations which is the goal of the League will at length be realized. The supporters of this tendency bear in mind that the effects of the War are still at work in the minds of men; the annihilation of four great states, the devastation of lands, the ruin of millions of families—all that is still too strong and too much alive. It would be wrong to follow a policy neglectful of these facts. . . .

'The second tendency is, in truth, directed towards the same end, but is based on the consideration that for their attainment entirely new procedures and policies are essential. While the supporters of the first tendency insist on gradual development, . . . the supporters of the second desire to break away rapidly and forcibly from the legacy of war—want to forget it instantaneously. They stress the necessity of immediate and unrestricted collaboration between all peoples. Their attitude with regard to the peace treaties is not so rigid. They do not distinguish between former allies and former enemies. . . . This tendency is avowedly pacifist. Its supporters demand general disarmament; they talk about it a great deal. They are, moreover, moderate with regard to reparations. This tendency is characterized also by a feeling of mistrust towards the small states, for a certain propaganda has given rise to the legend that small states are more chauvinistic and militaristic than the large. . . .

'Generally, though not always rightly, the first political tendency is identified with French policy; the second with British and Italian policy.'[1]

Dr. Benes' speech suggests some of the reasons why Great Britain failed to enlist the co-operation of France and her allies in a programme of economic reconstruction. The emphasis laid in British circles on the economic restoration of Germany as the first essential step to general European recovery alarmed them. Too little attention, they felt, was being paid to their own financial and economic problems. British insistence on the economic restoration of Germany was the more disturbing because accompanied by widespread criticism of the break-up of Europe into national states. 'In 1920,' commented a French economist, 'Europe and her frontiers and her quarrels were held responsible for unemployment in England and even in America. Nothing less than the entire political status instituted by the Treaties was questioned. Naturally this attitude of countries outside Europe contributed to the maintenance of a great nervous tension in the nations newly-born or resuscitated, for they felt that any wholesale reconstruction would be accomplished only at their expense.'[2] The economic difficulties of Europe which were the heritage of war and which could have

---

[1] Text in *L'Europe Nouvelle*, June 3, 1922.
[2] Aubert, L.: *The Reconstruction of Europe*, p. 64.

been mitigated only by the continuance of the war-time machinery of control and co-operation were, they considered, being mistakenly attributed to the political reorganization of Europe effected by the Treaties. Nor was Great Britain, in their view, prepared to play an adequate rôle in the construction of safeguards against the revival of German power which would result from German economic recovery.

The French could justly claim that the influence of France in Europe arose from the identity of interest between France and the small states of the Continent. Countries such as Belgium and Czechoslovakia ardently desired the continuance of the Anglo–French Entente as—to quote Masaryk's words and Benes' rider—the 'necessary authority in Europe' which provided 'the key for solving the European situation and for safeguarding the European peace for long decades ahead.' [1] Since Great Britain appeared to be turning her back on the Continent, and since from 1920 to the first months of 1924 the rift between Great Britain and France grew wider, they had no choice but to look increasingly to France. France alone seemed willing to provide the power necessary to check the revival of German political expansion. The purposes of French policy cannot be better described than in the words of André Géraud:

'The principal aims we must have in view are the consolidation of the little national states that were created or enlarged at the end of the war when the Habsburg Monarchy fell to pieces. . . . While making every effort to live peacefully with our German neighbours, and to settle all our differences with them, we must strive for the evolution of a European continent where the designs and achievements of Pan-Germanism will find no place. That expression, "Pan-Germanism," is not often heard nowadays. . . . Still, to-day as yesterday, it indicates the weakest spot in the structure of our Western civilization.

'By the term Pan-Germanism . . . I simply want to indicate the striving of the Berlin Government for domination over the belt of central and eastern Europe where German minorities are scattered among Slav masses whose national characteristics have missed for centuries, and perhaps still miss to-day, the support and protection of an efficient state organization. . . .

'It devolves upon the Western Powers, and upon all peaceably-minded people in Europe, to see to it that the eastern and central states are not interfered with by imperial ambitions while they are still in the process of settling down on their permanent national foundations.'

But, questioned the famous journalist, would France be willing and able for long to assume the burden that was falling upon her shoulders?

[1] Machray, R.: *The Little Entente*, pp. 189, 238.

'Unless backed up from the outside, France cannot be expected to retain all alone an abiding sense of European partnership, still less to act upon it. There will be no lack of advisers to tell her not to look beyond the Rhine just as Spain does not look beyond the Pyrenees, and to let central and eastern Europe take care of themselves. But if she listens to such counsellors, will the eventual retribution of Nemesis fall on her alone?' [1]

The second period of Anglo-French relations as regards the maintenance of the territorial settlement extended from the signature of the Locarno Treaties in October 1925 to the denunciation of the western Locarno Treaty in March 1936. The conclusion of the western Locarno Treaty, it has been suggested, emphasized the precarious character of the Polish-German and the Czech-German frontier, because Great Britain refused to underwrite those frontiers as she had the Franco-German—a refusal that was consistently maintained thereafter. Yet the validity of any such judgement is doubtful. The Locarno Treaties as a whole afforded Europe a measure of stability which Europe had failed to achieve during the preceding period. They constituted an ingenious compromise between the determination of Great Britain not to extend her commitments beyond western Europe, and the preoccupation of France with the maintenance of the territorial settlement in eastern Europe. The simultaneous conclusion of the western Locarno Treaty and of the Franco-Polish and the Franco-Czech treaties was not, as Briand realized full well, without its significance. The railing against France in Great Britain on account of the so-called encirclement of Germany died down. Moreover, the western Locarno Treaty itself was not devoid of import for the stability of eastern Europe. The ability of France to render aid and assistance to Poland and Czechoslovakia depended in large measure on the existence of the demilitarized zone, the maintenance of which was understood to have been guaranteed. Locarno may also be held to have marked the adoption by Great Britain of a more conservative attitude towards the problem of territorial change. 'I am certain,' declared Sir Austen Chamberlain shortly before the signature of the western Locarno Treaty, 'that whatever their intention, whatever their object, those who at this time raise these frontier questions, and keep the minds of the nations concerned unsettled and disturbed, are not serving the interests of peace or the renewal of the prosperity of Europe.' [2] Henceforward the tendency of British policy was to deprecate any raising of the issue of territorial revision. During the Locarno decade only one territorial question came definitely to the fore—that of the independence of Austria, which constituted

[1] Géraud, A.: 'French Responsibilities in Europe,' *Foreign Affairs*, January 1927.
[2] 185 *H.C. Deb.*, June 24, 1925, col. 1563.

for France, in Paul Boncour's words, 'the keystone of order in this part of Europe.'[1] Both in 1931, on the occasion of the Austro-German Customs Union proposal, and again in 1933–1934, when Austrian independence was jeopardized by the Nazi onslaught, the British Government ranged itself in effect on the side of the established order.[2]

The German reoccupation of the demilitarized zone on 7th March 1936 proved the starting-point of a third phase in British and French policy with regard to the territorial settlement. The reoccupation, it has been truly said, was in its consequences the most momentous single incident of the inter-war years. It let down an iron curtain between France and her allies in central Europe. The system on which France relied, and Great Britain also at a second remove, was thereby undermined.[3] Germany had finally regained the power to force through territorial changes in eastern and central Europe without effective intervention by France. No purpose would be served by relating again the intricate details of the successive crises—March 1938, September 1938, March 1939 —in the course of which Germany recast the map of Europe. Nor is there reason to linger here on the policy of appeasement, that final search, in the least advantageous circumstances, for a basis of understanding with those whom Stresemann had characterized as 'the Radicals of the Right, whom no man can satisfy, nor ever will.'[4]

A new and final phase opened on 17th March 1939 with the British Prime Minister's speech to the Birmingham Unionist Association, which presaged the abandonment of the policy of appeasement. In the following weeks Great Britain took the lead in extending guarantees to the countries of eastern and south-eastern Europe threatened by German or Italian aggression: to Poland on 31st March, to Greece and Roumania on 13th April. The guarantees constituted a belated recognition of the dangers to which Sir James Headlam-Morley had drawn attention in 1925:

'We cannot now be indifferent if Germany breaks through upon the east and there begins to acquire a new accession of territory and strength which would inevitably in the future be brought to bear upon the Rhine. . . . Has anyone attempted to realize what would happen if there were

---

[1] Quoted Ball, M. M.: *Post-War German-Austrian Relations*, p. 208.
[2] British policy with regard to Germany's eastern neighbours is excellently treated by Prof. A. Wolfers: *Britain and France between Two Wars*, ch. xvii.
[3] These phases are those of Huddleston, S.: 'France faces the Facts,' *Contemporary Review*, May 1938.
[4] *Stresemann*, ii, p. 246. For a fair appraisal of British policy in 1938–1939, see Medlicott, W. N.: *British Foreign Policy since Versailles*, chs. xii and xiii. For French policy, Knapton, E. J.: 'The Duel for Central Europe: Some Aspects of French Diplomacy, 1938–39,' *Journal of Central European Affairs*, April 1942.

to be a new partition of Poland, or if the Czechoslovak State were to be
so curtailed and dismembered that in fact it disappeared from the map
of Europe? The whole of Europe would at once be in chaos. There
would no longer be any principle, meaning, or sense in the territorial
arrangements of the Continent. Imagine, for instance, that under some
improbable condition Austria rejoined Germany; that Germany, using
the discontented minority in Bohemia, demanded a new frontier far over
the mountains, including Carlsbad and Pilsen, and that at the same time,
in alliance with Germany, Hungary recovered the southern slope of the
Carpathians. This would be catastrophic, and even if we neglected to
interfere in time to prevent it, we should afterwards be driven to
interfere, probably too late.' [1]

From March 1939 British policy was inspired by the conviction
that Great Britain could not watch with indifference the continued
elimination of the small states of eastern Europe. 'We know,'
declared Lord Halifax on 29th June, 'that if the security and
independence of other countries are to disappear, our own security
and our own independence will be gravely threatened.' [2] The
principles at stake in 1939 were those which British statesmen had
proclaimed in the first days of the Great War: the right of small
nations to freedom and security in the enjoyment of their independence, and the submission of disputes to friendly settlement by the
processes of negotiation and compromise. The issue upon which
Great Britain entered the present war cannot be better stated than
in these words: 'Britain is fighting to-day, as she has fought many
times before, to maintain on the Continent of Europe an orderly
society of independent nations free from the brutal domination of
a single overwhelming Power.' [3]

[1] Headlam-Morley, Sir J.: *Studies in Diplomatic History*, pp. 183-185.
[2] *Cmd.* 6106, p. 59.
[3] Carr, E. H.: *Britain*, p. 196.

INDEX